Acute Psychosis, Schizophrenia and Comorbid Disorders

Acute Psychosis, Schizophrenia and Comorbid Disorders

Recent topics from
Advances in Psychiatric Treatment Volume 1

Edited by Alan Lee

Gaskell

British Library Cataloguing-in-Publication Data

A catalogue record for this book is available from the British Library.

ISBN 1 901242 16 1

Distributed in North America
by American Psychiatric Press, Inc.

ISBN 0 88048 586 8

Gaskell is an imprint of the Royal College of Psychiatrists, 17 Belgrave Square, London SW1X 8PG

The Royal College of Psychiatrists is a registered charity (no. 228636).

The views presented in this book do not necessarily reflect those of the Royal College of Psychiatrists, and the publishers are not responsible for any errors of omission or fact. This volume is produced by the Publications Department of the College; it should in no way be construed as providing a syllabus or other material for any College examination.

Printed by Henry Ling Limited, Dorchester, Dorset.

Contents

Contributors vi

Preface. *A. Lee* ix

Introduction. *G. Morgan* 1

Management of a newly admitted patient with acute disturbance. *J. Cookson* 2

Guidelines for the management of patients with acute disturbance. *R. Macpherson,*
    B. Anstee & R. Dix 7
    Commentary. *T. Turner* 12

X High-dose antipsychotic medication. *A. V. P. Mackay* 14

Neuroleptic malignant syndrome. *D. Kohen & M. Bristow* 21

Pharmachological treatment of the newly diagnosed patient with schizophrenia.
    M. J. Travis & R. W. Kerwin 27

Treatment of the patient with long-term schizophrenia. *A. Mortimer* 35

Cognitive–behavioural treatments in schizophrenia. *G. Haddock & S. Lewis* 43

Deploying a community mental health team for the effective care of individuals
    with schizophrenia. *G. Strathdee* 49

Setting up an assertive community treatment service. *A. Kent & T. Burns* 58
    Commentary. *S. R. Hirsch* 64

Mental health nursing: issues and roles. *K. Gournay* 66
    Commentary. *R. Lingham* 71

Making care programming work. *D. Kingdon* 73

Management aspects of care for homeless people with mental illness. *P. Timms* 78

Substance misuse in severe mental illness. *R. Cantwell & G. Harrison* 86

Misuse of amphetamines and related drugs. *N. Seivewright & C. McMahon* 93

Psychiatric illness and learning disability: a dual diagnosis. *J. Bernal & S. Hollins* . . . 100

Treatment of psychoses in the elderly. *A. Phanjoo* 109

Risk and childbirth in psychiatry. *M. Oates* 116

Fit to be interviewed by the police? *K. J. B. Rix* 123

Preparing a medico-legal report. *R. Bluglass* 130

Index 137

Contributors

Bryan Anstee is a Consultant Psychiatrist at Llanarth Court Hospital, Llanarth, Raglan, Gwent NP5 2YD. He used to be Deputy Regional Adviser in Psychiatry for the South West Region and Consultant General/Rehabilitation Psychiatrist at Wotton Lawn Hospital, Gloucester.

Jane Bernal is Senior Lecturer in Psychiatry of Learning Disability at the Department of Psychiatry of Disability, St George's Hospital Medical School, Jenner Wing, Cranmer Terrace, London SW17 0RE. Her research interests include epilepsy, autism, adults with behavioural phenotypes and forensic psychiatry of learning disabilities. Her clinical work is for Wandsworth Community Health Trust providing specialist services to adults with learning disabilities and challenging/mental health needs, and to those with epilepsy.

Robert Bluglass, CBE is Emeritus Professor of Forensic Psychiatry at the University of Birmingham, and an Honorary Consultant in Forensic Psychiatry at the Reaside Clinic, Birmingham Great Park, Bristol Road South, Birmingham B45 9BE. He has over 30 years' experience of preparing medico-legal reports.

Michael Bristow is a Consultant/Senior Lecturer in General Psychiatry at Sutton Hospital (St Helier Trust, Surrey SM2 5NF). Together with Dr Kohen, he has helped establish the Neuroleptic Malignant Syndrome Database (mbristow@globalnet.co.uk) and works on different aspects of this syndrome.

Tom Burns is Foundation Professor of Community Psychiatry at St George's Hospital Medical School (Jenner Wing, Cranmer Terrace, London SW17 0RE). His current interests include provision of care for the severely long-term mentally ill, conducting a randomised controlled trial of assertive communtiy treatment, and the primary/secondary care interface. He was Chairman of the Social and Community Section of the Royal College of Psychiatrists and has chaired a College Working Party on in-patient provision.

Roch Cantwell is a Consultant Psychiatrist and Honorary Clinical Senior Lecturer at the University of Glasgow (University Department of Psychological Medicine, Gartnavel Royal Hospital, 1055 Great Western Road, Glasgow G12 0XH). He has a special interest in substance misuse in major mental illnes, including its epidemiology and impact on service provision.

John Cookson is a Consultant and Honorary Senior Lecturer in psychiatry at the Royal London Hospital (St Clement's) (2A Bow Road, London E3 4LL), with a catchment area in east London and responsibilities including the psychiatric intensive care unit, opened in 1988. His research interests are the use of drugs in psychiatry and particularly the treatment of manic–depressive illness.

Roland Dix is a Clinical Nurse Specialist in the Psychiatric Intensive Care Unit at Wotton Lawn, Horton Road, Gloucester GL1 3WL. He is Editor for the National Association of PICUs and a member of its Executive Committee. He is also a Visiting Lecturer on Aggression in Mental Health at the University of the West of England.

Kevin Gournay (Institute of Psychiatry, De Crespigny Park, Denmark Hill, London SE5 8AF) is a Chartered Psychologist and Registered Nurse, and is an affiliate of the Royal College of Psychiatrists. He has the largest portfolio of mental health nursing research in Europe, with 16 projects valued at £1.5 million, including studies of epidemiology, of dual diagnosis, violence in forensic settings, and several randomised controlled trials of treatment and training. Professor Gournay serves on several national initiatives, and is the author of 200 books, chapters, articles and papers.

Gillian Haddock is Senior Lecturer in Clinical Psychology at the University of Manchester and Honorary Consultant Clinical Psychologist for Tameside and Glossop Community and Priority Services NHS Trust (Mental Health Unit, Tameside General Hospital, Fountain Street, Ashton-under-Lyne, Lancashire OL6 9RW). She obtained her BSc in psychology at the University of York and her masters and PhD at the University of Liverpool.

Glynn Harrison is Norah Cooke Hurle Professor of Mental Health, University of Bristol (Department of Mental Health, 41 St Michael's Hill, Bristol BS2 8DZ). He qualified in medicine in Dundee and trained in psychiatry in Bristol, before becoming a Consultant Psychiatrist in Nottingham. He was appointed to the Foundation Chair of Community Mental Health in Nottingham in 1994, and took up his present post in Bristol in 1997. Clinically, he is a general psychiatrist with a special interest in the treatment of schizophrenia.

Steven R. Hirsch is Professor of Psychiatry at Charing Cross and Westminster Medical School, St Dunstan's Road, London W6 8RP.

Sheila Hollins is Professor in Psychiatry of Learning Disability at the Department of Psychiatry of Disability, St George's Hospital Medical School, Jenner Wing, Cranmer Terrace, London SW17 0RE. Her research interests include bereavement, psychotherapy in learning disabilities, and forensic psychiatry of learning disabilities. Her clinical work is for Wandsworth Community Health Trust providing a mental health service to adults with learning disabilities and a specialist psychotherpy service.

Andrew Kent is a Senior Lecturer in Community Psychiatry at St George's Hospital Medical School, Cranmer Terrace, London SW17 0RE.

Robert Kerwin is Head of the Section of Clinical Neuropharmacology at the Institute of Psychiatry (De Crespigny Park, Denmark Hill, London SE5 8AF). He has researched and published widely on the pharmacology of schizophrenia and was awarded the prestigious Joel Elkes International Award by the American College of Neuropsychopharmacology for outstanding contribution to psychopharmacology.

David Kingdon has been appointed Professor of Mental Health Care Delivery at the University of Southampton (Mental Health Group, Southampton University, Brintons Terrace, Southampton SO14 0YG). He has previously worked as Medical Director in Nottingham, Senior Medical Officer at the Department of Health and as an adult psychiatrist in Bassetlaw, Nottinghamshire. He has published articles and book chapters on the development of mental health services and cognitive therapy.

Dora Kohen is a Consultant in Adult General Psychiatry (East Wing, Homerton Hospital, Homerton Row, London E9 6SR) and Professor of Clinical Psychiatry in Istanbul, Turkey. She works on different aspects of psychopharmacology and especially side-effects of psychotropic medication. She has recently established a UK-wide Neuroleptic Malignant Syndrome database to widen interest in treatment and management of neuroleptic malignant syndrome, on which she is engaged in research.

Alan Lee is an adult general psychiatrist with a research interest in patients with affective disorders and their long-term outcomes. He works as a Consultant Psychiatrist and Special Senior Lecturer, University Hospital, Nottingham NG7 2UH.

Shôn Lewis is Professor of Psychiatry at the University of Manchester (School of Psychiatry and Behavioural Sciences, Department of Psychiatry, Withington Hospital, Nell Lane, West Didsbury, Manchester M20 8LR). He did his MRCPsych and MD at the Institute of Psychiatry in London.

Richard Lingham (10 St John's Terrace, Devoran, Truro, Cornwall TR3 6NE) qualified as a psychiatric social worker in 1967, having trained at London University and the London School of Economics. During the 1970s he worked in Aberdeen and Buckinghamshire as Deputy Director of Social Services, and was Director of Social Services for Cornwall and the Isles of Scilly (1979–1987). In 1989 he was appointed a member of the Mental Health Act Commission and in 1996 to the Mental Health Review Tribunal. He has been involved (as a member or chair) in six inquiries after homicides (1994–1998). In July 1998 he was appointed Chair of Cornwall and Isles of Scilly Health Authority.

Angus Mackay, OBE is Clinical Director for Mental Health, Argyll and Bute (Argyll and Bute Hospital, Blarburie Road, Lochgilphead, Argyll PA31 8LD), Member of the CSM, Chairman of the Mental Health Reference Group for Scotland; formerly Clinical Director of the MRC Neurochemical Pharmacology Unit and Lector in Pharmacology, Trinity College, Cambridge. Interests include the neurochemistry and neuropharmacology of schizophrenia.

Rob Macpherson is Consultant Rehabilitation/General Psychiatrist and Clinical Tutor at Wotton Lawn, Horton Road, Gloucester GL1 3WL. His MD thesis concerned patient education in schizophrenia. His ongoing research interests include various aspects of service provision and subjective patient experiences in severe mental illness.

Charles McMahon is a Consultant Psychiatrist in Substance Misuse at Renfrewshire Healthcare Trust, Dykebar Hospital, Grahamstone Road, Paisley PA2 7DE. He is particularly interested in the realtionships between drugs of misuse and psychiatric disorders, and in problems associated with chronic polydrug use.

Gethin Morgan is Director of Continuing Professional Development at the Royal College of Psychiatrists, 17 Belgrave Square, London SW1X 8PG.

Ann Mortimer became Foundation Chair in Psychiatry at the University of Hull (School of Medicine, Coniston House, East Riding Campus, Willerby HU10 6NS) in February 1996. Her research interests encompass a wide spectrum of psychosis, spanning genetic, neuropsychological, social and treatment issues. Management of schizophrenia with atypical neuroleptics and its consequences in terms of functional outcome is a particular focus of her work.

Margaret Oates is Senior Lecturer and Honorary Consultant in Psychiatry at the Queen's Medical Centre, University Hospital, Nottingham NG7 2UH. She runs a service for women suffering from psychiatric disorders associated with childbirth.

André Phanjoo graduated from Edinburgh University in 1966 and did his postgraduate training in psychiatry and the Royal Edinburgh Hospital and Department of Psychiatry, Edinburgh University. He is Clinical Director for the Care of the Elderly Unit in the Edinburgh Healthcare NHS Trust (Jardine Clinic, Royal Edinburgh Hospital, Morningside Terrace, Edinburgh EH10 5HF) and is Honorary Senior Lecturer in the Department of Psychiatry. His main research interests are in the pharmacological treatment of Alzheimer's disease and depression in the elderly.

Keith Rix is a Consultant Forensic Psychiatrist in Leeds (High Royds Hospital, Menston, Ilkley, West Yorkshire LS29 6AQ) and visiting consultant at HM Prison, Leeds. He is a member of the Association of Police Surgeons and frequently gives evidence on the reliability of police interviews.

Nicholas Seivewright is a Consultant Psychiatrist in Substance Misuse at Community Health Sheffield NHS Trust, Norfolk House, 4 Norfolk Street, Sheffield S1 2JB. For many years he has had two parallel interests, in research into personality disorders and in the clinical treatment of drug misuse. In addition to developing services in Sheffield, his current clinical and academic interests include benzodiazepine misuse, cocaine, and pharmacological treatments in addictions.

Geraldine Strathdee is currently a Consultant Psychiatrist working in a primary health care group locality in south London (Laurel House Commumnity Mental Health Centre, 2 Blean Grove, Maple Road, Penge SE20 8QU). She is also Director of the Implemens Network, a network of clinicians and managers actively engaged in developing effective and efficient mental health services. Service development and research interests include clinical effectiveness, primary care mental health, community psychiatry, and services for those with dual diagnosis.

Philip Timms is Senior Lecturer in Community Psychiatry at Guy's, King's and St Thomas's Medical School. He is a consultant psychiatrist with the START Team (1st Floor, Master's House, Dugard Way, London SE11 4TH), which provides mental health services for homeless people in south-east London. He is Editor of the Royal College of Psychiatrists' factsheets and 'Help is at Hand' leaflets and has an interest in clinical information systems and liaison with voluntary sector agencies.

Michael Travis is a Lecturer in the Section of Clinical Neuropharmacology at the Institute of Psychiatry (De Crespigny Park, Denmark Hill, London SE5 8AF) and Locum Consultant on the psychiatric intensive care unit at the Maudsley Hospital. He is supported by the Medical Research Council and is involved in research investigating the effects of psychotropic medication on neuroreceptors using single photon emission tomography.

Trevor Turner was appointed Consultant Psychiatrist at St Bartholomew's and Hackney Hospitals in 1987. He has a special interest in the problems of acute care in the inner city, with publications on Section 136, community care and the management of schizophrenia. He was Medical Director of the City and Hackney Community Services NHS Trust (1994–1998) and is based at the Department of Psychiatry, Homerton Hospital, Homerton Row, London E9 6SR.

Preface

Alan Lee

This collection is the first in a series which will bring together the most popular articles from the Royal College of Psychiatrists' Continuing Professional Development journal, *Advances in Psychiatric Treatment*. Although primarily aimed at senior psychiatrists, many of the journal's articles have enjoyed an unexpectedly wide circulation among trainees preparing for the membership (MRCPsych) examinations, as well as specialist registrars and non-medical mental health professionals. The articles reproduced here have been chosen on the basis of demand from this wider readership, and focus mainly on themes relevant to the general adult psychiatrist. They have been updated to provide a systematic, well-referenced and authoritative account of key clinical topics relating to modern therapeutic practice.

There is a natural tension between the aspirations of evidence-based medicine and the realities and uncertainties of day-to-day clinical psychiatry. Psychiatric trainees are often caught in the centre of this, and can doubt whether there is any middle ground where theory and practice can be integrated so that textbook learning can translate directly and meaningfully to the job at hand. *Advances in Psychiatric Treatment* was developed to help bridge this gap for senior psychiatrists, and it is hoped that this new book series will do the same for a wider audience. It should be a useful adjunct to the College Seminars titles for those preparing for examinations and their future careers.

Although each chapter stands alone, there is a continuity to this volume, and little overlap, so that the book tells a story which can be read from cover to cover. The result is a *Pilgrim's Progress* of psychosis, describing many of the vicissitudes which can mark the natural histories of patients with severe mental disorders. Psychiatry is indeed more than a science, and this is a moving account of how general adult psychiatry is struggling to stand alongside sufferers, their carers and the community. At a time when some fear that general psychiatry has entered a no-man's land, and others have predicted its early demise, readers may find inspiration and leadership here. What follows is an exciting portrayal of how modern psychiatric teams are responding in a practical, evidence-based and professional way to some of the most difficult clinical challenges of the post-asylum era.

This is a book that I would have liked to have been able to read before the MRCPsych examinations. I hope it will be useful to candidates, their teachers and their examiners alike. It is also a book to revisit in some of those soul-searching moments, when maintaining high standards of service in the face of limited resources can seem an improbable dream. That the writing can bridge the ideal standards of professional examinations and the realities of inner-city psychiatry is a great tribute to its authorship.

Thanks are due to the busy clinicians, many of whom are leaders in their various fields, who have generously shared their knowledge and expertise and produced such clear and accessible accounts of their practice. Thanks are also particularly due to Professor Andrew Sims for his energy and breadth of vision as the founding editor of *Advances in Psychiatric Treatment*, and to members of the Editorial Board who have ensured the high standard of articles throughout the journal. The publications team at the Royal College of Psychiatrists is to be congratulated; in particular, Andrew Morris, as Scientific Editor, and Louise Whalley, whose efficiency, tact and good sense as Editorial Assistant has made such a major contribution to the success of *Advances in Psychiatric Treatment* in its first four years.

Alan Lee
October 1998

Introduction

Gethin Morgan

The contributions to this, the first of a new series of books, address some of the most demanding situations encountered by the clinician. The broad subject range, including acute psychosis, schizophrenia and comorbid disorders, will undoubtedly be appreciated by clinicians in the light of their own specific interests and needs, but I venture here to offer a personal response to them. In reviewing them I quickly appreciated their succinct and direct approach to practical problems. The style of presentation, in which key points are summarised, helps the reader confirm what has been learnt, and indeed focuses attention very effectively.

The early chapters concern perhaps the most challenging of all situations we meet – the management of acutely disturbed behaviour, with particular attention to problems relevant to schizophrenic illnesses. The face-to-face approach in assessment and management helps to pinpoint the hazards that should be checked out and the management options which need to be considered. In such a crisis situation it can be so difficult to know which drug to use, and step-by-step guidance on both this and more general aspects of management is very helpful. Should we be tempted to escalate or resort to high-dose medication we are reminded of the many hazards which accompany such a strategy. Welcome guidance is given regarding assessment of the neuroleptic malignant syndrome, particularly with regard to its early detection in hospital ward settings.

The clinical task does not, of course, always end when treatment of the acute phase of schizophrenia is over and we are reminded that at most only 15% of patients in Western countries remain free of relapse after a first episode. And so there follows a series of articles on management of schizophrenic illness in the long term, with particular emphasis on pharmacological and psychological treatments, social and family factors as well as organisation of services. Prevention of relapse is not the only task

because there is much to be done in the management of unresolved symptoms and social defect. Factors which influence compliance with treatment are very usefully evaluated. Particularly welcome in these articles is a 'feet on the ground' approach, whereby the practical applicability of therapies in the reality of clinical care situations is never lost from sight.

The next group of articles deals with key strategic components in the development of community care services. They include how to organise a community mental health team, and the setting up of an assertive community treatment service. Without doubt much energy and, indeed, courage has been invested in developing treatment services in this way. We are rightly reminded that the care programme approach is the mainstay of how we should organise our clinical efforts.

Later articles are concerned with other aspects of acute clinical care. They are equally well directed at common yet important challenges in our day-to-day work. Comorbidity such as substance misuse, psychiatric aspects of childbirth, psychological illness in the elderly or problems related to learning disabilities – all these present their own special challenges and they are well addressed here. Finally, should our clinical duties take us to the police station or courts, we are provided with useful guidance on how to proceed and document our findings.

Throughout this volume the vigour with which psychiatrists are facing the new and immense challenges presented by the present-day clinical scene is writ large. It should be a useful source of guidance and encouragement to all clinicians – those who are in training as well as consultants established in their field – not only to remain abreast of the latest developments, but also to feel confident that their speciality encompasses expertise which is based firmly on a well-researched scientific foundation.

Management of a newly admitted patient with acute disturbance

J. Cookson

Case history

A 25-year-old Bengali man was taken to casualty by relatives who were concerned about his unpredictable and dangerous behaviour. He lived close to his parents and five younger siblings, and there was no family history of mental disorder.

He had been born in Bangladesh and came to the UK at the age of 12 and completed his schooling. He had worked in the restaurant trade until two years earlier when he left his job after an argument with his employer. He had married at 22; his wife, who spoke little English, was pregnant and they had one son. He had been less regular in his attendance at the Mosque in the previous two years and recently had stopped altogether.

According to his father, he had started to behave strangely two years earlier when he stayed out of his home and neglected his family; he had accused his wife of infidelity. His father had persuaded him to return to Bangladesh where they stayed with an uncle in Sylhet and visited an Imam. They had also attended the psychiatrist at the town's medical college and he had received injections of fluphenazine decanoate and tablets of trifluoperazine and procyclidine. After four months, he had returned to England, and his family had noticed a marked improvement.

In the past four weeks he had again been staying out from home. He accused his brothers of trying to break up his marriage, and had been violent in his father's home; in a seemingly unprovoked attack he had tried to strangle his brother. He had at times sat motionless for long periods, and at others had appeared over-active, talking excitedly about his plans to take up a college course. His wife reported that she heard him shouting to himself during the night. He said that he had taken tablets obtained from a private general practitioner.

In the casualty department he was examined in a quiet area with a psychiatric nurse from the ward present, in keeping with the hospital's policy for the management of violence. When examined, he sat quietly with a tendency to a fixed gaze and was largely uncommunicative. He appeared tense and preoccupied, but laughed suddenly at times. He was abusive about his brothers, and thought that the doctor was aware of all his personal circumstances: "You know all about me. Don't ask more questions". He expressed plans to study and become a solicitor. He denied hearing voices, and no description of first-rank symptoms of schizophrenia was elicited. He said he felt fine and did not consider he had any health problems, but was willing to remain in hospital. He was unable to name the day of the week, but was otherwise orientated.

Physical examination

An examination showed a tachycardia of 115, blood pressure 140/95, and a temperature of 38°C. His skin was hot and sweaty. He had a moderate degree of rigidity in the upper limbs, but no 'cogwheeling' or tremor.

The provisional assessment was of an acute psychotic illness with suspected auditory hallucinations, persecutory and grandiose ideas and an irritable and elated affect that was rather incongruous. The occurrence of rigidity was noted, and led the admitting doctor to include neuroleptic malignant syndrome (NMS) in the list of diagnostic possibilities, which included schizophrenia and bipolar disorder, and catatonia which might also be symptomatic of these. Although the clouding of consciousness and fever might be manifestations of NMS, he was thought to require additional physical investigations to exclude possible infections.

Initial management

Admission to hospital was necessary for further psychiatric assessment, and to carry out investigations. It was decided to avoid antipsychotic medication until the diagnosis was clearer. He was admitted to a side-room on an open psychiatric ward with a nurse assigned to be with him continuously at first. Referral was made by the hospital psychiatric social worker to the district's Bengali Social Work Team, with a request for them to liaise with the wife and family.

Investigations

Blood tests were taken for full blood count, urea and electrolytes, liver function tests, creatine kinase, and thyroid function tests, and a urine specimen was obtained for microscopy and culture and for a drug screen. These investigations were all normal with the exception of creatine kinase which was raised at 900 units/l. On the advice of the physicians, an electroencephalogram and CAT brain scan were performed and showed no abnormality. It was concluded that he probably had the early stages of NMS, but was otherwise physically well, and that he had a psychotic illness which might include catatonic symptoms.

Further observation

'As required' medication with oral diazepam 10–20 mg was prescribed to a maximum of 60 mg daily. Further information was to be sought about his recent medication.

On the ward his behaviour was unpredictable and he failed to settle at night. He was given two doses of diazepam 20 mg. The following morning he awoke and suddenly seized the nurse who was sitting with him, saying that she was interfering with him. He had to be restrained. His management was reviewed by the doctor and nurses and a request was made that he should be transferred to the psychiatric intensive care unit (PICU), a small locked ward with a higher staff : patient ratio, and staff trained in techniques of control and restraint. His temperature had been normal since admission, but his blood pressure fluctuated. Although admission to the PICU did not in itself require compulsory detention, he was made subject to an order under Section 2 of the Mental Health Act 1983 because it had been necessary to restrain him for the protection of other people.

Within the PICU he was initially nursed in his own room, observed by two nurses; diazepam was given orally and he slept for long periods. On waking, however, he was apprehensive, highly aroused and impulsively violent to those around him. It was thought that he was having auditory hallucinations, but his speech was rambling and fragmented with a paranoid content. He was afebrile and his creatine kinase level was lower three days after admission.

Post-admission assessment

At the post-admission meeting under the Care Programme Approach (CPA), the history and assessment were reviewed. His general practitioner did not attend, but it was confirmed that he had been prescribed trifluoperazine 5 mg three times daily two weeks prior to admission, and according to his wife he had taken most of this. It was decided that he required antipsychotic medication for the treatment of his psychosis, and that in order to reduce the risk of NMS recurring, phenothiazines should be avoided, and creatine kinase and temperature should be monitored. Oral haloperidol was to be given, initially in a dose of 5 mg. Procyclidine 5 mg was to be given with each dose of haloperidol to reduce the risk of acute dystonia, to which young males in particular are liable.

The meeting identified the community psychiatric nurse who would be involved in the patient's aftercare, and who should be invited to the next CPA meeting. The patient was considered to have a risk factor (serious aggressive behaviour during relapse) which would probably make him suitable for inclusion on the supervision register prior to discharge.

Drug treatment

The junior doctors responsible for urgent decisions about psychotropic medication were aware of the 'Guidelines for the pharmacological management of violent psychiatric patients' – a document produced with collaboration between the psychiatric department and the hospital pharmacist. The document summarises the advantages and disadvantages of different classes of drugs (antipsychotics, benzodiazepines and amylobarbitone), and different routes of administration (oral, intramuscular, intravenous or depot) in the management of acute behavioural disturbance. It provides detailed advice on doses for individual antipsychotics (chlorpromazine, haloperidol and zuclopenthixol), benzodiazepines (diazepam, lorazepam and clonazepam) and amylobarbitone. Junior doctors are introduced to this document as part of their induction course on joining the psychiatric department.

In this case, the use of diazepam was favoured by the patient's willingness to accept oral medication (diazepam is less rapidly absorbed by the intramuscular than the oral route); otherwise, lorazepam might have been used intramuscularly (or either diazepam or lorazepam intravenously).

The shorter duration of action of lorazepam was considered a disadvantage. Some benzodiazepines are effective in the longer-term control of mania (e.g lorazepam in high doses), but others (clonazepam and diazepam) benefit mania and schizophrenia mainly by virtue of their short-term sedative and anxiolytic properties. The choice of antipsychotic lay mainly between haloperidol, zuclopenthixol and sulpiride. Sulpiride was not favoured because of the lack of parenteral formulations. Haloperidol was preferred as being available by oral, intravenous and depot formulation; if the patient had consistently refused oral medication after being given an injection (of a benzodiazepine), then zuclopenthixol would have been preferred because of the availability of the short-acting depot acetate formulation, which can be used to avoid repeated confrontations with reluctant or struggling patients. In this case, in view of the risk of NMS, haloperidol was thought preferable as its duration in the body would be shorter than zuclopenthixol acetate. Haloperidol blocks mainly dopamine but also noradrenaline alpha-1 receptors. Zuclopenthixol differs from haloperidol also in having a broader spectrum of pharmacological activity and being more sedative; it is not available for intravenous use.

On commencing antipsychotic medication, the symptoms which were targeted (for monitoring the patient's response) were the apparent auditory hallucinations and unpredictable aggressive behaviour, the incongruous laughter and the abnormalities of speech which made the patient difficult to understand. These positive symptoms tend to improve slowly (from 2 to 6 weeks) in schizophrenia, but more quickly in mania. In addition, it was expected that the use of an antipsychotic would contribute a more immediate sedative effect, reducing hostility and overactivity.

On commencing haloperidol there was no increase in body temperature and no return of muscular rigidity. Creatine kinase level measured after one and three days showed no elevation. It was therefore decided to increase the dose of haloperidol to 5 mg three times daily together with procyclidine 5 mg three times daily. Two days later, the patient remained unpredictably aggressive and was still being given diazepam up to 60 mg daily. The dose of haloperidol was increased from 15 to 30 mg and later 40 mg daily.

Further progress

Two weeks after commencing haloperidol, the patient was still in need of close observation, but less diazepam (given 'as needed') was being used to reduce the risk of his sudden impulsive

behaviour. He had established a relationship of trust with nurses and had reported auditory command hallucinations telling him to attack people. He did not feel the nurses were hostile to him. His speech was more normal in speed and less disjointed. A grandiose content remained and his mood was still elated. Full blood count and liver function tests were repeated to detect any idiosyncratic hepatic or bone marrow reaction to the antipsychotic. It was considered whether to increase the dose of haloperidol or to change to another drug. The same dose was continued in order to allow the anti-schizophrenic effect a full 4–6 weeks to develop.

After six weeks of antipsychotic treatment the patient remained on the PICU, but did not require continuous individual nursing attention. His sleep remained brief and he continued elated and grandiose. He was no longer showing evidence of auditory hallucinations and his speech was less disjointed. In view of the residual manic symptomatology and the tendency to impulsive behaviour he was commenced on carbamazepine. The dose of haloperidol – which might otherwise have been reduced at this time – was maintained, because of the tendency of carbamazepine to induce liver enzymes which metabolise other drugs including haloperidol. Treatment with lithium was also considered, but in view of the atypical or schizoaffective pattern of his illness, it was considered less likely to be useful, and the patient was reluctant to have regular blood tests. He and his family were informed of the nature of carbamazepine, the rare risk of serious allergic reactions including agranulocytosis, and the importance of reporting rashes, sore throats or fevers. Blood was to be taken after 2–3 weeks for a blood count, to provide early detection of a delayed hypersensitivity reaction affecting the bone marrow; liver function tests were also to be performed, as were urea and electrolytes to detect hyponatraemia.

The dose of carbamazepine was increased gradually from 100 to 600 mg daily over the course of two weeks, to reduce early side-effects such as nausea, dizziness, drowsiness and headaches. After two weeks there was further improvement, particularly in the patient's elation, impulsivity and grandiosity; unescorted leave in the hospital grounds was satisfactory, and plans were made for his transfer to an open ward, from where he might begin to have leave from the hospital.

Follow-up

He continued to improve but was thought to have some residual negative symptoms. Prior to discharge a community psychiatric nurse was introduced to him, and a member of the Bengali social work team was assigned to be his keyworker. He was placed on the supervision register. He was advised that he should continue on carbamazepine and haloperidol, with the possibility that depot antipsychotic medication might be more helpful in the future. He returned to live with his wife, and attended out-patients.

Comment

The case, which is fictitious, is presented not as a model of good practice, but as a vignette to illustrate important decision points that are likely to arise (Box 1).

Management of such a case will vary according to local circumstances which will have brought about development in particular areas, according to prevailing needs and resources. Box 2 lists local policies which may be useful in the management of acutely disturbed patients. The following may merit further discussion or commentary from readers.

Management of violence

Hospitals should have a written procedure for the prevention and management of violence. There should also be a policy setting out criteria for different levels of nursing supervision, and systems for reviewing and recording the level required. The development of an intensive care unit can benefit the whole hospital by encouraging expertise in the provision of care to patients during acute exacerbations of their illness with less reliance on sedative medication (Hyde & Harrower-Wilson, 1994). Again, a written operational policy is useful to ensure that appropriate patients are admitted. Restraint and seclusion may also be necessary (Fisher, 1994). The Royal College of Psychiatrists' Research Unit (1998) has published guidelines on *Management of Imminent Violence*.

Box 1. Discussion points

Differential diagnosis
Role of psychiatric intensive care unit
Rapid tranquillisation; choice of drug and dose
Carbamazepine
Use of supervision register
Ethnic aspects

Box 2. Useful policies in the management of acute behavioural disturbance

Hospital policy on management of violence
Intensive care unit: operational policy
Policy on level of nursing observation
Pharmacy policy on prescribing for acutely disturbed patients
Care Programme Approach implementation policy
Policy for supervision register

Drugs for rapid tranquillisation

The relative merits of antipsychotics and benzodiazapines were discussed by Dubin (1988). A number of psychiatrists favour a combination of haloperidol and diazepam (Pilowski *et al*, 1992). The majority of studies of randomised trials of haloperidol in compliant patients have found no advantages, in terms of eventual control of schizophrenic symptoms, in exceeding standard doses (10–20 mg/day), and that very high doses (100–240 mg/day) are associated with more side-effects and the risk of sudden death (see King, 1994).

For rapid tranquillisation however, higher doses may provide a greater degree of sedation; in this situation the more sedative drugs, such as zuclopenthixol and chlorpromazine, may be helpful, by virtue of their histamine and alpha-1 receptor blocking effects. The *Drug and Therapeutics Bulletin* (1991) stated that intramuscular chlorpromazine should be avoided as it crystallises in the tissues; this was retracted in the subsequent issue. But chlorpromazine can produce serious hypotension. Droperidol, a drug with potent dopamine and noradrenaline alpha-1 receptor blocking actions, is also liable to lower blood pressure, especially in a dehydrated patient.

High-dose antipsychotic medication

The Royal College of Psychiatrists' consensus statement on high-dose antipsychotic treatment does not address the use of antipsychotics for acute tranquillisation, but rather the longer-term management of psychosis (Thompson, 1994). However, it is relevant in its recommendation that care must be taken if exceeding the upper limit of doses specified by the *British National Formulary* (BNF) and, in turn, in the data sheets produced by the Association of the British Pharmaceutical Industry (ABPI). Following a change in the data sheet for haloperidol, the upper limit for severe or resistant cases of psychosis or dangerously impulsive behaviour in adults is now given as 5 mg three times daily. In adolescents, however, the dose may be up to 60 mg daily and in people with treatment-resistant schizophrenia the dose may be up to 120 mg daily. In the face of such conflicting information, the clinician must also follow the advice (Thompson, 1994) that a consultant's opinion should be obtained before the upper limit is exceeded, and a note should be made of the reasons for doing so. The use of very high doses should be a last resort when other means of treatment have failed (Hirsch & Barnes, 1994).

There is no known pharmacological rationale for the efficacy of high-dose antipsychotics (Mackay, 1994), but our understanding of the mechanism of drugs such as clozapine in schizophrenia remains incomplete.

Sudden unexplained deaths

One of the reasons for caution in the use of medication for the acutely disturbed patient is the number of reports of sudden unexplained deaths in this situation. In some cases, deaths have been associated with high blood levels of antipsychotics (Jusic & Lader, 1994). However, some cases have involved standard doses of drugs including haloperidol or chlorpromazine, given parenterally, sometimes combined with benzodiazepines or amylobarbitone. Young men and those with physical illness (e.g. diabetes) are particularly vulnerable. Cardiac arrhythmias may be responsible in some cases, but in others, respiratory depression (by accumulated doses of barbiturates or benzodiazepines) or laryngeal dystonia causing stridor and hypoxia may be involved.

In the struggling or highly aroused patient, high levels of catecholamines (noradrenaline and adrenaline), which increase myocardial excitability, may be dangerous if the repolarisation process in the heart (due to activation of potassium conductance and inactivation of calcium conductance) is prolonged. Abnormal repolarisation may be evident in the electrocardiogram as a prolonged Q–T interval or abnormal T waves. Certain antipsychotics (e.g. pimozide and thioridazine) are known to interact with calcium or calmodulin in the heart to interfere with repolarisation, causing prolongation of the Q–T interval and abnormal T waves. Many other antipsychotics (phenothiazines and butyrophenones, but less so benzamides and thioxanthines) are known to have membrane-stabilising effects at very high doses. These effects (also known as quinidine-like, local anaesthetic, or type-1 antiarrhythmic) involve blockade of sodium channels. In this regard, the antipsychotics resemble tricyclic antidepressants and would be expected to cause atrioventricular or intraventricular conduction delays including AV block or bundle branch block.

It remains unclear how standard doses of these antipsychotics might interact with states of excitement or exhaustion to produce fatal arrhythmias. When high doses of antipsychotics are used, or if the intravenous or parenteral route is used for sedation, the patient should not be left unattended. The nurse assigned to them should check and record the pulse, blood pressure and respiration and should be sufficiently trained to recognise symptoms of respiratory depression, dystonia or dysrhythmia. In case of respiratory depression, they should be able to provide oxygen through a mask or an Ambu bag, and be aware of the need to alert medical staff.

Initiating carbamazepine

Care is required in the use of carbamazepine because of the risk of allergic reactions. The current ABPI data sheet recommends that blood tests be carried out before starting treatment and periodically during treatment, but that clinical monitoring is of primary importance. Earlier data sheets had advised more frequent blood counts. Although the license extends only to the prophylaxis of lithium-resistant manic–depressive psychosis, the drug is also useful in combination with haloperidol in excited patients with psychosis (Klein *et al*, 1984).

References

Drug and Therapeutics Bulletin (1991) Management of behavioural emergencies. *Drug and Therapeutics Bulletin, 29*, 62–64.

Dubin, W. R. (1988) Rapid tranquillisation: antipsychotic or benzodiazepines? *Journal of Clinical Psychiatry*, **49** (suppl. 12), 5–11.

Fisher, W. A. (1994) Restraint and seclusion: a review of the literature. *American Journal of Psychiatry*, **151**, 1584–1591.

Hirsch, S. R. & Barnes, T. R. E. (1994) Clinical use of high-dose neuroleptics. *British Journal of Psychiatry*, **164**, 94–96.

Hyde, C. E. & Harrower-Wilson, C. (1994) Psychiatric intensive care: principles and problems. *Hospital Update*, 287–295.

Jusic, N. & Lader, M. (1994) Post-mortem antipsychotic drug concentrations and unexplained deaths. *British Journal of Psychiatry*, **165**, 787–791.

King, D. J. (1994) The use of high doses of neuroleptics: the current situation. *International Clinical Psychopharmacology*, **9**, 75–78.

Klein, E., Bental, E., Lerer, B., et al (1984) Carbamazapine and haloperidol v. placebo and haloperidol in excited psychoses. *Archives of General Psychiatry*, **41**, 165–170.

Mackay, A. V. P. (1994) High dose antipsychotic medication. *Advances in Psychiatric Treatment*, **1**, 16–23.

Pilowski, L. S., Ring, H., Shine, H. G., et al (1992) Rapid tranquillisation. A survey of emergency prescribing in a general psychiatric hospital. *British Journal of Psychiatry*, **160**, 831–835.

Royal College of Psychiatrists' Research Unit (1998) *Management of Imminent Violence. Clinical Practice Guidelines to Support Mental Health Services*. Occasional Paper OP41. London: Royal College of Psychiatrists.

Thompson, C. (1994) The use of high dose antipsychotic medication. *British Journal of Psychiatry*, **164**, 448–458.

Guidelines for the management of patients with acute disturbance

Rob Macpherson, Bryan Anstee & Roland Dix

Treatment of acutely disturbed patients is a stressful area of psychiatric practice. Castle *et al* (1994) found that MRCPsych Part II trainees expressed a general dissatisfaction with training in the management of violence, and in our experience junior trainees are even less confident in the treatment of the disturbed patient. A survey by Cunnane (1994) found that no consensus exists among consultant psychiatrists on which drug treatment is most appropriate for the management of the aggressive, acutely disturbed patient with psychosis. There was uncertainty as to optimal management, low expectation of quick results, unwillingness to express an opinion and the use of drug cocktails of dubious rationale.

The Royal College of Psychiatrists' report (1993) on high-dose antipsychotic treatment gave no specific guidance in the area of managing acutely disturbed patients. However, a subsequent survey (Palmer, 1996) by the Clinical Practice Guidelines Steering Group of the Royal College of Psychiatrists found that 50% of all professionals and service users considered "risk assessment and management of deliberate self-harm and dangerousness" to be a priority area for guideline development. Subsequently, the Royal College of Psychiatrists' Research Unit (1998) has produced a systematic review including clinical practice guidelines on the management of violence.

In this context, and in collaboration with colleagues in the Severn NHS Trust, we produced a general set of principles to cover general aspects of the management of the acutely disturbed patient, as well as drug treatment. These guidelines were not intended to be a rigid protocol but represent a tried and tested line of management. They are based on a review of the literature and refer specifically to medication schedules produced by Tardiff (1992) and Dubin & Feld (1989).

Rapid tranquillisation

Rapid tranquillisation with antipsychotics has demonstrated efficacy in acute behaviour disturbance secondary to schizophrenic psychosis (Tupin, 1985) and in controlling agitation of diverse aetiology including personality disorder, alcohol intoxication and delirium (Clinton *et al*, 1987). Because of the risk of severe side-effects with high-dose antipsychotics, particularly the risk of sudden death, it is best practice to keep doses as low as possible (Royal College of Psychiatrists, 1993). Doses as low as 10 mg haloperidol daily have been shown to be effective in treating acute schizophrenic breakdown (Rifkin *et al*, 1991).

Sudden cardiorespiratory collapse associated with antipsychotic treatment, especially during a period of extreme physiological arousal, is well known (Lader, 1992), and a recent survey identified 15 of 206 deaths in detained patients as 'iatrogenic' (Banerjee *et al*, 1995). These authors raised concerns about the use of massive doses of medication or mixed drug combinations, in too frequent boluses, by inexperienced nurses and unsupervised trainee psychiatrists. The lack of subsequent untoward incident inquiry or agreed clinical protocol for treatment of aggression was highlighted.

Rapid tranquillisation with antipsychotics is generally effective in controlling behaviour, but the antipsychotic effect (i.e. versus delusions and hallucinations) is often delayed for several weeks (Donlon *et al*, 1980). Both benzodiazepine and antipsychotic treatment are effective in acute behaviour disturbance, the choice of treatment being determined largely by clinical presentation and drug side-effect profiles (Table 1).

Patients with respiratory disease who are retaining CO_2 should be treated with antipsychotics in preference to benzodiazepines, which can cause respiratory failure. A further potential problem with benzodiazepine treatment is behavioural

Table 1. The main side-effects in emergency treatment of disturbed patients

	Sedation	Postural hypotension	Parkinsonism	Neuroleptic malignant syndrome	Respiratory depression	Withdrawal syndrome	Ataxia
Chlorpromazine, thioridazine	Present	Present	Present	Present			
Haloperidol			Present	Present			
Droperidol	Present		Present	Present			
Benzodiazepine	Present				Present	Present	Present

disinhibition, which may occur particularly with short-acting drugs as the effects wear off.

Theoretically, in treating mania or acute psychosis, a two-step approach which allows initial trial of moderate dose antipsychotic treatment, and then introduces benzodiazepines in the event of non-response, allows for maximum benefits but minimises risk due to cumulative drug effects. Dubin (1988) recommends the first-line use of antipsychotic treatment in schizophrenia, and where severe agitation occurs in substance misuse. Benzodiazepines have demonstrated a useful role in the treatment of mania (Chouinard, 1985), mild behaviour disturbance secondary to substance misuse (Dubin, 1988), and in treating acute schizophrenic hyperarousal (Mendoza *et al*, 1987). They may be of particular value in treating disturbed patients where the underlying diagnosis is not yet clear, pending determination of whether further treatment, aimed at psychotic symptoms, is needed. The antipsychotic side-effect akathisia has been associated with physical assault (Crowner *et al*, 1990), and the presence of this may be important in deciding between antipsychotic or benzodiazepine (or both concurrently) interventions for short-term behavioural control.

The survey by Cunnane (1994) showed that standard management in the UK in this area does not usually follow protocols suggested for rapid tranquillisation. Intermittent or fixed dosage regimes are commonly used, and in order to avoid drug accumulation with the frequent dosing regimes advocated in most rapid tranquillisation policies, it is clearly best practice to switch as soon as possible to regular, fixed-dose regimes, which can then be adjusted according to response, towards a regime appropriate for longer-term treatment (in the case of schizophrenia, possibly including the establishment of intramuscular depot medication). For similar reasons, we have included in the guidelines the schedule for administration of intramuscular zuclopenthixol acetate, a widely used treatment which has the advantages of lower dosing frequency.

In these authors' view, because of the risk of cardiopulmonary collapse, intravenous treatment should be avoided. It can only be given if medical staff skilled in resuscitation and resuscitation equipment are available (*Drug and Therapeutics Bulletin*, 1995).

Psychological and environmental factors

Although these factors play a crucial part in determining the outcome of treatment, there is surprisingly little research in this area. A literature review (Shugar & Rehaluk, 1990) found no empirical studies of the value of continuous observation. Most studies were completed by nurses in an area which is perhaps inappropriately viewed as representing nursing, rather than multidisciplinary, practice. However, Davies (1989) has produced an excellent overview of the issues that are important in preventing assault on professional helpers. Stevenson (1991) reviewed 'de-escalation', a range of theoretical techniques which aim "by redirecting the patient towards a calmer personal space", to reduce anxiety, maintain control and avoid aggressive acting out. Attention to personal issues in staff and efforts to avoid creating guilt and shame in clinicians by discussing difficulties without laying blame is likely to help in understanding and preventing repeated aggression (Vincent & White, 1994). Theoretical frameworks which aim to understand and predict aggressive behaviour may be of value (Boettcher, 1983), particularly in units such as the psychiatric intensive care unit which commonly deal with potentially aggressive or violent patients. Training and education in aggression management and control and restraint techniques are available, and nursing staff with the ENB 956 clinical course in the assessment and management of the acutely disturbed patient are likely to make a particular contribution to care planning.

These guidelines are aimed, in a climate of increasing medico-legal concern, at incorporating theory around best practice and recognising the value of practice recommended and sanctioned by a group of consultant psychiatrists, mental health professionals from other disciplines and pharmacists. The authors hope that these guidelines will be subjected to clinical audit so that it may be possible to validate particular treatments for specific subgroups of patients and clinical situations.

Assessment of patients

Taking a full history from the patient is not usually possible in the acute situation, and it is often necessary to accept some degree of diagnostic uncertainty in the early stages of treatment. Obtain:

(a) as full a history as possible from the patient, family, old case notes and information from the police/GP; and
(b) a comprehensive mental state examination, with particular attention to hostility, aggression and withdrawal, and their relationship to manic and psychotic symptoms.

Make a provisional diagnosis of:

(a) acute psychosis or mania;
(b) acute confusional state; or
(c) acute stress reaction in a vulnerable individual.

Initial management is broadly similar, but if the diagnosis is confusional state, investigate medically and start physical treatment as well as psychiatric management.

Management of patients

Environment

Patients usually respond best in a quiet, unstimulating environment with consistent nursing staff present. Early involvement of the psychiatric intensive care unit staff (ideally including discussion prior to admission) is advisable, with a view to rapid transfer of aggressive patients.

In units which use seclusion for the management of severe aggression, a formal seclusion policy should be fully operational, and this must be understood and followed by all staff.

The level of nursing supervision should be determined by multi-disciplinary assessment, and reviewed at least each nursing shift. Supervision should be reduced as soon as possible, by consultation between the nurse in charge and the responsible medical officer (RMO)/duty doctor. Close observation should only be carried out by nurses trained in appropriate techniques. The levels of observation are:

level 1– 'special' observation: one-to-one contact continuously
level 2 – 15-minute checks (documented), plus continuous awareness of whereabouts
level 3 – awareness of whereabouts at all times.

Prolonged 'special' observation can exacerbate behaviour disturbance. The value of inobtrusive monitoring, as opposed to direct observation, should always be considered. Intermittent rather than regular fixed time checks may be more effective.

Staff safety

The following suggestions will help to reduce the occurrence and severity of assaults on staff.

(a) When interviewing a patient who has a potential for aggressive behaviour, always inform nursing staff of your intentions and location.
(b) Try to conduct joint medical and nursing assessments to protect interviewers and reduce stimulation to the patient.
(c) Request the hand-held assault alarm available on each ward and keep this on your person throughout the interview.
(d) Sit at an angle to the patient, at a safe distance, in close proximity to the exit. Always avoid interviewing with the patient between you and the door.

Remember to put safety of people first. If a situation is escalating beyond the capacity of the hospital team to cope with it, call the security services or the emergency services on (9) 999. Do not attempt restraint unless there is sufficient back-up (usually a three-person control and restraint specialist nursing team).

Psychological approaches

A calm, consistent approach by the nurses and other staff is needed. Talking down, distraction and other de-escalation techniques are useful. Skilled, confident staff experienced in this area, ideally who already have a trusting relationship with the patient, are likely to be most effective.

Explain that it is the aggressive/threatening behaviour which is the problem, and that the patient is not being punished or harmed by the treatment. Remember that aggressive patients are usually frightened and anxious so they need explanations of what is being done to them, and why. They should be involved as much as possible in their treatment plan.

Separation from stressful family relationships is often helpful in reducing anxiety and over-stimulation.

Mental Health Act status

If a patient is resisting and aggressive, and refusing treatment or threatening to leave the ward, and still informal, the RMO or duty consultant should be called to make a Mental Health Act assessment. Use of Section 5 (II) may be necessary to prevent a patient from leaving the ward, although it does not allow treatment without the patient's consent.

A patient on Section 2 or 3 can be given intramuscular treatment with antipsychotics including zuclopenthixol acetate without consent.

In an emergency situation, a dangerous patient can be given intramuscular medication under common law, that is without Section, to calm and make safe, while a Section assessment is awaited.

Drug treatment

Drug treatment is needed when behaviour is out of control, and should be given early and consistently, in sufficient doses to bring the situation under control.

It is necessary to review the drug history to find the drug of choice and any contraindications. If not available, consider the following immediate management strategies.

Option A (intramuscular zuclopenthixol acetate)

In treating acute psychosis, providing no contra-indications exist (these include being antipsychotic naïve), give zuclopenthixol acetate 100 mg intra-muscularly and a further 50 mg after 2–4 hours if no improvement. Further zuclopenthixol acetate up to 150 mg intramuscularly may be administered the following day if sedation and acute symptom control is insufficient (maximum accumulated dose 400 mg intramuscularly over three days).

Note In order to judge whether a patient will maintain refusal to cooperate with oral treatment, it is generally preferable when instigating treatment to give at least one intramuscular injection of a shorter-acting drug.

Table 2. Daily oral antipsychotic maximum doses	
Drug	Oral maximum daily (mg)
Chlorpromazine	1000
Clozapine	900
Droperidol	120
Flupenthixol	18
Fluphenazine	20
Haloperidol	200
Loxapine	250
Methotrimeprazine	1000
Pericyazine	300
Prochlorperazine	100
Pimozide	20
Risperidone	16
Sulpiride	2400
Thioridazine	600 (800 up to 4 weeks)
Trifluoperazine	80
Zuclopenthixol	150

Option B (rapid tranquillisation)

Oral Give chlorpromazine 50 mg test dose by mouth and observe for postural hypotension. If this is not a problem, give oral chlorpromazine 100 mg at 30- to 60-minute intervals until the patient is calm or sleep is induced (maximum daily dose 600 mg).

Alternatively, give haloperidol 10 mg orally at 30- to 60-minute intervals until the patient is calm and behaviour is settled (maximum daily dose 60 mg).

Intramuscular Give intramuscular haloperidol 5–10 mg test dose. Observe for postural hypotension. If this is not a problem, give intramuscular haloperidol 10 mg every 30 minutes until the patient is calm (maximum daily dose 60 mg).

Alternatively, use intramuscular droperidol 5 mg test dose. Observe for postural hypotension. If this is not a problem, give intramuscular droperidol 5–10 mg up to four-hourly until the patient is calm (maximum dose 60 mg).

Option C (fixed-dose regimes)

Repeating medication administration half-hourly or hourly may only be practical if accepted orally, and if repeatedly enforced is likely to result in greater conflict, re-escalating aggression and hostility to staff, and undermining of the thera-peutic relationship. In all cases, the treatment should move towards a regular, fixed-dose oral/depot regime as soon as possible, and this will often be possible from the beginning of a treatment episode.

Commonly used fixed-dose regimes of the various drugs are as follows, but determining the effective treatment dosage will always depend on individual response: (a) chlorpromazine 50–200 mg oral three times daily; (b) haloperidol 5–10 mg oral three times daily; (c) droperidol 5–10 mg oral three times daily.

Cumulative antipsychotic dose, including as-required doses, should be kept within maximum daily limits, as in Table 2 (refer to *British National Formulary* if in doubt). Polypharmacy with more than one antipsychotic preparation should be avoided. As sudden, large increases in anti-psychotic dose can cause serious problems, dose titration is very important.

Suggested treatment in the event of non-response to option A, B or C

Always discuss this situation with the consultant. It is necessary to review the diagnosis and environmental factors. Treatment options include the following.

Benzodiazepines   Add lorazepam oral/intra-muscular 2–4 mg every 1–2 hours (maximum daily dose 10 mg). Or diazepam 10 mg oral four-hourly (maximum daily dose 40 mg)

Barbiturates   Consider only where a full trial of antipsychotic and benzodiazepine treatment has failed *and* severely disturbed behaviour persists; add intramuscular amylobarbitone sodium 200 mg every 1–2 hours. Consider oral amylobarbitone sodium 200 mg as needed.

Patients treated acutely with benzodiazepines/barbiturates should be monitored for respiratory depression. If respiratory rate drops below 10 per minute while on benzodiazepine treatment, give flumazenil intravenously 200 µg over 15 seconds, then 100 µg at 60-second intervals, and seek medical support.

For elderly/debilitated patient

Reduce recommended doses by 50%. Drugs of choice for the elderly are thioridazine, starting with 10–25 mg orally, or haloperidol, starting with 0.5–1 mg orally/intramuscularly, with careful monitoring of blood pressure and physical state.

Side-effects

See Table 1 for an overview of the main side-effects in emergency treatment.

Neuroleptic malignant syndrome (NMS) usually presents with muscular rigidity, pyrexia and confusion, but partial syndromes are common. If suspected, substitute benzodiazepines for antipsy-chotics and check white cell count and creatinine kinase (both usually raised in NMS). Neuroleptic malignant syndrome is a medical emergency and requires urgent medical advice/admission.

Physical support

Ensure that a balanced diet and adequate fluids are offered to the patient. Consider charting fluid intake if problematic. For patients on recently increased high dose antipsychotics, six-hourly temperature, pulse and respiration should be checked, and consider serial electrocardiograms. A screen of blood tests is helpful, to exclude serious coexisting or underlying pathology.

Staff support

Inform consultant early and discuss regularly thereafter. Multi-disciplinary team meetings are an essential focus for management planning. Regular, daily review of drugs/environmental regime is necessary. Involvement of the patient's family may be useful, particularly to ensure that the frequency of visiting is not causing problems of excess stimulation.

Remember the stress of being exposed to aggression and paranoid criticism/hostility, and try to support colleagues and admit to personal frailties, anxieties and feelings of helplessness.

Management after an aggressive incident

Despite preventive and coping strategies, incidents will nevertheless happen, and there is a risk of compounding difficulties by unhelpful criticism. Victims need sympathy, support and reassurance, not just in the short term. Support may helpfully involve the spouse in some cases, and in a severe reaction the possibility of professional counselling should be considered. The issue of whether to prosecute the aggressor is one for the victim, who may be helped by talking this through with colleagues or managers.

For professionals who are assaulted, it is advisable to return to work as soon as possible (perhaps taking no time off), to prevent the 'incubation of fear' which can occur.

In the management of a severe aggressive incident, immediate safety must be secured prior to any investigation. The investigation should attempt as sensitively as possible to compile detailed reports around the incident so as to understand its causes, context and consequences, in staff and patient groups. The aim should be to generate a positive, constructive atmosphere in which the incident can be reviewed honestly and openly, and constructive lessons learned for the future.

References

Banerjee, S., Bingley, W. & Murphy, E. (1995) *Deaths of Detained Patients.* London: Mental Health Foundation.

Boettcher, E. G. (1983) Preventing violent behaviour. An integrated theoretical model for nursing. *Perspectives in Psychiatric Care,* **2,** 54–58.

Castle, D., Reeve, A., Ivinson, L., *et al* (1994) What do we think about our training? *Psychiatric Bulletin,* **18,** 357–359.

Chouinard, G. (1985) Anti-manic effects of clonazepam. *Psychosomatics,* **26,** 7–12.

Clinton, J. E., Sterner, S., Steimachers, Z., *et al* (1987) Haloperidol for sedation of disruptive emergency patients. *Annals of Emergency Medicine,* **16,** 319–322.

Crowner, M., Douyon, R., Convit, A., *et al* (1990) Akathisia and violence. *Psychopharmacology Bulletin,* **26,** 115–118.

Cunnane, J. G. (1994) Drug management of disturbed behaviour by psychiatrists. *Psychiatric Bulletin,* **18,** 138–139.

Davies, W. (1989) The prevention of assault on professional helpers. In *Clinical Approaches to Violence* (eds K. Howells & C. R. Hollin), pp. 311–328. Chichester: Wiley.

Donlon, P. T., Hopkin, J. T., Tupin, J. P., *et al* (1980) Haloperidol for schizophrenic patients: an evaluation of three oral regimes. *Archives of General Psychiatry,* **37,** 691–695.

Drug and Therapeutics Bulletin (1995) The drug treatment of patients with schizophrenia. *Drug and Therapeutics Bulletin,* **33,** 81–86.

Dubin, W. R. (1988) Rapid tranquillisation: antipsychotics or benzodiazepines? *Journal of Clinical Psychiatry,* **49,** 5–11.

—— & Feld, M. D. (1989) Rapid tranquillization of the violent patient. *American Journal of Emergency Medicine,* **7,** 313–320.

Lader, M. (1992) *Expert Evidence. Committee of Inquiry into Complaints about Ashworth Hospital.* Cm 2028. London: HMSO.

Mendoza, R., Djenderedjian, A. H., Adams, J., *et al* (1987) Midazolam in acute psychotic patients with hyperarousal. *Journal of Clinical Psychiatry,* **48,** 291–292.

Palmer, C. (1996) Clinical practice guidelines: the priorities. *Psychiatric Bulletin,* **20,** 40–42.

Rifkin, A., Doddi, S., Karajgi, B., *et al* (1991) Dosage of haloperidol for schizophrenia. *Archives of General Psychiatry,* **48,** 166–170.

Royal College of Psychiatrists (1993) *Consensus Statement on the Use of High Dose Antipsychotic Medication.* CR 26. London: Royal College of Psychiatrists.

Royal College of Psychiatrists' Research Unit (1998) *Management of Imminent Violence. Clinical Practice Guidelines to Support Mental Health Services.* Occasional Paper OP41. London: Royal College of Psychiatrists.

Shugar, G. & Rehaluk, R. (1990) Continuous observation for psychiatric inpatients: a critical evaluation. *Comprehensive Psychiatry,* **30,** 48–55.

Stevenson, S. (1991) Heading off violence with verbal de-escalation. *Journal of Psychosocial Nursing and Mental Health Services,* **29,** 6–10.

Tardiff, K. (1992) *Concise Guide to Assessment and Management of Violent Patients.* Washington, DC: American Psychiatric Press.

Tupin, J. P. (1985) Focal neuroleptization: an approach to optimal dosing for initial and continuing therapy. *Journal of Clinical Psychopharmacology,* **6,** 210–222.

Vincent, M. & White, K. (1994) Patient violence toward a nurse: predictable and preventable? *Journal of Psychosocial Nursing and Mental Health Services,* **32,** 30–32.

Commentary

Trevor Turner

There has long been considerable individual variation in the regimes for managing acutely disturbed patients, in terms of the drugs used, routes of administration and the dosages given. We all tend to learn from 'accepted' practice in the units in which we train, and the lack of good-quality controlled trials, published in leading and accessible journals, compounds the problem. Given the importance of this issue, when concerns about sudden death in the context of high dose regimes are generating considerable publicity (for example, Mind is calling for a blanket ban on dosages greater than those given in the *British National Formulary*), the need for rigorous research has never been greater. Guidelines have, however, become established in a number of units, and this clear summary by Macpherson *et al* is therefore to be welcomed, as is the recent publication on the *Management of Imminent Violence* (Royal College of Psychiatrists' Research Unit, 1998).

The authors have, understandably, concentrated on medication issues but their comments on staffing and environment are equally pertinent. There is evidence that increased proportions of agency staff are associated with increased levels of violence on a unit. Training and experience, as well as personal knowledge of patients (and vice versa) when they are well, can often prevent outbursts or alleviate disturbed situations. Being aware of predictors of violence in terms of previous history, symptoms, and levels of arousal (e.g. posture, sweating/respiration, eye contact) can ensure appropriate staffing levels and the early use of medication. We probably also undervalue the impact of environment. In Hackney our untoward incident rates on the wards, and the use of Section 5 (2), dropped by up to 50% when we moved from an old workhouse unit to new, purpose-built wards built around the principles of space and light.

In terms of the practical aspects of what to do, it may often seem impossible to carry out a true mental state assessment on a mute or screaming patient who is being restrained in a side room. Inexperienced trainees may feel that trying to clarify symptoms, while frustrated nurses are hanging on to the patient and expecting something to be done, is not worth the delay. Such assessments need a fine judgement, and an immediate clarification of who is in charge of a disturbed incident. Explaining to all, amidst a mêlée, what you are doing, why you are doing it, and what the treatment plan will be, can ensure good team work and coordinated activity. Visitors, other patients and family usually need to be kept out of the way. The straightforward act of constantly reassuring the patient that you are doctors and nurses, and here to help, seems obvious but is often forgotten. Documenting behavioural and mental state details, treatment plans, and medications given in clearly timed and dated notes are essential. It also gives one time to think, to clarify treatment steps, for example while awaiting responses to medication, and to ensure that other colleagues can easily acquaint themselves with what has happened. The doctor supervising acutely disturbed patients should stay on hand until the nurses feel assured that the situation is safe.

Given that most disturbed patients are well known to treatment units, and will not be neuroleptic naïve, it is vital that notes or summaries are easily accessible. We regularly reinstate depot, along with zuclopenthixol acetate and lorazepam if necessary, when a potentially violent patient is admitted on relapse. Two or three days' relative sedation, under good observation, is in the best interests of the patient, the family and the staff. The plea of an old patient, "doctor, don't let me get like that again", indicates the mental anguish of manic or confused sufferers. Likewise the use of liquid oral preparations, rather than tablets, for the suspiciously hostile, or the use of zuclopenthixol acetate (we have used it even at home with the support of the general practitioner, community nurses and the willing family) can ensure continued stabilisation.

Crucially, these guidelines outline the key need for much better audit and research of acute treatment approaches, and should be most useful in generating this process. Whether, however, we can provide the necessary numbers and quality of trained staff, in properly designed and therapeutic environments, is unfortunately much less certain. Resource limitations abound, and the shortage of trained mental health nurses requires thoughtful recruitment policies locally and nationally. Additional pay scales for staff in psychiatric intensive care units will have to equal the forensic lead available in most medium secure units now. Historically, psychiatry has been judged by its management of the 'furiously mad', and intensive care unit experience should be a *sine qua non* of both medical and nursing training.

Reference

Royal College of Psychiatrists' Research Unit (1998) *Management of Imminent Violence. Clinical Practice Guidelines to Support Mental Health Services*. Occasional Paper OP41. London: Royal College of Psychiatrists.

High-dose antipsychotic medication

A. V. P. Mackay

The dopamine hypothesis for the mode of action of antipsychotic drugs has been with us for 30 years and has, by and large, withstood the test of time. It simply states that antipsychotic drugs owe their therapeutic effects to an ability to block central dopamine receptors. This has given us a working and testable explanation for the effects of these drugs and has prompted the synthesis of new agents. While so-called antipsychotic drugs (otherwise known as neuroleptics or major tranquillisers) are known to be effective in schizophrenia and related psychoses, mania, and the agitation associated with severe depressive illness or organic disorder, this chapter is only concerned with the pharmacotherapy of schizophrenia.

Expose the brains of patients suffering from schizophrenic illness to a D_2 dopamine receptor blocker, and in seven cases out of ten there will be a useful amelioration of positive psychotic symptoms, usually within two months.

What do we do about the three patients out of ten who do not get better? Most clinicians edge the dose of antipsychotic medication up – sometimes past the point at which Parkinsonian signs become prominent, and usually within the dose maxima specified in the product licence as reproduced in the published ABPI Data Sheet Compendium and largely reflected in the *British National Formulary* (BNF) (Table 1). That would seem reasonable as a strategy to take account of individual differences in absorption, metabolism and elimination. However, still faced with therapeutic failure, the clinician sometimes pushes the dose further, into the realm of high-dose or 'mega-dose' therapy. Terminology here is loose, but the term 'high dose' is probably applicable at daily doses greater than 1000 mg chlorpromazine or 100 mg haloperidol, or equivalent (see Table 1), and the term 'conventional dose' will be used here to mean doses lower than these. It must be remembered that the pharmacological effect of more than one antipsychotic agent should be considered to be additive. Thus, in calculating whether or not the patient's medication should be considered 'high dose', the combined daily dose (expressed in mg equivalents) should be worked out.

Clinicians are commonly faced with patients suffering from schizophrenia who do not respond to conventional doses of antipsychotic drugs. Given that the upper dose limits specified in the data sheets and BNF have been chosen from available evidence on the risks and benefits, the clinician embarking on doses higher than these would do well to consider whether the benefits outweigh the possible risks and whether preferable alternatives exist. Before considering the issues relevant to these questions, it is necessary to have a working understanding of the current view on the mode of action and clinical use of antipsychotic drugs.

Table 1. Advisory maximum daily oral doses from the *British National Formulary*	
Drug	Dose (mg)
Sulpiride	2400
Chlorpromazine	1000
Clozapine	900
Thioridazine	800
Loxapine	250
Droperidol	120
Haloperidol	100
	(rarely 120)
Pimozide	20
Risperidone	16
Olanzapine	20

Mechanism of action

The dopamine hypothesis was derived largely from observations which we now know relate to one subtype of dopamine receptor, the D_2 receptor. This receptor is found in all brain areas to which dopamine-containing neurons project. They are richest in striatal areas such as caudate and putamen, and are also found in mesolimbic areas such as the amygdala, nucleus accumbens, cingulate and prefrontal cortex. It has been assumed that antipsychotic effects are mediated through actions at dopamine receptors in limbic areas.

All known antipsychotic drugs are antagonists at D_2 receptors, but their selectivity and potency vary considerably. By 'selectivity' is meant the 'cleanliness' of their pharmacology – which receptors other than D_2 receptors the drug might block.

'Potency' is a complex property, reflecting the bioavailability of the drug at strategic sites, and the affinity of the drug for the receptor; a drug with a high affinity will occupy a high percentage of receptors at relatively low drug concentration.

Antagonism at D_2 receptors is responsible for extrapyramidal side-effects and hyperprolactinaemia. Inference about the degree of D_2 receptor blockade in the basal ganglia from clinical extrapyramidal signs is complicated by the fact that coincidental blockade at acetylcholine and/or serotonin receptors will minimise or abolish the motor effects of D_2 blockade.

Other side-effects, such as sedation, postural hypotension, dry mouth, cardiotoxicity, and so on, are a result of the ability of many, if not most, antipsychotic drugs to act as antagonists at receptors other than D_2 and to affect membrane channels for ions such as Na^+ and Ca^{2+}. For example, H_1 and α_1 noradrenaline blockade may be associated with sedation and (in the latter case) with hypotension; acetylcholine receptor blockade is associated with dry mouth and other atropinic effects, and ion channel blockade may be the cause of disturbance in excitable tissue such as the myocardium.

To what extent the other receptor actions contribute to the antipsychotic effect originally credited to D_2 receptors remains a matter of fierce debate. The dopamine receptor family has now grown to comprise five clearly defined subtypes (D_{1-5}). Data on effects at D_2 receptors are by far the most plentiful, but information is growing on the action of antipsychotics at other dopamine receptors, notably D_3 and D_4, which appear to be particularly enriched in mesolimbic areas of the brain.

Clinical use of antipsychotics

The place of these agents is based predominantly on their ability to ameliorate the positive symptoms of schizophrenic illness, with associated behavioural improvement. A beneficial effect on negative symptoms is much less dependable. A fair degree of success is achieved in approximately 70% of patients suffering from schizophrenic illness, with benefits usually evident on diagnostic psychotic features within four to eight weeks.

However, antipsychotic drugs are also used routinely for a much less specific purpose: the control of disturbing and/or dangerous behaviour in the patient with acute psychosis. This effect is often sought in emergencies and during the early stages of treatment, before the onset of the truly antipsychotic action. Such behavioural control is often achieved only with accompanying sedation and possibly extrapyramidal impairment. (Sedation is not confined to antipsychotic drugs, as reduced arousal is a marked effect of benzodiazepines.)

Resort to high doses can occur in clinical situations of essentially two sorts:

(a) the subacute or chronic failure of the patient to experience any reduction in core psychotic symptoms; or
(b) the failure of conventional doses to ameliorate disturbing or dangerous behaviour.

While the issues considered below are relevant mainly to the problem of chronic treatment resistance, the principles also apply, to some extent, to the need for behavioural control.

Efficacy of high doses

There is no published evidence for the efficacy of high-dose medication as a generally effective strategy either to accelerate therapeutic response or to increase the number of patients who respond satisfactorily to medication – indeed, current opinion generally favours the use of quite modest doses of haloperidol (Hilton *et al*, 1996). Nor is there any evidence that escalating doses produce a response in chronically resistant patients (Kane, 1994).

Systematic studies of high-dose antipsychotics tend, naturally, to draw conclusions from averages, which may fail to reveal statistically significant differences while obscuring perhaps dramatic individual responses. Studies on treatment-resistant patients tend to involve small samples, and this could lead to type 2 statistical errors, through which differences are missed.

Despite the lack of support from the literature, there is a belief among clinicians that high doses may evoke a response where conventional doses have failed; this belief probably owes more to anecdotal experience than systematic study – we all tend to remember the occasional patient who did respond to high doses, but we should consider carefully the questions posed in Box 1.

Dangers of high doses

The possible dangerous results of high-dose antipsychotic medication are listed in Box 2.

Sudden death

The possibility that antipsychotic drugs, especially when used at higher than conventional doses, may be associated with sudden death has excited interest and concern within the media. It is a concern shared by the Royal College of Psychiatrists and the Committee on the Safety of Medicines, and definitive studies are being mounted in the UK to examine the issue. Unexpected, probably cardiac, deaths have been reported in psychiatric units (Simpson *et al*, 1987; Mehtonen *et al*, 1991) for which antipsychotic drugs have been blamed. In the latter study, from Finland, sudden deaths were associated with so-called low-potency drugs, such as the phenothiazines. It has been said that as many as 50 sudden deaths per year may be occurring in the UK among patients on antipsychotic drugs, but the precise figure and the identification of a causal link must await further study.

Suspicion is justified, since pharmacologically plausible mechanisms can be suggested for such a danger. The ability of some antipsychotics to produce profound hypotension has long been known, and probably relates to antagonism at noradrenaline receptors peripherally. A more sinister and covert action at sodium and calcium channels may result in severe cardiac dysrhythmias, even at conventional doses. Such effects may underlie the prolongation of the Q–T interval on electroencephalography, which has been reported with pimozide, and may also produce T wave changes and *torsades des pointes* (pleomorphic ventricular tachycardia).

Ion channel effects are particularly relevant to the question of high-dose medication since, unlike occupancy of transmitter receptors, effects at ion channels are effectively non-saturable; the higher the concentration of drug to which tissue is exposed, the higher the percentage of channels affected.

Extrapyramidal disorder

High dosing is associated with severe Parkinsonism and akathisia, but dystonias are less clearly dose

---

Box 1. Doctors contemplating the use of high-dose antipsychotic drugs consider

Are high doses effective?
What are the dangers?
What is the pharmacological rationale?
What are the alternatives?

Box 2. Dangers of high antipsychotic doses

Sudden death (through hypotension or cardiac dysrhythmia)
Severe extrapyramidal impairment
Neuroleptic malignant syndrome (related to rate of dose escalation)
'Paradoxical' deterioration of behaviour

---

related. Excessive dosing may even raise the probability of tardive dyskinesia.

Neuroleptic malignant syndrome

The risk of this potentially lethal syndrome is probably more closely related to the rate of dose escalation rather than the size of the dose *per se*.

Paradoxical/violent behaviour

Barnes & Bridges (1980) have reported the emergence of 'paradoxical' disordered behaviour in patients as the dose of antipsychotic rises. Severe akathisia may be expressed as a dramatic disturbance of behaviour. High doses of drugs with atropinic effects (such as thioridazine) may cause toxic confusional states due to blockade of central acetylcholine receptors.

It has also been suggested (Hirsch & Barnes, 1994) that a danger exists of 'withdrawal' rebound in behavioural disturbance during dose reduction following high doses.

Rationale for high doses

Despite the absence of firm evidence for efficacy and in the light of very real dangers, the case for the occasional use of high-dose medication in selected patients might be supportable if some *a priori* pharmacological justification could be provided.

It is well established that systemic concentrations of antipsychotic drugs, and in some cases active metabolites, vary considerably between people on the same oral dose. This variation probably arises out of differences in compliance, in first-pass metabolism (enzymatic breakdown in gut wall and liver), and in elimination. In most patients there is some sign or symptom signifying entry of pharmacologically active amounts of drug into the brain – be it extrapyramidal disorder or sedation – before the conventional dose ceiling is reached.

In the absence of any effect whatsoever within the conventional dose range, it may be reasonable to suspect a problem of absorption or elimination and to increase the dose until some effect on the central nervous system appears. If impaired oral bioavailability is suspected, or even non-compliance, then a trial of intramuscular medication might be considered (such as the relatively short-acting depot preparation, zuclopenthixol acetate). For those with access to such assays, measurement of plasma drug concentrations may provide a crude check on compliance and bioavailability.

Assuming that pharmacologically active concentrations of drug are being achieved in the systemic circulation (and this is likely in the vast majority of compliant patients within the conventional dose range), then there remain three theoretically possible justifications for high-dose exposure in resistant psychosis (see Box 3):

(a) conventional doses have not blocked a sufficient proportion of D_2 receptors generally in the brain; *or*

(b) conventional doses have not blocked D_2 receptors in the right place; *or*

(c) blockade at receptors *other* than D_2 is progressively recruited as the drug concentration rises, implying a lower affinity of the drug for other receptors which might contribute to the psychosis.

Incomplete D_2 blockade

Until recently it has not been possible to do anything other than guess at the percentage of D_2 receptors which might be blocked anywhere in the human brain at conventional doses of antipsychotic. An educated guess could have been made from the work of Hornykiewicz and his colleagues, who showed, from clinicopathological

deduction, that neurological signs appear in Parkinson's disease only after some 80% of dopamine cells are lost from the substantia nigra. A crude extrapolation might suggest, therefore, that some 80% of dopamine receptors might have to be blocked before Parkinsonian signs appear with antipsychotic medication.

This crude guess has been largely borne out by work using sophisticated isotope imaging techniques such as positron emission tomography (PET). Work, mainly from the Karolinska Institute, has shown the degree of D_2 blockade in the putamen of patients exposed to antipsychotic drugs. Parkinsonian signs were apparent in patients once 75–80% of D_2 receptors were blocked, and this happened in the majority of patients at doses of haloperidol below 15 mg per day (Farde *et al*, 1992). This is a most important reference point, since it means that substantial D_2 blockade is occurring, on average, at a dose some six times lower than the BNF ceiling.

Earlier studies had also suggested that over 80% of D_2 receptors are usually blocked well within the conventional dose range (Farde *et al*, 1988). A curvilinear relationship between receptor occupancy and drug concentration is evident, revealing that a very shallow part of the curve relating receptor occupancy to drug concentration is reached at around 80% receptor occupancy. Increases in drug dose thereafter appear to have a greatly decreased incremental effect on receptor blockade.

The conclusion of Farde *et al*, that past a certain point increased doses achieve little extra D_2 receptor blockade, has been confirmed by Wolkin *et al* (1989*a*). Wolkin and colleagues went further to explore with PET D_2 receptor blockade in people responsive and non-responsive to haloperidol. No difference in occupancy was found (Wolkin *et al*, 1989*b*).

Thus, overall, no support is evident from work on the basal ganglia for the use of high doses on the basis of blocking more D_2 receptors.

D_2 receptors in strategic areas

For increasing dose to produce D_2 blockade in certain brain areas, it must be postulated either that a barrier to drug distribution exists in some brain areas, or that D_2 receptors in, say, limbic fields have a lower affinity for antipsychotic drugs than in basal ganglia. Neither possibility seems likely. No site-specific barriers have been found for these drugs, and in any case antipsychotic drugs are highly lipid soluble.

Differential affinity between brain sites also appears unlikely; Leysen and colleagues have investigated the differential affinity of haloperidol and risperidone for limbic and striatal areas of

Box 3. Does giving high doses make any pharmacological sense?

Suggestion	Verdict
More complete D_2 receptor block	Unlikely
Blockade of D_2 receptors in inaccessible but important sites	Unlikely
Blockade of receptors other than D_2	Possible

mammalian brain *ex vivo*, and have found that the affinity of each drug for D_2 receptors in limbic areas is almost identical to its affinity in striatum (Schotte *et al*, 1993).

Increasing the dose above conventional limits seems unlikely to reach D_2 receptors in more useful places.

Non-D_2 receptors

It is possible that in some patients the neurochemical expression of schizophrenic illness is different from that in the majority; perhaps for these patients D_2 blockade is insufficient (or even unnecessary) to achieve a therapeutic response. Maybe in this minority the dopamine hypothesis does not hold true.

By increasing the dose are we recruiting blockade at receptors other than D_2? The answer is probably yes, but many candidates exist (Box 4).

Most antipsychotic drugs have a lower affinity at receptors other than D_2, but this is not the case for the currently popular 'atypical' antipsychotics. Much attention has recently been directed at the affinity of atypical drugs for 5-HT$_2$ and D_3/D_4 dopamine receptors. The latter are D_2-like but with quite distinct properties and distributions, which may help to explain the relative preference of clozapine for mesolimbic DA receptor fields, in contrast to typical antipsychotics (Pilowsky *et al*, 1997).

To visualise what happens when the dose of a drug is systematically increased, we have to be aware of the receptor profile of the drug – an image of the rank order of receptor affinities, or, in other words, which new receptors start to be blocked as the dose rises. Figure 1 represents a semi-quantitative attempt to draw dose–occupancy profiles for a small range of popular antipsychotic agents. These profiles might be seen as the receptor signature for each antipsychotic, and it can be seen that each signature is different.

A clinical reference point is the dose at which Parkinsonian signs appear – at that dose some 80% of D_2 receptors are likely to be blocked (Farde *et al*, 1992), although this inference is not possible with drugs having strong anticholinergic or antiserotonergic actions. The prototype antipsychotic, chlorpromazine, is remarkable for the range of receptors it blocks within a tight dose range (Fig. 1). Thioridazine has a similarly broad spectrum of action within a few dose multiples, in contrast to sulpiride, pimozide or haloperidol, which are relatively selective (Fig. 1). Clozapine, the prototype atypical neuroleptic, is distinguished by its relatively low affinity for D_2 receptors and remarkably high affinity for H$_1$, 5-HT$_2$, D_4 and α_1 noradrenaline receptors. Risperidone has extremely

---

> **Box 4. Receptors popularly associated with antipsychotic drug action**
>
> **Dopamine – D_1, D_2, D_3, D_4, D_5**
> **Noradrenaline – α_1**
> **Histamine – H_1**
> **Serotonin – 5-HT$_2$**
> **Acetylcholine (muscarinic) – ACh$_m$**

---

high affinity for 5-HT$_2$ and α_1 noradrenaline receptors, and also a high affinity for D_2 receptors. Ozanzapine, a recently marketed atypical, shows high affinity for 5-HT$_2$, H$_1$ histamine and D_2 receptors and, like clozapine but unlike risperidone, a high affinity for acetylcholine muscarinic receptors (Fig. 1).

Examination of these profiles can lead to many provisional deductions and suggestions, but some general conclusions might be permissible in relation to the use of high doses:

(a) high-dose medication is probably not required for substantial blockade of D_2 receptors; and

(b) high doses are not required for blockade of any of the receptor types shown in Figure 1; by selecting a particular antipsychotic according to its receptor profile, receptor blockade can be achieved within conventional dose ranges.

D_4 receptors

D_4 receptors have caused excitement through the publication by Seeman *et al* (1993) which reports a sixfold increase in the density of D_4 receptors in post-mortem brain tissue from people with schizophrenia compared with various controls. If D_4 is the target at which antipsychotic medication is unwittingly aimed, then sulpiride, thioridazine or clozapine should all be particularly effective drugs. While a special place for clozapine has been identified in the treatment of treatment-resistant schizophrenic illness (Kane *et al*, 1988; Baldessarini & Frankenburg, 1991), this has not yet been shown to be the case with other drugs capable of blocking D_4 receptors. Suggestions have similarly been made that atypical agents may be particularly effective because they block 5-HT$_2$ or D_1 receptors. However, as can be seen from Fig. 1, chlorpromazine has a relatively high affinity for both 5-HT$_2$ and D_1 receptors.

Other types of blockade

Sadly, these inconsistencies prompt yet another two suggestions which might accommodate a

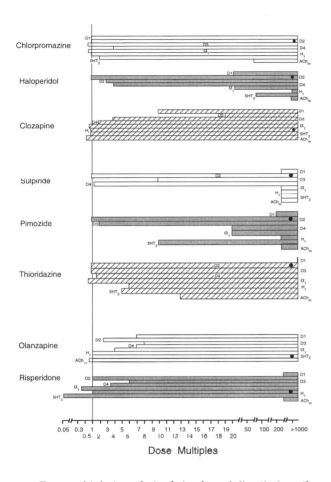

'Dose multiples' are derived simply and directly from the average rank order of affinities for the various receptor types. The horizontal bars, one for each receptor type (dopamine receptors D_1, D_2, D_3, D_4, α_1 adrenergic receptors, H_1 histamine receptors, 5-HT$_2$ serotonin receptors and ACh$_m$ muscarinic acetylcholine receptors, respectively, for each drug), illustrate relative receptor occupancy by a drug as its concentration rises. This simplified illustration was derived from various sources of published data. Within each published data set the affinity constant for each drug at each receptor type was expressed as a whole-number ratio of its affinity at an internal reference receptor (●). These ratios for various receptors were averaged across the published data sets for each particular drug. The result is a number of average potency ratios calculated from the following literature sources: Snyder *et al* (1974); Seeman (1990); Sokoloff *et al* (1990); Sanchez *et al* (1991); Van Tol *et al* (1991); Leysen *et al* (1992); Reynolds (1992); Leysen (1993); Schotte *et al* (1993); Goldstein (1995).

Fig. 1   Dose–occupancy profiles of some popular antipsychotic drugs

---

pharmacological justification for the use of high doses in resistant cases.

First, it may be that in some patients the therapeutic response is not related specifically to blockade at any one receptor type, but rather to the pattern of blockade at a whole series of receptors –

Box 5. High doses are not necessary to block any of the individual receptors currently felt to be important in the therapeutic action of antipsychotic drugs

patterns of the sort shown in Fig. 1. It has been established that complex 'cross-talk' takes place between receptors within the neuronal membrane, and the net effect on neuronal excitability will derive from a combination of effects at various receptor types which will vary in both intensity and quality. Although perhaps unlikely, the wrong signature may be converted into the correct one by escalating the dose. Understanding such an effect might be possible with the use of drug receptor profiles such as those shown in Fig. 1, but would undoubtedly require a level of sophistication in our knowledge and application of synaptic pharmacology which is far beyond the present position.

The second and perhaps associated possibility, that high doses may allow the drugs to occupy receptors of which we are ignorant (either unknown types or known receptors with subtle changes associated with the psychotic trait), is clearly impossible to test at present.

Conclusions

From the available evidence on receptor affinities, it would appear that any of the commonly researched receptors can be blocked by the use of conventional doses of a particular drug, or modest combination of drugs. The lack of any pharmacological rationale for the use of high doses is entirely consistent with the lack of published evidence for clinical efficacy. It must be stressed, however, that these must be treated as no more than provisional conclusions. Failure to secure a therapeutic response with conventional doses in some patients undoubtedly reflects our ignorance of the neurochemical processes involved. Until we understand the reason for this failure, the use of high doses, with a low probability of success, must be approached with due caution. What is quite clear is that escalating doses run the risk of more serious side-effects, regardless of the drug, and perhaps the most dangerous are those caused by interference with ion channels in the heart.

For excellent summaries of the clinical alternatives to the use of high doses in treatment-refractory patients and the safeguards which should be taken if high-dose therapy is contemplated, the reader is referred to the consensus statement from the Royal College of Psychiatrists (Thompson, 1994) and to the *Psychiatric Bulletin* article by Hilton *et al* (1996).

References

Baldessarini, R. & Frankenburg, F. R. (1991) Clozapine, a novel antipsychotic agent. *New England Journal of Medicine*, **324**, 746–754.

Barnes, T. R. E. & Bridges, R. K. (1980) Disturbed behaviour induced with high dose antipsychotic drugs. *British Medical Journal*, **281**, 274–275.

Farde, L., Wiesel, F.-A., Halldin, C., *et al* (1988) Central D_2-dopamine receptor occupancy in schizophrenic patients being treated with antipsychotic drugs. *Archives of General Psychiatry*, **45**, 71–76.

——, Nordstrom, A.-L., Wiesel, F.-A., *et al* (1992) Positron emission tomographic analysis of central D_1 and D_2 dopamine receptor occupancy in patients treated with classical neuroleptics and clozapine. *Archives of General Psychiatry*, **49**, 538–544.

Goldstein, J. M. (1995) Pre-clinical pharmacology of new atypical antipsychotics in late stage development. *Expert Opinion on Investigational Drugs*, **4**, 291–298.

Hilton, T., Taylor, D. & Abel, K. (1996) Which dose of haloperidol? *Psychiatric Bulletin*, **20**, 359–362.

Hirsch, S. R. & Barnes, T. R. E. (1994) Clinical use of high dose neuroleptics. *British Journal of Psychiatry*, **164**, 94–96.

Kane, J. M. (1994) The use of higher-dose antipsychotic medication. *British Journal of Psychiatry*, **164**, 421–432.

——, Honigfeld, F., Singer, J., *et al* (1988) Clozapine for the treatment resistant schizophrenic: a double-blind comparison with chlorpromazine. *Archives of General Psychiatry*, **45**, 789–796.

Leysen, J. E. (1993) Risperidone: receptor occupancy profile and pharmacological activity. *Schizophrenia Review*, **1**, 9–10.

——, Janssen, P. M. F., Gommeren, W., *et al* (1992) *In vitro* and *in vivo* receptor binding and effects on monoamine turnover in rat brain regions of the novel antipsychotics risperidone and ocaperidone. *Molecular Pharmacology*, **41**, 494–508.

Mehtonen, O. P., Aranko, K., Malkonen, L., *et al* (1991) A study of sudden death associated with the use of antipsychotic or antidepressant drugs. *Acta Psychiatrica Scandinavica*, **84**, 58–64.

Pilowsky, L. S., Mulligan, R. S., Acton, P. D., *et al* (1997) Limbic selectivity of clozapine. *Lancet*, **350**, 490–491.

Reynolds, G. (1992) Developments in the drug treatment of schizophrenia. *Trends in Pharmacological Sciences*, **13**, 116–121.

Sanchez, C., Arnt, J., Dragsted, N., *et al* (1991) Neurochemical and *in vivo* pharmacological profile of sertindole, a limbic-selective neuroleptic compound. *Drug Development Research*, **22**, 239–250.

Schotte, A., Janssen, P. F. M., Megens, A. A. H. P., *et al* (1993) Occupancy of central neurotransmitter receptors by risperidone, clozapine and haloperidol measured *ex vivo* by quantitative autoradiography. *Brain Research*, **631**, 191–202.

Seeman, P. (1990) Atypical neuroleptics: the role of multiple receptors, endogenous dopamine and receptor linkage. *Acta Psychiatrica Scandinavica*, **82** (suppl. 358), 14–20.

——, Guan, H.-C. & Van Tol, H. H. (1993) Dopamine D4 receptors elevated in schizophrenia. *Nature*, **365**, 441–445.

Simpson, G. M., Davis, J., Jefferson, J. W., *et al* (1987) *Sudden Deaths in Psychiatric Patients: The Role of Neuroleptic Drugs*. APA Task Force Report, No. 27. Washington, DC: APA.

Snyder, S. H., Greenberg, D. & Yamamura, H. I. (1974) Anti-schizophrenic drugs: affinity for muscarinic cholinergic receptor sites in the brain predicts extrapyramidal effects. *Journal of Psychiatric Research*, **11**, 91–95.

Sokoloff, P., Giros, B., Martres, M.-P., *et al* (1990) Molecular cloning and characterisation of a novel dopamine receptor (D3) as a target for neuroleptics. *Nature*, **347**, 146–151.

Thompson, C. (1994) Consensus statement. The use of high-dose antipsychotic medication. *British Journal of Psychiatry*, **164**, 448–458.

Van Tol, H. H. M., Bunzow, J. R., Guan, H.-C., *et al* (1991) Cloning of the gene for a human dopamine D4 receptor with high affinity for the antipsychotic clozapine. *Nature*, **350**, 610–614.

Wolkin, A., Brodie, J. D., Barouche, F., *et al* (1989a) Dopamine receptor occupancy and plasma haloperidol levels. *Archives of General Psychiatry*, **46**, 482–483.

——, Barouche, F., Wolf, A. P., *et al* (1989b) Dopamine blockade and clinical response: evidence for two biological subgroups of schizophrenia. *American Journal of Psychiatry*, **146**, 905–908.

Neuroleptic malignant syndrome

D. Kohen & M. Bristow

Neuroleptic malignant syndrome (NMS) is a severe and acute dysregulation of vegetative processes such as thermoregulation and control of the autonomic nervous system associated with blockade of dopaminergic synapses either by the use of antagonists or the sudden withdrawal of agonists. It is associated with high and/or frequently administered doses of neuroleptics.

It is important to draw attention to NMS because although mortality rates have declined it is a potentially lethal illness and may cause rapid multi-system failure. Its early stages may be missed on psychiatric wards because of lack of attention to physical observations such as temperature and the misattribution of equivocal signs, such as drowsiness or incontinence, to other causes.

Although a rare form of 'lethal' catatonia, involving high temperature and rigidity, was first described long before the advent of neuroleptic drugs, Delay's description (1960) of a *syndrome malin* in 1960 is usually regarded as the first recognition of this syndrome. Over the next 20 years the number of case reports grew and the appearance of reviews such as Caroff's in 1980 marked the birth of the NMS. Reported incidence rates vary by up to 50-fold, possibly due to differences in diagnostic criteria, and mortality reports are similarly variable. Although it is debatable whether it is a rare, severe idiosyncrasy or one of many neuro-muscular side-effects of dopamine antagonists (Levinson & Simpson, 1986), most clinicians regard it as a serious but recognisable risk of neuroleptic treatment which merits further attention.

Aetiology

Despite its superficial resemblance to malignant hyperthermia, it is likely that NMS is a central disturbance of dopamine metabolism. The evidence for this is manifold. First, all the drugs involved with NMS have dopamine blockade in common, especially D_2 blockade. This includes drugs such as tetrabenazine, which is not strictly a neuroleptic. The incidence of NMS with cessation of dopamine agonists in Parkinsonism also suggests dopaminergic transmission. Further evidence comes from studies of dopamine metabolites in NMS sufferers. In several cases, the dopamine metabolite homovanillic acid has been found to be decreased in the cerebrospinal fluid, suggesting central depletion of dopamine.

Osman & Khurasani (1994) have proposed a "dopamine shut-down" hypothesis for NMS suggesting that neuroleptic blockade in sufferers leads to massive central depletion of dopamine with adverse effects on temperature regulation in the hypothalamus. Drawing attention to the similarity between NMS and catatonia, they suggest that lethal catatonia is a spontaneous depletion of central dopamine often preceded by a period of intense dopaminergic overactivity and perhaps caused by a phase of presynaptic inhibition; NMS is seen as an iatrogenic version of this.

Notwithstanding the connection with dopaminergic transmission, the rarity of NMS suggests that other factors may be involved. The relationship of dopamine to other neurotransmitter activity has come under scrutiny with suggestions that serotonin, acetylcholine or N-methyl-D-aspartate-type glutamate receptors may be crucially involved in destabilising dopaminergic activity. Some studies have found noradrenaline metabolites to be increased in the body fluids of those suffering NMS and a link has been made between dopamine blockade and noradrenergic overactivity. It has been suggested that several of the symptoms of NMS could represent noradrenergic overactivity (hypertension, tachycardia, leucocytosis). Alternatively, these phenomena and that of noradrenergic overactivity could be an effect, rather than a cause, of the profound physiological disruption caused by impaired thermoregulation.

Epidemiology

Incidence and mortality

The reported incidence of NMS has varied widely, between 0.07 and 3%. Some of the highest incidences have resulted from retrospective surveys in which the precision of diagnosis is suspect. Large-scale prospective studies on neuroleptic-treated in-patients using clearly defined criteria suggest that the true incidence is at the lower end of this range. Thus, Keck *et al* (1991) suggest an incidence of four out of 2695 patients (0.15%), Modestin *et al* (1992) found no cases in 335 patients, Deng *et al* (1990) 12 out of 9792 (0.12%) and Gelenberg *et al* (1991) one out of 1450 (0.07%).

However, some prospective studies show higher rates, for example Hermesh *et al* (1992) found five cases in 223 and Naganuma & Fuji (1994) found 10 cases in 564 patients. In both studies the diagnostic criteria seem rigorous (although the second study weights creatine phosphokinase elevation to an extent greater than is recommended in DSM–IV; American Psychiatric Association, 1994) and it is difficult to reconcile these findings with those quoted above except by observing that their smaller size makes them statistically more suspect. We would support Caroff & Mann (1993) who give a pooled incidence rate of about 0.2% while acknowledging that local variations in both neuroleptic usage and awareness of the syndrome may contribute to some variation in the incidence.

As well as a decrease in the incidence there has been a decrease in the reported mortality. In the earliest studies it was quoted as up to 30%, in studies quoted after 1984 it was 11% and in most recent studies it has the status of a rare event. This is probably due to the earlier recognition of the syndrome and prompt recourse to corrective measures.

Risk factors

Psychiatric diagnosis

Neuroleptic malignant syndrome occurs in neuroleptic-treated patients from all psychiatric diagnostic groups. More than one study of NMS sufferers has found a preponderance of patients with a diagnosis of bipolar disorder, but many studies fail to confirm this. It is possible that mania may promote agitation (see below), a more reputable risk factor. Rosebush & Stewart (1989) reported 24 cases of NMS of which 43% had computed tomography brain scan abnormalities,

a much higher than expected proportion in psychiatric disorder.

The link with established central nervous system compromise is strengthened by reports of NMS in Parkinson's disease after withdrawal of dopamine agonists, and in Huntington's disease after starting tetrabenazine. There have also been case reports of NMS in sufferers from severe learning disability or quadriplegia when treated with neuroleptics, although prospective studies on these groups have not been carried out.

Drug treatment

Neuroleptic malignant syndrome has been described in association with all neuroleptics in current usage. This includes the selective D_2 blockers, like sulpiride, as well as risperidone with its mild extrapyramidal side-effects. It is also reported in drugs such as perphenazine and metoclopramide when used as anti-emetics. Lithium has also been reported to cause NMS both alone and in combination with neuroleptics, as have tricyclics (trimipramine and amoxapine) and selective serotonin reuptake inhibitors (SSRIs) (fluoxetine). But reports of NMS in the latter two groups are rare and in the case of the SSRI may have been the serotonin syndrome (see below). Haloperidol and fluphenazine decanoate have been cited in some of the larger studies as being especially associated with the onset of the disorder, but this may reflect their widespread usage.

Clozapine has been suggested by some authors to be free from the potential to cause NMS and even advocated as the treatment of choice for those who have suffered the syndrome. However, there are reports of an NMS-like syndrome in association with clozapine (Thornberg & Ereshefsky, 1993), although several of the cases described were atypical and clozapine has been described as producing a benign hyperthermia in the absence of other symptoms.

Most authors conclude that the first two weeks after starting or changing a neuroleptic drug

---

Box 1.   Risk factors for neuroleptic malignant syndrome

History – previous NMS, known cerebral compromise

Mental state – agitation, overactivity, catatonia

Physical state – dehydration

Treatment – intramuscular therapy, 'rapid neuroleptisation', high doses, high-potency neuroleptics regime are the most risky, but NMS has been reported to occur several months after starting drugs. There has been one case report of the development of severe NMS after cessation of long-term depot medication (Cape, 1994) and we know of a case where presentation occurred several days after the last dose of oral medication. It is worth drawing attention to the fact that risks from neuroleptic drugs may exist over a longer time span than their half-lives in the peripheral circulation.

Circumstantial factors

These seem to be the most consistently associated with the genesis of NMS, both in epidemiological and case-control studies (Box 1). In particular, dehydration, agitation or overactivity in the patient and the use of intramuscular preparations are found to predispose to NMS (Keck *et al*, 1989). Higher doses are also implicated. Keck *et al* (1989) found that the average dose of neuroleptic in cases was nearly twice that of controls (671 mg chlor-promazine *v.* 388 mg) but the association is not simple. Many of these factors, such as overactivity and dehydration or agitation and intramuscular injection, may be covariables. There is no evidence that hot weather or high ambient temperature are predisposing factors.

Demographic factors

Neuroleptic malignant syndrome occurs most frequently in young men. However, it is possible that this reflects patterns of neuroleptic usage such as the more frequent use of high-dose or intramuscular preparations in young males. There is no evidence of ethnic or demographic predisposition.

Heredity

Unlike malignant hyperthermia, NMS carries little or no familial risk and it is rare for case reports to show more than one family member to be affected. Sufferers from NMS show negative results on the halothane–caffeine test which is used to diagnose susceptibility to malignant hyperthermia in probands' relatives.

Biochemical variables

Although dehydration is a likely risk factor, it is difficult to ascertain whether any of the other metabolic disturbances associated with NMS are cause or effect. However, one abnormality that has attracted increasing attention is the finding of low serum iron in sufferers from NMS (Rosebush & Mazurek, 1991). It has been suggested that low serum iron may reduce the number of functional dopamine receptors, while also leading to the restlessness that is described as a risk factor. However, evidence for the presence and relevance of low serum iron in NMS is inconclusive.

Previous NMS

Recrudescence of NMS has been commonly described after early re-challenge with neuroleptics and one series suggests that as many as 17% of NMS sufferers have had previous episodes (Caroff & Mann, 1993).

Diagnosis

Symptoms

For practical purposes there are four symptom types: fever, rigidity, autonomic disturbance and alteration in consciousness.

According to Velamoor *et al* (1994), the earliest symptom is usually alteration in consciousness. This is likely to be missed, especially if persistent drowsiness is ascribed to the sedative effect of neuroleptics. Autonomic instability may produce variations in blood pressure, tachycardia, diaphoresis, salivation or incontinence. Some of these symptoms may also be ascribed to direct drug side-effects unless especial vigilance is maintained. Hypertension should raise suspicion, as should urinary incontinence (the latter may easily be ascribed to 'behavioural' problems in a disturbed individual).

Rigidity may take the form of cogwheel or lead pipe rigidity. It tends to be impervious to treatment with anticholinergics. In most cases it involves the limbs but has been occasionally described as localised to head and neck. There are rare reports of cases where rigidity is absent. Other specific movement disorders such as opisthotonus, myoclonus, dysphagia or dysarthria sometimes occur. Fever is present in 98% of cases and in the majority rises above 38°C. In a small minority, hyperpyrexia (temperature >41°C) occurs. This is associated with a high rate of mortality, as are the complications of severe rigidity, such as myoglobinuria and renal failure.

Laboratory investigations

There are no changes that are pathognomonic of NMS. Creatine kinase is frequently elevated and often exceeds 1000 units/l. (The upper limit of most reference ranges is 200 units/l.) Creatine kinase is widely distributed in body tissue and has three isoenzymes. Most laboratories will measure the whole enzyme and also the myocardial isoenzyme (as part of their cardiac enzyme assay). In NMS, the pooled enzyme level is generally highly elevated with only a small amount of elevation in the myocardial isoenzyme. However, creatine kinase is sensitive to disruption by many factors including intramuscular injections, muscular injuries and exertion. It is also liable to be raised in those treated with neuroleptics who become febrile for other reasons (O'Dwyer & Sheppard, 1993). Hence, it is not a very reliable diagnostic test. Serial estimations in documented cases indicate that rises and falls tend to correspond to fluctuations in the clinical state, so it may be considered a reasonably good marker for clinical progression of the syndrome.

A leucocytosis is found in the majority of cases and, less commonly, mild elevation of enzymes such as lactate dehydrogenase, alkaline phosphatase and transaminases. Other biochemical findings may be hypo- or hypernatraemia or metabolic acidosis. In severe cases there may be uraemia. Reports of darkening of urine should raise suspicion of myoglobinuria.

Computed tomography scanning reveals no abnormality or non-specific findings, nor does lumbar puncture. Magnetic resonance imaging findings in one case were said to resemble those of hypertensive encephalopathy.

Post-mortem findings

As fatal cases generally involve hyperpyrexia, coagulopathies, renal failure or other serious systemic complications, it is difficult to tease out the effects of these from the effects of NMS *per se*. Cerebellar degeneration and anterior hypothalamic infarction have been reported, as have 'non-specific changes'.

Differential diagnosis

Although many drugs and toxins may cause hyperthermia, and NMS-like symptoms may occur as part of generalised cerebral disorder, the important differentials for a psychiatrist to consider are listed below.

Heat exhaustion   Sufferers from heat exhaustion have been exposed to high ambient temperature and may have hyperpyrexia and agitation. Muscle rigidity is unlikely, as are the autonomic disturbances of NMS, especially diaphoresis.

Atropinism   Anticholinergics are commonly used in psychoses and in high doses may cause pyrexia and confusion. They are unlikely to be associated with diaphoresis or autonomic instability.

Extrapyramidal symptoms with intercurrent fever   This is probably the most important differential, both because it is the most common and because stoppage of neuroleptics is not indicated. One study suggests that up to a third of cases provisionally diagnosed as NMS may have intercurrent infections causing the fever (Sewell & Jeste, 1992). It has been shown that consumption of neuroleptics in the presence of a febrile illness can lead to rises in serum creatine kinase. Chest or urinary tract infections are the most common sources.

Catatonia   There is some overlap of the symptoms of NMS with catatonia and some authors consider them to be variants of the same syndrome (White, 1992). Circumstantial evidence to support the relationship between NMS and catatonia comes from the usefulness of electroconvulsive therapy in both catatonia and NMS. While the resemblance is very strong for the 'lethal' variant of catatonia, where pyrexia and rigidity are the rule, there is no evidence to suggest that every case of acute catatonia becomes 'lethal', nor that every case of NMS is associated with catatonic symptoms. It is probably reasonable to assume that full-blown NMS and 'lethal' catatonia are an identical final common pathway and that catatonia is a significant risk factor for the development of this final common pathway (White & Robins, 1991; Raja *et al*, 1994). For this reason caution in the use of neuroleptics in the treatment of catatonia is urged.

Serotonin syndrome   This can resemble NMS (Ames & Wirshing, 1993), with fever and fluctuating blood pressure being prominent symptoms together with diaphoresis, changes in mental state and tremor. Serotonin syndrome typically occurs with the use of drugs increasing the availability of serotonin, such as combinations of monoamine oxidase inhibitors and tricyclics, SSRIs and tryptophan, etc. It should be considered in cases where SSRIs and dopamine blocking agents are used together. In the initial stages, management would consist of supportive measures and withdrawal of medication similar to the course of action in NMS. The similarity of NMS to the serotonin syndrome has led to the suggestion (Fink, 1996) that they are variants of a general neurotoxic syndrome related to catatonia. Increasing awareness among clinicians of the serotonin syndrome will probably enable this hypothesis to be tested in due course.

Partial NMS (forme fruste NMS, extrapyramidal symptoms with fever, etc)   Several authors describe cases of neurotoxicity following neuroleptic treatment which fall short of the DSM–IV criteria for NMS. There is some debate about whether such cases should be included under the rubric of NMS (Adityanjee, 1991) but, whatever the conceptual argument, the clinician needs to be aware that such phenomena occur and are probably more common than full-blown NMS.

Other disorders   Rare disorders that may mimic NMS include thyrotoxic crises, phaeochromocytoma and cerebral disorders such as encephalitides, lupus or tumours. Collateral evidence for these disorders is usually available.

Clinical course

Neuroleptic malignant syndrome usually appears within a week of starting or changing the dose of neuroleptic drugs. If drugs are withdrawn and supportive measures instituted, symptoms persist for an average of one week, although there is wide variation either side of this figure. Persistent morbidity is rare although there have been case reports of persisting neurological sequelae and even dementia following severe cases.

Management

General measures

It is generally agreed that on diagnosis or strong suspicion of NMS neuroleptics should be stopped immediately. It is probably also advisable to stop lithium, given its association with NMS and other forms of neurotoxicity. The role of antidepressants in the causation of NMS is more doubtful but since tricyclics affect the autonomic nervous system and some SSRIs are thought to have dopamine blocking potential (and may cause a similar syndrome to

---

NMS) their use may be considered hazardous. Benzodiazepines may be used for sedation and electroconvulsive therapy is considered safe for the treatment of severe psychosis. Carbamazepine is also reportedly safe.

Supportive measures are of great importance, especially rehydration and cooling. Advice from physicians should be sought early as there are reports of established cases deteriorating rapidly, even over hours. In most cases transfer to a medical ward is desirable (see Box 2).

Specific measures – bromocriptine and dantrolene

Because NMS is a rare and sporadic condition treatment tends to be empirical. Two measures that have achieved some degree of popularity are the use of the dopamine agonist bromocriptine, given in divided doses orally or parenterally in amounts up to 60 mg per day, and the muscle relaxant dantrolene. Although the aetiology of NMS is unknown, both measures have intuitive backing. One study (Rosenberg & Green, 1989) retrospectively compared cases where these agents have been used with cases where supportive measures alone were used and suggested that the time to symptom resolution is hastened. This view is debatable and Rosebush & Stewart (1989), using a similar method, have suggested that the use of these agents is actually associated with greater morbidity. One caveat to this view is that the more serious cases are less likely to be treated with supportive measures alone, leading to selection bias.

Until this debate is resolved, a sensible approach would be to use the agents selectively; thus, dantrolene would be indicated where rigidity was severe and bromocriptine where other symptoms such as hyperthermia and autonomic instability are more salient. However, this is the physician's concern and we would not encourage psychiatrists to manage the established syndrome themselves. Parenteral treatment with L-dopa has also been suggested but few data exist on its efficacy.

Neuroleptic re-challenge

An important question facing the clinician when treating a patient with psychosis who has had NMS is when and how to reintroduce neuroleptics. It is suggested (Rosebush *et al*, 1989) that the risk of recrudescence is appreciably lower if a gap of about two weeks is left between recovery from NMS and the reintroduction of neuroleptics. One study suggests that large doses and intramuscular and depot preparations be avoided. It is also

---

Box 2.   Management of NMS

Measure white blood cell count, electrolytes and urea, liver functions and creatine kinase
Correct dehydration and pyrexia
Withdraw neuroleptics, lithium and antidepressants
Electroconvulsive therapy and benzodiazepines are not contraindicated
Specific remedies (bromocriptine, dantrolene) are probably useful
Refer to medical team

considered wise to avoid high-potency drugs with extrapyramidal side-effects such as the butyrophenones and thioxanthines.

Management of milder forms of neuroleptic toxicity

Little is known about the natural history of these milder reactions. Addonizio *et al* (1986) describe them as "abating without cessation of neuroleptic treatment" but their outcome is difficult to predict in advance. Some clinicians have suggested an algorithm for the management of neuroleptic toxicity (Gratz *et al*, 1992), whereby different symptoms are treated in different ways and stopping medication is not advised until a certain threshold of severity is crossed. Although the consequences of stopping neuroleptics in a patient with psychosis may be far-reaching, we would recommend that clinicians are cautious about neuroleptic usage in equivocal cases until NMS can be definitely ruled out.

References

Addonizio, G., Susman, V. & Roth, S. D. (1986) Symptoms of neuroleptic malignant syndrome in 82 consecutive inpatients. *American Journal of Psychiatry*, **143**, 1587–1590.

Adityanjee, M. D. (1991) The myth of elevated serum creatine phosphokinase level and neuroleptic malignant syndrome. *British Journal of Psychiatry*, **158**, 706–707.

American Psychiatric Association (1994) *Diagnostic and Statistical Manual of Mental Disorders* (4th edn) (DSM–IV). Washington, DC: APA.

Ames, D. & Wirshing, W. C. (1993) MDMA, serotonin syndrome and neuroleptic malignant syndrome – a possible link? *Journal of the American Medical Association*, **269**, 869.

Cape, G. (1994) The neuroleptic malignant syndrome – a cautionary tale and a surprising outcome. *British Journal of Psychiatry*, **164**, 120–123.

Caroff, S. N. (1980) The neuroleptic malignant syndrome. *Journal of Clinical Psychiatry*, **41**, 79–83.

—— & Mann, S. C. (1993) The neuroleptic malignant syndrome. *Medical Clinics of North America*, **77**, 185–202.

Delay, J., Pichot, P., Lemperiere, T., *et al* (1960) Un neuroleptique majeur non phenothiazinque et non reserpinque, l'haloperidol, dans le traitment des psychoses. *Annales Medico Psychologique*, **118**, 145–152.

Deng, M. Z., Chen, G. Q. & Phillips, M. R. (1990) Neuroleptic malignant syndrome in 12 out of 9792 Chinese inpatients exposed to neuroleptics. *American Journal of Psychiatry*, **147**, 1149–1155.

Fink, M. (1996) Toxic serotonin syndrome or neuroleptic malignant syndrome? *Pharmacopsychiatry*, **29**, 159–161.

Gelenberg, A. J., Bellinghausen, B., Wocjik, J. D., *et al* (1991) A prospective study of neuroleptic malignant syndrome. *American Journal of Psychiatry*, **145**, 517–518.

Gratz, S. S., Levinson, D. & Simpson, G. (1992) The treatment and management of neuroleptic malignant syndrome. *Progress in Neuropharmacology and Biological Psychiatry*, **16**, 425–443.

Hermesh, H., Aizenberg, D., Weizman, A., *et al* (1992) Risk for definite neuroleptic malignant syndrome. *British Journal of Psychiatry*, **161**, 254–257.

Keck, P., Pope, H., Cohen, B. M., *et al* (1989) Risk factors for neuroleptic malignant syndrome. *Archives of General Psychiatry*, **46**, 914–918.

——, —— & McElroy, S. L. (1991) Declining frequency of neuroleptic malignant syndrome in a hospital population. *American Journal of Psychiatry*, **148**, 880–882.

Levinson, D. F. & Simpson, G. M. (1986) Neuroleptic induced extrapyramidal symptoms with fever. *Archives of General Psychiatry*, **43**, 839–848.

Modestin, J., Toffler, G. & Drescher, J. (1992) Neuroleptic malignant syndrome: results of a prospective study. *Psychiatry Research*, **44**, 251–256.

Naganuma, H. & Fuji, I. (1994) Incidence and risk factors for neuroleptic malignant syndrome. *Acta Psychiatrica Scandinavica*, **90**, 424–426.

O'Dwyer, A-M. & Sheppard, N. (1993) The role of creatine kinase in the diagnosis of neuroleptic malignant syndrome. *Psychological Medicine*, **23**, 323–326.

Osman, A. A. & Khurasani, M. (1994) Lethal catatonia and neuroleptic malignant syndrome – a dopamine receptor shutdown hypothesis. *British Journal of Psychiatry*, **165**, 548–550.

Raja, M., Altavista, M., Cavallari, S., *et al* (1994) Neuroleptic malignant syndrome and catatonia. *European Archives of Psychiatry and Clinical Neuroscience*, **243**, 299–303.

Rosebush, P. & Stewart, T. (1989) A prospective analysis of 24 episodes of neuroleptic malignant syndrome. *American Journal of Psychiatry*, **146**, 717–725.

——, —— & Gelenberg, L. (1989) Twenty neuroleptic rechallenges after fifteen cases of NMS. *Journal of Clinical Psychiatry*, **50**, 295–298.

—— & Mazurek, I. (1991) Serum iron and neuroleptic malignant syndrome. *Lancet*, **338**, 149–151.

Rosenberg, M. R. & Green, M. (1989) Neuroleptic malignant syndrome. *Archives of Internal Medicine*, **149**, 1927–1931.

Sewell, D. & Jeste, D. (1992) Distinguishing NMS from NMS like acute medical illnesses. *Journal of Neuropsychiatry and Clinical Neuroscience*, **4**, 265–269.

Thornberg, S. & Ereshefsky, L. (1993) Neuroleptic malignant syndrome associated with clozapine monotherapy. *Pharmacotherapy*, **13**, 510–513.

Velamoor, V., Norman R. M. G., Caroff S. N., *et al* (1994) Progression of symptoms in neuroleptic malignant syndrome. *Journal of Nervous and Mental Disorders*, **182**, 168–173.

White, D. A. C. (1992) Catatonia and the neuroleptic malignant syndrome – a single entity? *British Journal of Psychiatry*, **161**, 558–560.

—— & Robins, A. H. (1991) Catatonia – harbinger of the neuroleptic malignant syndrome. *British Journal of Psychiatry*, **158**, 419–421.

Pharmacological treatment of the newly diagnosed patient with schizophrenia

Michael J. Travis & Robert W. Kerwin

The early treatment of newly diagnosed schizo-phrenia has ramifications for the future psychiatric and social well-being of the patient. Changes in care structures and care delivery mechanisms, in addition to financial constraints and outcome targets, provide an additional incentive to ensuring that any intervention is both successful and cost-effective.

Although it has long been acknowledged that the mainstay of treatment in schizophrenia is pharmacological, and involves the use of anti-psychotic neuroleptic medication, there have been few attempts to devise a treatment protocol for first-onset patients that can be evaluated as part of a randomised controlled trial (RCT). Never-theless, there is some evidence to guide prescribing practice.

Acute treatment of the newly diagnosed patient with schizophrenia will vary considerably according to the patient's clinical state and the need to prevent harm to self or others. Medium-term treatment should involve optimisation of therapy to the minimum effective dose and frequency. This phase of treatment should also entail a rigorous assessment of treatment resistance. This would enable patients who would benefit from clozapine to receive it early in the course of their illness. Long-term maintenance treatment of first-onset schizophrenia is a more vexing issue and involves a careful clinical risk–benefit analysis. As over two-thirds of first-onset patients will suffer a subsequent relapse without further treatment, it is an area with vast scope for minimising the morbidity associated with schizophrenia.

Importance of first presentation

There is increasing evidence that the nature and character of an individual's schizophrenic process is established in the first few years of illness. Neuropsychological function appears to be affected in those with schizophrenia, compared with healthy controls, at illness onset, but few studies have shown any deterioration in the patients' cognitive ability over time (Goldberg *et al*, 1993). This is in accordance with the vast majority of neuroimaging studies, which consis-tently report little effect of illness duration on the extent of morphological brain changes.

The first two years of illness may be crucial to long-term outcome. Two studies have reported findings in accordance with previous suggestions that deterioration plateaus early in schizophrenia. Thara *et al* (1994) reported on 90 patients pro-spectively followed-up for 10 years. The quarter of their sample who remained affected by positive and negative symptoms had stabilised by the second year, with no evidence of further deterior-ation. In accordance with this, 'course type' over the two years after onset is strongly associated with course over the subsequent 10 years (Harrison *et al*, 1996).

It is tempting to think that with early, appropri-ately aggressive treatment some amelioration of the long-term effects of schizophrenia may be achieved. There is some evidence that early treatment does have significant effects on outcome.

Importance of early treatment

There have been two excellent recent reviews of the rationale behind the early identification and treatment of schizophrenia (McGlashan & Johannessen, 1996; Birchwood *et al*, 1997). The evidence that a longer duration of illness prior to treatment is detrimental to various measures of treatment outcome is based on a number of retrospective analyses and three prospective studies (see Box 1).

Box 1. Importance of early treatment

Neuropsychological and neuropathological changes are evident early in the course of schizophrenia and change little with time

The first two years from symptom onset characterise the subsequent course of illness

In retrospective studies of first-onset patients a longer duration of illness prior to pharmacotherapy is associated with poorer outcome

In prospective studies of first-onset patients longer duration of prodrome and pre-treatment psychotic symptoms predicts a lower level of remission, and longer duration of pre-treatment psychotic symptoms is associated with a longer time to remission

---

Outcome before and after introduction of neuroleptics

Wyatt (1991) reviewed a series of 19 studies, of primarily first-onset patients, which compared the outcome of those treated before the introduction of chlorpromazine with those treated subsequently. He noted that the use of medication increased the chances for a better long-term course. This conclusion was reinforced by Opjordsmoen (1991), who compared first-admission delusional cases (*n*=151), half of whom were admitted prior to neuroleptic treatment and half afterwards. Despite the fact that all of Opjordsmoen's cohort received neuroleptics at some point in the course of their illness, the author described significantly worse outcome for the patients who did not receive neuroleptics as their first treatment.

Retrospective studies

In a review of 10 studies relating to the first wave of patients treated with neuroleptics, Angrist & Schulz (1990) reported that in six out of 10 the response to pharmacotherapy correlated negatively with duration of illness. Results supporting these findings have been noted in studies from China (Lo & Lo, 1977), Japan (Inoue *et al*, 1986) and Iceland (Helgason, 1990). The latter study split a group of 107 on the basis of illness duration of greater than or less than one year pre-treatment. Over 18 years of follow-up, the group with pre-treatment illness duration greater than one year had a higher re-admission rate. In a smaller but significant study of 20 patients over three years, it was demonstrated that the ongoing treatment for patients with illness duration greater than six months pre-treatment cost twice as much as ongoing treatment for those who received treatment within six months of the onset of symptoms (Moscarelli *et al*, 1991).

Prospective studies

Three major prospective studies focusing on the duration of pre-treatment illness have all found an association between longer duration of illness and poorer outcome.

In the smaller study reporting this association, Rabiner *et al* (1986) investigated a sample of 36 first-episode patients with psychosis over one year, and reported a correlation between relapse or poor outcome and longer duration of pre-treatment illness in the group with schizophrenia. In a larger study, Johnstone *et al* (1986) reported on a sample of 253 first-onset patients with schizophrenia followed-up for two years. In that sample patients with a longer duration of illness had a higher frequency of relapse. That this effect appears to continue whether patients were included in the placebo or active treatment wing of a controlled trial emphasises the importance of early treatment (Crow *et al*, 1986).

In a widely quoted two-year follow-up study, Loebel *et al* (1992) carefully and intensively investigated 70 first-episode patients diagnosed with either schizophrenia or schizoaffective disorder (mainly schizophrenia) who were included in an antipsychotic treatment protocol. They separated duration of illness prior to treatment into two components: the first included the duration of the prodrome plus the duration of psychotic symptoms, and the second the duration of psychotic symptoms alone. They reported that a lower level of remission was associated with a longer duration of both psychotic symptoms and prodrome prior to treatment. The longer the duration of pre-treatment psychotic symptoms, the longer the time to remission. Importantly, time to remission was not related to other factors, although a lower level of remission was associated with poorer premorbid functioning and an earlier age at onset. This finding of an association between better treatment response and shorter duration of pre-treatment psychosis has been replicated by Szymanski *et al* (1996).

Treatment

Treatment of the newly diagnosed patient involves a three-pronged approach using all of the skills of the multi-disciplinary team. Social and occupational therapy are an important part of helping the patient to re-establish their lives after an episode of psychosis. Psychological therapies, including family work and cognitive–behavioural therapy (CBT), are becoming increasingly well validated and may be a useful adjunct to medication (Kuipers, 1996). However, the cornerstone of schizophrenia treatment is pharmacological (Kane & Marder, 1993), which will be the focus of this article.

Pharmacotherapy for schizophrenia can best be considered in terms of acute, medium-term and long-term maintenance treatment. No consensus yet exists in any of these three areas with regard to type or dose of drug and duration of treatment. Nevertheless, significant research contributions have been made. The re-introduction of clozapine in 1990 and the advent of several new antipsychotics over the past four years have renewed interest and optimism in the treatment of schizophrenia. These new antipsychotics have, for want of a better term, been classified as 'atypical' antipsychotics, a term which has a variety of definitions, tells us little about the pharmacology of the drug, and does not aid the clinician with prescribing. We propose a new classification (Box 2). The new atypical antipsychotics are better called 'third-generation' antipsychotics. The rationale for this is that the first-generation antipsychotics were developed from the known pharmacology and structure of chlorpromazine and share high D_2 occupancy as their primary mode of action. Second-generation antipsychotics include drugs such as sulpiride, thioridazine and remoxipride. Using current definitions these may be classified as atypical antipsychotics. They still appear to exert their effects via D_2 receptor antagonism and yet do not seem to confer the benefits of the third-generation drugs. The third generation of antipsychotics has been developed using clozapine, rather than chlorpromazine, as a prototype. Although they have a variable pharmacology they may exert their effects via other receptors, such as the 5-HT_{2A} receptor, in addition to the D_2 receptor. The third-generation drugs may be subdivided further on the basis of their relative affinities for a range of receptors into 'broad-spectrum third-generation', such as olanzapine and quetiapine, and 'serotonin–dopamine antagonist third-generation', such as risperidone, sertindole and ziprasidone.

Box 2. The classification of antipsychotics

First-generation antipsychotics (formerly known as typical antipsychotics). Based on the structure and pharmacology of chlorpromazine – i.e. chlorpromazine, haloperidol, zuclopenthixol, trifluoperazine, etc.

Second-generation antipsychotics. Next stage in drug development, may be 'atypical' by some definitions – i.e. sulpiride, remoxipride, thioridazine

Third-generation antipsychotics (formerly the 'atypical' antipsychotics). Based on the structure and/or pharmacology of clozapine – i.e. *broad spectrum*: olanzapine, quetiapine; *serotonin–dopamine antagonist*: risperidone, sertindole, ziprasidone

---

General principles

The ideal situation, for both patient and clinician, is for the patient to be receiving medication at the minimum effective dose, with a minimum of side-effects, and to be compliant with this medication. If these criteria are met, then the cost for the care of the patient is minimised, both in terms of in-patient stays and community care. It is perhaps a function of the heterogeneity of schizophrenia and the vagaries of political and health care systems that relatively little prospective research has been directed towards these issues.

Acute treatment

The acute phase is best thought of as the period between the commencement of treatment and the onset of antipsychotic effect, usually 7–14 days. Good clinical practice is to start a patient on one type of antipsychotic medication and maintain it so that they may have an adequate trial of treatment. The drug used may be crucial as it will often be the patient's first experience with medication likely to have serious side-effects and which they may have to take for many years. The choice of medication regime will depend on the patient's clinical presentation, likely compliance and the need for sedation.

Increasingly, third-generation antipsychotics, such as risperidone, olanzapine, quetiapine and sertindole, are advocated for the first-line treatment of newly diagnosed patients with schizophrenia (Lieberman, 1996). These drugs exhibit reduced rates of neurological side-effects in comparison with first- and second-generation antipsychotics at therapeutic doses (Casey, 1996). The issue of side-effects is particularly relevant to first-episode patients as they appear to be more sensitive to extrapyramidal side-effects, high levels of which reduce compliance. All of the third-generation antipsychotics are equally effective in comparison with first- and second-generation antipsychotics and may share with clozapine reduced rates of tardive dyskinesia and enhanced efficacy against secondary negative symptoms. Although further work remains to be completed, a recent double-blind comparison of risperidone (mean dose 6.1 mg) and haloperidol (mean dose 5.6 mg) in first-episode patients has shown equal efficacy with significantly reduced extrapyramidal side-effects in the risperidone-treated group (McCreadie, 1996).

The optimum doses of third-generation antipsychotics is still an area of debate. It has been suggested that the optimum dose for risperidone is between 6 and 8 mg per day (Marder, 1994). Olanzapine and sertindole are still under scrutiny and the doses outlined in their respective data sheets should be followed.

The first presentation of schizophrenia is variable, however the most clinically challenging presentation is that of the potentially violent or self-harming patient with florid positive symptoms. Sedation is often required, but in order to produce sedation with antipsychotics relatively high doses may need to be used. This increases the risk of akathisia and acute dystonic reactions with any generation of antipsychotic (Malhotra et al, 1993). This is problematic as akathisia may paradoxically make the patient more agitated and acute dystonic reactions and parkinsonian side-effects may have disastrous consequences for future compliance (Frances & Weiden, 1987).

Often in the past such patients have received high doses of sedative first-generation antipsychotics from the outset, with a reluctance to reduce doses once recovery has occurred (Thompson, 1994). However, low doses of a first-generation antipsychotic, such as haloperidol 5–15 mg per day, are equally effective against psychotic symptoms in comparison with higher doses and carry a reduced risk of side-effects (Kane & Marder, 1993). The available evidence suggests that third-generation antipsychotics reduce the risk of side-effects even further and therefore this is a primary justification for using them as first-line treatments. In patients requiring sedation it is strongly suggested that this is achieved by the addition of a benzodiazepine such as lorazepam or clonazepam rather than by the addition of a sedative first-generation antipsychotic.

For all newly diagnosed patients, the choice of antipsychotic is in itself a matter of personal preference and experience. It should be borne in mind that there is little evidence supporting the use of polypharmacy (Thompson, 1994) and that using a single neuroleptic for an entire therapeutic trial ensures that the patient receives the treatment most likely to produce symptomatic relief in the shortest time. Careful thought must therefore be given to the use of a neuroleptic, such as droperidol, which is not licensed for long-term maintenance treatment.

Medium-term treatment

This is the time from the expectation of first treatment response to the point when the patient may be considered a responder or non-responder to a medication. The dose and duration of a medication that a patient should receive before a change is considered are still sources of some debate; however, there are some guidelines. Treatment resistance is usually defined as lack of satisfactory clinical improvement despite the use of two antipsychotics from different chemical classes prescribed at an adequate dose for an adequate duration. Stricter criteria may be adopted as in the Kane criteria. If, as suggested, a third-generation antipsychotic is used first-line, it would seem logical to use either a broad-spectrum or a serotonin–dopamine antagonist for greater than six weeks at the recommended dose, and if this was not successful then to switch the patient to a drug from the other third-generation antipsychotic class as a second-line treatment, again for a six-week minimum period.

If a first- or second-generation antipsychotic is used, the patient should be treated for greater than six weeks at a minimum dosage of >500 mg chlorpromazine equivalence per day. If satisfactory improvement has not occurred, then switch to a drug of different chemical class for a further six weeks. When a patient has failed to respond to two antipsychotics from different chemical classes, clozapine treatment should be seriously considered.

With the advent of the Clozaril Patient Monitoring Service, the risks associated with clozapine-induced agranulocytosis have been minimised. In addition, the need for early use of clozapine in treatment resistance is becoming clearer. As already discussed, the pattern of illness is established early for the majority of patients. Up to a third of patients receiving standard neuroleptics will be resistant to such treatment. If the supposition that psychosis itself is toxic is true, then every effort must be made to give patients an effective treatment as early as possible in the course of their illness. Up to a half of treatment-resistant patients will respond to clozapine (for review see Travis, 1997).

Rehabilitation and psychological therapies should be considered during this phase of treatment, carrying over into the long-term treatment phase. Rehabilitation should focus on four key areas: the need for comprehensive and long-term therapy; individually tailored treatment programmes based on individual needs; active participation in treatment by patient and family; and possible limitations that the patient may suffer as a direct result of their illness (Bellack & Mueser, 1993). As with any rehabilitation programme, the aim should be to maximise the patients' strengths and help to redevelop their abilities. In view of the correlation between social isolation and increased relapse rates, social skills training has an important part to play in any rehabilitation. As most patients return to their families after a hospital stay, it is surprising that there has not been greater enthusiasm for the use of family intervention strategies. A variety of modes of intervention have been shown to have a robust effect on relapse prevention. Most of these methods involve family education, improving communication, 'here and now' problem-solving and attempts at helping emotional processing within families (Kuipers, 1996). A combination of social skills training with family education and medication may significantly reduce subsequent relapse rates, in comparison with any other combination (Hogarty *et al*, 1991).

Recent research has indicated the usefulness of CBT in schizophrenia. Therapy centres around enhancing coping strategies, goal-setting and the modification of hallucinations and delusions. This is particularly indicated to promote psychological adjustment and insight and for patients who have medication-resistant hallucinations and delusions. Cognitive–behavioural therapy has also been advocated in the treatment of acute psychosis (Drury *et al*, 1996*a,b*)

Long-term maintenance treatment

The use of maintenance antipsychotics for first-onset schizophrenia is an under-researched area. Studies focusing on prophylactic antipsychotic medication in chronic schizophrenia have shown an almost 75% 6–24 month relapse rate in patients who were switched to placebo after a year symptom-free. This is in contrast to a relapse rate of 23% in patients on continuous antipsychotic medication (Hegarty *et al*, 1994). Recent research in similar populations has shown that effective prophylaxis can be achieved with doses of first-generation (typical) antipsychotic medication lower than the standard prescribed dose, provided this is combined with relatively close follow-up. There was also a corresponding reduction in side-effects and negative symptoms in the low-dose groups (for review see Carpenter & Carpenter, 1996). The use of low-dose depot medication (as opposed to oral medication) may have additional benefits in terms of relapse prevention (Davis *et al*, 1994).

It would seem logical that in well-characterised patients with a first diagnosis of schizophrenia similar clinical issues will dictate prescribing practice, and that these rates will be mirrored, at least in part. Unfortunately, few prospective studies in newly diagnosed cohorts have been reported.

It is still unclear how long effective treatment should be continued after the first onset of schizophrenia. In view of the consistent finding that at least a quarter of first-episode patients recover without subsequent relapse, it would seem sensible to limit the amount of time that newly diagnosed patients spend on medication, for fear of causing unnecessary harm to a substantial minority of patients who do not require prophylactic medication. There is, as yet, no convincing body of evidence to allow a clear decision, although the literature does indicate that first-episode patients gain the maximal benefit from neuroleptic therapy after about six months of treatment (Carpenter & Carpenter, 1996). It would be wise, therefore, to suggest a six-month treatment period at minimum effective dose, followed by a further six months of progressive dose reduction. This would require close clinical supervision, but would be expected to reduce adverse effects and perhaps enhance compliance. Close collaboration with patients over medication doses and strategies may also enhance their therapeutic engagement and increase the likelihood that they will approach services and accept treatment earlier in the course of a subsequent relapse.

The question of depot medication for first-episode patients is a difficult one. While there is support for enhanced relapse prevention in chronic patients given depot antipsychotics, the generalisability of this to first-episode patients is unclear.

At the current level of knowledge the use of depot neuroleptics for this group should be reserved for patients who have been shown to gain significant clinical benefit from first-generation antipsychotic medication but have shown consistent difficulties with compliance.

The use of the novel third-generation antipsychotics, risperidone, sertindole, olanzapine and quetiapine, for prophylactic treatment has not yet been fully validated by RCTs in populations with newly diagnosed or chronic schizophrenia. Clozapine, the prototypical third-generation antipsychotic, similarly has not been investigated in RCTs of maintenance therapy. This is because of the restrictions imposed on its use. However, clozapine's clinical efficacy in relapse prevention is well established, naturalistically, at 1–2 years of treatment , and there have been naturalistic reports of good maintenance efficacy for up to 17 years of treatment (for review see Travis, 1997).

There are several other reasons to make the assumption that third-generation antipsychotics should be effective in prophylaxis. All antipsychotics investigated so far as part of controlled trials have been shown to be equally effective maintenance treatments. As the third-generation are at least as efficacious as first-generation antipsychotics in acute treatment, it might follow that they will also be adequate long-term treatments; initial data with risperidone are encouraging (Lindstrom *et al*, 1995). Based on preliminary data, it may well be that the third-generation antipsychotics will be shown to be better for long-term therapy (see Weiden *et al*, 1996). Although we still do not know precisely how clozapine exerts its effect, all of the third-generation antipsychotics share a high 5-HT_{2A} : striatal D_2 receptor blockade ratio as part of their pharmacodynamic profile. It has been suggested that this is why these drugs exhibit a lower incidence of neurological side-effects and secondary negative symptoms at optimum doses (Kapur & Remington, 1996). It may be hypothesised that if adverse effects and negative symptoms are indeed minimised with the third-generation antipsychotics, then compliance and re-hospitalisation rates will be lower than with first-generation antipsychotic maintenance treatment (see Weiden *et al*, 1996).

Psychosocial rehabilitation and cognitive psychotherapy are an integral part of long-term

---

Box 3. Pharmacological treatment

Acute phase
Use of a third-generation (atypical) antipsychotic at a therapeutic dose (6–8 mg/day for risperidone; refer to manufacturers' data sheets for others)
If a first-generation (typical) antipsychotic is used, a dose of roughly 500 mg chlorpromazine equivalents is adequate
Benzodiazepines for sedation (i.e. lorazepam 2–4 mg, clonazepam 2–8 mg)

Medium term
Six weeks' treatment on drug of first choice at therapeutic doses (6–8 mg/day for risperidone; refer to manufacturers' data sheets for other third-generation antipsychotics)
For a first-generation antipsychotic doses should be maintained between 250 and 750 mg chlorpromazine equivalents for six weeks
If this is ineffective, then six weeks' treatment on a medication of a different chemical class at therapeutic dose/similar dose equivalents. (Consider switching from a serotonin–dopamine antagonist to a broad-spectrum third-generation antipsychotic or vice versa)
If this is ineffective, then consider treatment with clozapine

Long-term maintenance
Maintenance on first effective antipsychotic at minimal therapeutic dose for six months
Slow reduction of medication over six months with close clinical review
If there are residual deficits but acceptable clinical improvement, then consider longer-term maintenance
If the patient relapses, then restart medication at full therapeutic dosage
If the patient requires clozapine, then it is unlikely that any attempt to stop medication in the future will be successful

maintenance treatment, where appropriate. Family and patient education regarding the ramifications of the patient's illness and the need for treatment has been shown to be effective in reducing subsequent relapse and enhancing the therapeutic relationship between patients, carers and professionals. This may have implications for early recognition and treatment of incipient relapses (for review see Kuipers, 1996). The problem of social isolation should be addressed by encouraging the patient to become involved in locally provided services or rehabilitation resources.

Most recent reviews in this area have made an assertion that one of the best ways of reducing morbidity and hospitalisation for newly diagnosed patients is the early recognition of relapse (Carpenter & Carpenter, 1996; Birchwood *et al*, 1997). Therefore, of overriding importance is the integration of pharmacological and psychosocial treatments in the framework of available care networks. This should strengthen communication and allow a more proactive approach to be taken to treatment needs.

Conclusions

In comparison with the efforts that have been made in biological and epidemiological research in patients with newly diagnosed schizophrenia, prospective studies of treatment have been scarce. Advances in neuropharmacology and psychological therapies should allow a more eclectic and hypothesis-driven approach to research in this area than has hitherto been possible.

The relative importance of the first episode of psychosis in terms of the patients' experience of psychiatric services and treatments cannot be over-emphasised. The evidence that delaying effective treatment will reduce the extent of future remission provides an impetus to the need for clear guidelines over the pharmacological and psychosocial management of the newly diagnosed patient with schizophrenia.

A framework for the medication treatment of a newly diagnosed patient with schizophrenia is summarised in Box 3.

Although this (or any other) framework remains to be evaluated in an RCT, the pharmacotherapy of schizophrenia has developed markedly over the past decade. The confirmation that reduced doses of first-generation antipsychotics are therapeutically effective has already begun to alter prescribing practices in the UK. Prescribing practice should be profoundly altered by the re-introduction of clozapine, the advent of risperidone, sertindole, olanzapine and quetiapine and the imminent arrival on the market of other novel third-generation antipsychotics such as ziprasidone. The rationale for using third-generation antipsychotics as first-line treatment for the newly diagnosed patient with schizophrenia is very strong. These medications promise great hope for the future of schizophrenia treatment as they provide psychiatrists, for the first time since the advent of antipsychotics, with the opportunity to offer effective treatments with minimal side-effects. This optimism is reinforced by the increasingly evidence-based use of effective psychosocial treatments for schizophrenia.

However, without a treatment consensus based on well-conducted trials the benefits seen with these treatments are likely to be patchy at best and the ability of clinical psychiatrists to justify resource allocation requirements will be severely impaired.

References

Angrist, B. & Shulz, S. C. (eds) (1990) *Introduction to the Neuroleptic Non-Responsive Patient: Characterization and Treatment.* Washington, DC: American Psychiatric Press.

Bellack, A. S. & Mueser, K. T. (1993) Psychosocial treatment for schizophrenia. *Schizophrenia Bulletin*, **19**, 317–336.

Birchwood, M., McGorry, P. & Jackson, H. (1997) Early intervention in schizophrenia. *British Journal of Psychiatry*, **170**, 2–5.

Carpenter, W. T. & Carpenter, W. T., Jr. (1996) Maintenance therapy of persons with schizophrenia. *Journal of Clinical Psychiatry*, **57** (suppl. 9), 10–18.

Casey, D. E. (1996) Extrapyramidal syndromes and new antipsychotic drugs: findings in patients and non-human primate models. *British Journal of Psychiatry*, **168** (suppl. 29), 32–39.

Crow, T. J., MacMillan, J. F., Johnson, A. L., *et al* (1986) A randomised controlled trial of prophylactic neuroleptic treatment. *British Journal of Psychiatry*, **148**, 120–127.

Davis, J. M., Metalon, L., Watanabe, M. D., *et al* (1994) Depot antipsychotic drugs: place in therapy. *Drugs*, **47**, 741–773.

Drury, V., Birchwood, M., Cochrane, R., *et al* (1996a) Cognitive therapy and recovery from acute psychosis: a controlled trial. I: Impact on psychotic symptoms. *British Journal of Psychiatry*, **169**, 593–601.

—, —, —, *et al* (1996b) Cognitive therapy and recovery from acute psychosis: a controlled trial. II: Impact on recovery time. *British Journal of Psychiatry*, **169**, 602–607.

Frances, A. J. & Weiden, P. (1987) Promoting compliance with outpatient drug treatment. *Hospital and Community Psychiatry*, **38**, 1158–1160.

Goldberg, T. E., Hyde, T. M., Kleinman, J. E., *et al* (1993) Course of schizophrenia: neuropsychological evidence for a static encephalopathy. *Schizophrenia Bulletin*, **19**, 797–804.

Harrison, G., Croudace, T., Mason, P., *et al* (1996) Predicting the long term outcome of schizophrenia. *Psychological Medicine*, **26**, 697–705.

Hegarty, J. D., Baldessarini, R. J., Tohen, H., *et al* (1994) One hundred years of schizophrenia: a meta-analysis of the outcome literature. *American Journal of Psychiatry*, **151**, 1409–1416.

Helgason, L. (1990) Twenty years' follow-up of first psychiatric presentation for schizophrenia: what could have been prevented? *Acta Psychiatrica Scandinavica*, **81**, 231–235.

Hogarty, G. E., Anderson, C. M., Resii, D. J., *et al* (1991) Family psychoeducation, social skills training and maintenance chemotherapy in the aftercare treatment of schizophrenia. II: Two year effects of a controlled trial on relapse and adjustment. *Archives of General Psychiatry*, **48**, 340–347.

Inoue, K., Nakajima, T. & Kato, N. (1986) A longitudinal study of schizophrenia in adolescence. I: The one to three year outcome. *Japanese Journal of Psychiatry and Neurology*, **40**, 143–151.

Johnstone, E. C., Crow, T. J., Johnson, A. L., *et al* (1986) The Northwick Park Study of first episodes of schizophrenia. I: Presentation of the illness and problems relating to admission. *British Journal of Psychiatry*, **148**, 115–120.

Kane, J. M. & Marder, S. R. (1993) Psychopharmacological treatment of schizophrenia. *Schizophrenia Bulletin*, **19**, 287–302.

Kapur, S. & Remington, G. (1996) Serotonin–dopamine interaction and its relevance to schizophrenia. *American Journal of Psychiatry*, **153**, 466–476.

Kuipers, E. (1996) The management of difficult to treat patients with schizophrenia, using non-drug therapies. *British Journal of Psychiatry*, **169** (suppl. 31), 41–51.

Lieberman, J. A. (1996) Atypical antipsychotic drugs as a first-line treatment of schizophrenia: a rationale and hypothesis. *Journal of Clinical Psychiatry*, **57** (suppl. 11), 68–71.

Lindstrom, E., Eriksson, B., Hellgren, A., *et al* (1995) Efficacy and safety of risperidone in the long-term treatment of patients with schizophrenia. *Clinical Therapetics*, **17**, 402–412.

Lo, W. H. & Lo, T. (1977) A ten-year follow-up study of Chinese schizophrenics in Hong Kong. *British Journal of Psychiatry*, **131**, 63–66.

Loebel, A. D., Lieberman, J. A., Alvir, J. M. J., *et al* (1992) Duration of psychosis and outcome in first-episode schizophrenia. *American Journal of Psychiatry*, **149**, 1183–1188.

Malhotra, A. K., Litman, R. E. & Pickar, D. (1993) Adverse effects of antipsychotic drugs. *Drug Safety*, **9**, 429–436.

Marder, S. R. (1994) Risperidone in the treatment of schizophrenia. *American Journal of Psychiatry*, **151**, 825–835.

McCreadie, R. G. (1996) Managing the first episode of schizophrenia: the role of new therapies. *European Neuropsychopharmacology*, **6**, S2-3–S2-5.

McGlashan, T. H. & Johannessen, J. O. (1996) Early detection and intervention with schizophrenia: rationale. *Schizophrenia Bulletin*, **22**, 201–222.

Moscarelli, M., Capri, S. & Neri, L. (1991) Cost evaluation of chronic schizophrenic patients during the first three years after first contact. *Schizophrenia Bulletin*, **17**, 421–426.

Opjordsmoen, S. (1991) Long-term clinical outcome of schizophrenia with special reference to gender differences. *Acta Psychiatrica Scandinavica*, **83**, 307–313.

Rabiner, C. J., Wegner, J. T. & Kane, J. M. (1986) Outcome study of first episode psychosis: relapse rates after 1 year. *American Journal of Psychiatry*, **143**, 1155–1158.

Szymanski, S. R., Cannon, T. D., Gallacher, F., *et al* (1996) Course and treatment response in first episode and chronic schizophrenia. *American Journal of Psychiatry*, **153**, 519–525.

Thara, R., Henrietta, M., Joseph, A., *et al* (1994) Ten-year course of schizophrenia – the Madras longitudinal study. *Acta Psychiatrica Scandinavica*, **90**, 329–336.

Thompson, C. (1994) The use of high-dose antipsychotic medication. *British Journal of Psychiatry*, **164**, 448–458.

Travis, M. J. (1997) Clozapine. A review. *Journal of Serotonin Research*, **4**, 125–144.

Weiden, P., Aquila, R., Standard, J. (1996) Atypical antipsychotic drugs and long-term outcome in schizophrenia. *Journal of Clinical Psychiatry*, **57** (suppl. 11), 53–60.

Wyatt, R. J. (1991) Neuroleptics and the natural course of schizophrenia. *Schizophrenia Bulletin*, **17**, 325–351.

Treatment of the patient with long-term schizophrenia

Ann Mortimer

At most, 15% of patients in Western countries remain free of relapse after their first episode of schizophrenia (Crow *et al*, 1986). Like many chronic illnesses, schizophrenia can be controlled by appropriate treatment, but there may be a gradual deterioration over time. This encompasses problems such as: loss of self-care, communication and community skills; negative symptoms of poverty of affect and ideation; cognitive impairment; behaviour problems such as aggression; and poorly controlled positive symptoms.

Deterioration often appears consequent upon repeated relapse. Indeed, the prognosis of schizophrenia may have improved significantly following the introduction of neuroleptics (see McKenna, 1994) because of their marked prophylactic effect in preventing relapse. One analysis of 24 placebo-controlled studies of continuing antipsychotic treatment showed that patients relapsed more frequently on placebo than on active medication: active treatment over three years reduced the risk of relapse almost threefold (Davis, 1975).

Two issues are, therefore, germane to the long-term treatment of schizophrenia. The first is the prevention of relapses, most of which are caused by non-compliance (Davis *et al*, 1994), and the second is the management of unresolved symptoms and social deficits. Optimal management should include a spectrum of approaches from sophisticated use of medication to appropriate psychotherapy. Its rationale is essentially rehabilitative, comprising assessment of individual difficulties plus targeted interventions. If the patient cannot be returned to adequate function, ongoing support and care are necessary.

Continuous management of this nature is best facilitated by a multi-disciplinary framework, currently exemplified by the Care Programme Approach (CPA).

Relapse prevention

Relapse rates, neuroleptic prophylaxis and compliance

After an acute episode, 8–16% of patients per month relapse without medication (Davis *et al*, 1994). The figure is similar if medication is withdrawn after several years' successful maintenance. Intermittent treatment targeted at prodromal symptoms and 'drug holidays' is relatively unsuccessful and cannot be recommended (Anonymous, 1994; Christison *et al*, 1991).

Up to 60% of patients in the community are, at least episodically, non-compliant: relapse rates could possibly be halved if compliance were significantly improved (Kissling, 1994). The causes of non-compliance resemble those in non-psychiatric disorders: lack of information and understanding about illness, difficulty managing complex regimens of medication, denial, forgetfulness, inconvenience, expense, side-effects, lack of active symptoms, and fear of long-term harm or addiction. Schizophrenia adds to this list poor, or fluctuating, insight and stigma. These difficulties, however, suggest several approaches to improve compliance.

First or subsequent acute episodes

Information about illness and treatment should be imparted to and discussed with patients and carers as soon as possible (Anonymous, 1994). Learning objectives of this process of 'psychoeducation' include: understanding the origins and significance of the episode; acceptance of vulnerability and dependence on psychotropic medication; recognition of links between stressful events and exacerbation of illness; and understanding the distinction between the patient's personality and their schizophrenia. The success of psycho-education rests upon a constructive relationship between professionals and family.

For patients nearing discharge a process of gradually increasing responsibility for medication should occur, ideally with patients becoming fully self-medicating prior to discharge. Step-wise practice towards this goal begins with the patient asking for medication at the relevant time, and culminates in the patient taking complete responsibility, with regular or random checks of pill numbers. It is advisable to implement or change drug regimens gradually: many rapid alterations may be confusing for both patient and doctor.

After discharge

Follow-up of patients should be assertive: non-attenders should be traced. The time to intensify follow-up is when the patient insists on non-compliance, because relapse may be anticipated within the next few months. For patients subject to supervised discharge or listed on the super-vision register, there may be a lower threshold for attempting to return the patient to hospital.

Patients should be encouraged to participate in their own care. It is important to discuss medic-ation with each patient, so that they feel involved in decision-making. One randomised controlled trial of 'compliance therapy' (motivational interviewing and cognitive therapy) found that the compliance therapy group improved significantly compared with a non-specific counselling group regarding insight, attitudes to medication and compliance six months after discharge: there was a trend towards improved social functioning (Kemp *et al*, 1996). The finding that these advan-tages may be lost at 12 months underlines the need for such interventions to continue.

Maintenance in the community

In maintenance treatment the simplest regimen of medication at the minimum effective dose is appropriate, ideally a neuroleptic taken once daily or by depot administration. Written instructions may be useful for patient and carer. Tailoring the regime to patients' daily activities is advisable.

Depot injections are only advantageous com-pared with oral neuroleptics in out-patient studies; the advantage of decreased relapse is lost when in-patient groups are compared (Davis *et al*, 1994).

Depot formulations may ensure that the patient who will not comply with oral treatment continues to receive a neuroleptic, but awareness that the patient has defaulted may be the only tangible benefit. Depot administration circumvents 'first pass' metabolism, which may result in worse side-effects; some patients find it painful and demeaning.

Patients should always be observed for, and questioned specifically about, unwanted side-effects. These (particularly Parkinsonism and akathisia (Anonymous, 1994), sexual dysfunction, sedation and weight gain) are a major cause of non-compliance. Side-effects should be managed by dose reduction (preferably), a change to a drug with milder side-effects such as an atypical neuroleptic, or the addition of a specific antidote.

It is important to give positive feedback when medication has been used appropriately.

Unresolved positive symptoms

Differential diagnoses and simple solutions

Poorly controlled positive symptoms constitute one criterion for treatment resistance. They may also be encountered in patients who cannot tolerate a therapeutic dose of neuroleptic without unac-ceptable side-effects (Box 1).

Other causes of psychosis, such as sub-stance misuse, certain forms of severe personality disorder, and organic psychosis, should be ruled out, as should the possibility of non-compliance. The impact of high levels of stress within the family and their repercussions should not be underestim-ated. Skilled nursing observation, urinary screen-ing for drugs of misuse, serum prolactin levels, psychometric assessment and discussion with the patient and family may all contribute to accurate evaluation of unresolved psychosis.

A substantial minority of patients respond very poorly to medication, and this tends to be more of a problem with increasing chronicity. A thorough

---

Box 1. Unresolved positive symptoms

Assess compliance
Assess living situation
Optimise medication
Consider cognitive–behavioural strategies
Consider family work to reduce stress

review of the patient's current and previous medication should take place, with the objective of rationalising over-medication or polypharmacy and identifying regimes which did or did not work previously. Simple adjustments, such as reducing neuroleptic treatments and dosages, dealing with troublesome side-effects (particularly akathisia) and drug interactions, can be worthwhile. Anticholinergics should be stopped if possible since they can antagonise the antipsychotic effects of neuroleptics. High-dose neuroleptics may worsen the patient's condition and may be unsafe (Mortimer, 1994).

Lithium has been shown to benefit up to half of all patients (Siris, 1993). Predictors of response to lithium include affective symptoms, aggression and family history of affective disorder; improvements are not limited to predictor symptoms. Benzodiazepines are likely to be helpful when psychosis is accompanied by marked anxiety, or to control behaviour disturbance in acute relapse. Evidence that other adjuvants are worth trying is much less convincing: carbamazepine may treat side-effects since it reduces circulating levels of neuroleptics by up to 50%, while propranolol may relieve akathisia that is being mistaken for psychotic agitation.

Atypical neuroleptics

Several atypical neuroleptics are now available (discussed in Kerwin *et al*, 1998). They aim to combine the same, or improved, efficacy as conventional neuroleptics with milder side-effects, particularly extrapyramidal side-effects (EPS). Pharmacologically, they fall into two categories: those which preferentially block dopamine (D_2) and serotonin (5-HT_2) receptors, and those which block multiple receptors (Gerlach & Peacock, 1995). The first group includes risperidone, sertindole and ziprasidone. At recommended doses, risperidone has few EPS and may be advantageous in the treatment of negative symptoms. Sertindole trials report EPS and prolactinaemia at placebo level, but owing to prolongation of cardiac conduction electrocardiogram monitoring is indicated. Efficacy is very similar to haloperidol for positive and negative symptoms, there being statistically significant advantages over haloperidol for negative symptoms. Ziprasidone is still undergoing clinical trials: it may cause fewer EPS than conventional treatments.

The second group includes olanzapine, quetiapine, zotepine, and clozapine; zotepine remains under trial. Olanzapine induces EPS at placebo

rates: antipsychotic efficacy may be superior for negative symptoms. Quetiapine appears equivalent in efficacy to conventional antipsychotics, while compared with conventional treatment EPS are reported as similar to placebo level. Zotepine may cause fewer EPS than conventional neuroleptics and has equivalent efficacy for positive symptoms.

Evidence of superior benefit is greatest for clozapine: 30–60% of treatment-resistant patients respond to this drug (Anonymous, 1994). Extrapyramidal side-effects are conspicuous by their absence. There is a body of opinion that despite its drawbacks – the risk of neutropenia and inconvenience of white cell monitoring – clozapine should be used much earlier in the course of the illness than it generally is (Kerwin *et al*, 1998). Clozapine can be used safely with lithium, benzodiazepines and anticonvulsants (apart from carbamazepine). Sodium valproate may be given to patients on 600 mg of clozapine or more per day owing to lowered seizure threshold at higher doses.

Cognitive therapies for positive symptoms

Cognitive–behavioural therapy (CBT) assumes that schizophrenia emerges in individuals who tend to employ dysfunctional cognitive models of themselves and their environment: these models may be amenable to interventions which utilise learning theory. Cognitive–behavioural therapy identifies and quantifies target symptoms and behaviours, examines their antecedents and consequences, intervenes in these if possible, and with the patient formulates alternative explanatory models for the target symptoms. Changes in symptoms and behaviour are evaluated (Turkington, 1996). For hallucinations, approaches include focusing on them or distraction from them, enhancement of coping skills and reducing the patients' belief in their omnipotence and omniscience (Chadwick & Birchwood, 1994). Patients who are able to respond more constructively to their voices, without the usual anger or withdrawal, may gain a degree of control over them. Critical collaborative analysis of voices (Turkington & Kingdon, 1994) explores their origin and rationale, supplanted by behavioural experiments such as patients making a tape-recording when voices are heard, or taping their own rational responses which can be played back when voices are troublesome. Such interventions should not take place without adequate training and supervision.

Regarding delusions, it is well known that confrontation does not work. It may be possible to modify the belief through exploring the implications of the delusion as if it were absolutely true, and to test these out with behavioural homework. Reducing anger and anxiety associated with delusions is likely to be beneficial. However, there may be a risk of depression if delusions which preserve self-esteem are attenuated.

Importance of high expressed emotion and its management

Aspects associated with relapse (critical comments, hostility and emotional over-involvement) have been widely enumerated: a review of prevalence reported by North American and European studies (Kavanagh, 1992) found the percentage of high expressed emotion (EE) families to be at least 45%. Expressed emotion had substantial support as a predictor of positive symptoms. The median relapse rate in high-EE environments was 48%, versus 21% in low-EE environments.

Of seven studies which examined the effect on relapse of lowering EE in patients' relatives, five found a significant effect. The largest study followed 103 patients for two years. Four intervention groups were evaluated: routine care (including medication); routine care plus social skills training; routine care plus family psychoeducation and interpersonal problem-solving training; and routine care, social skills training, family psychoeducation and interpersonal problem-solving training. At two years the relapse rates for the four groups were 66, 42, 32 and 25%, respectively. The difference in relapse rate was found to depend on the lowering of high EE.

Conclusions

Skilled medication management can make a large difference to the resolution of positive symptoms in schizophrenia. However, it is naïve to assume that other factors have no influence: fraught, tense households are likely to be deleterious to all sorts of illnesses and this effect may be magnified in the case of mental illnesses. Questions remain concerning the specific therapeutic factors pertaining to these strategies. Is high EE a valid entity, or are reductions in relapse rate a result of increased time and attention being given to patients and their families, improving compliance in drug-taking and other behaviours in all parties (including the doctor)? Regarding CBT, does improvement of isolated symptoms impinge on overall outcome? Unresolved positive symptoms afford such potential for relapse that these therapies are definitely worth trying, notwithstanding poorly understood mechanisms of action.

Unresolved negative symptoms

Definition and differential diagnosis

Negative symptoms can be conceptualised as a failure to respond to stimuli, either externally or internally generated. Core negative symptoms are flatness of affect and poverty of ideation. Poverty of speech and drive, diminished expressive behaviour, self-care and personal function may be secondary to these core symptoms. They are considered prognostically unfavourable and relatively unresponsive to conventional neuroleptics. They may be an inevitable consequence of severe chronic illness, but differential diagnosis remains important.

Patients who are withdrawn owing to preoccupation with positive symptoms may appear to have negative symptoms (Box 2). Useful clues include inappropriate affect, fragments of thought disorder, abnormal involuntary movements and hallucinatory behaviour. Extrapyramidal side-effects, especially mask-like face and bradykinesia, are easily mistaken for real negative symptoms: other Parkinsonian phenomena should be assessed. Over-sedated patients often have little drive, and complain about it or appear drowsy or asleep for long periods. Depressed patients may be misdiagnosed, although there is no correlation between depression and negative symptoms. These patients can be encouraged to convey distress, whereas the patient with truly flat affect will maintain indifference. Other useful clues are diurnal variation, early wakening and depressive ideation. Depression is very common in patients with schizophrenia, ranging from an insightful response to emerging disability, to a genuine schizoaffective state. Standard treatment for depression is indicated: the management of suicidal ideation requires particular care.

Many patients have a history of prominent schizoid traits of social inactivity, difficulty expressing emotion and eccentricity. Whether such

---

Box 2. Differential diagnosis of negative symptoms

Excess medication – Parkinsonism/over-sedation
Unresolved positive symptoms
Depression
Schizoid premorbid personality

a personality is a way station on the road to schizophrenia (part of the illness) or a risk factor for schizophrenia (causing experiences to be misconstrued) is unclear. These traits are unlikely to be modified by psychiatric treatment.

Treatment of negative symptoms

One classic study of the effectiveness of rehabilitation (Wing & Brown, 1970) found that an increase in time spent by patients occupied in activities on wards was paralleled by clinical improvements in flatness of affect, social withdrawal and other negative symptoms. The implication is that patients retain some capacity to respond to external stimuli and give appropriate interaction. Every clinician will have come across patients who appear to be quietly institutionalised at home or in residential care: good outreach support for relatives and carers, respite periods and other rehabilitation provision perhaps constitute the best management strategy for the remediation of negative symptoms. However, there is evidence that clozapine and certain other atypical drugs do ameliorate negative symptoms. Patients should always be offered these drugs, particularly clozapine, as they may become much more amenable to rehabilitation as a consequence.

Behaviour problems

Scope of behaviour problems

Behaviour problems include self-harm, harming others, destroying property, sexual disinhibition, and socially embarrassing behaviours. Behaviour problems may ameliorate as part of the general process of getting better, in parallel with reduction of positive and negative symptoms: one study of patients on clozapine suggested this to be the case (Dye *et al*, 1996).

Violence

Violence, secondary to delusions, constitutes a particular danger. Patients who misuse drugs or alcohol are significantly more likely to commit violent offences: very high rates of comorbid substance misuse have been reported in schizophrenia. A minority of patients are responsible for a disproportionate amount of violence: the best predictor of future violence is past violence. Such patients require more intensive monitoring of

mental state and compliance than usual, and there should be contingency plans in case deterioration or defaulting from treatment occurs. Assessment of risk involves a consideration of not only the patient, but also his/her environment and potential victims.

Medication for specific problems

The role of medication in the management of specific behaviour problems is not well defined. Lithium and anticonvulsants may be used for their anti-aggressive properties (Siris, 1993). The use of anti-libidinal drugs in sexually disinhibited men with schizophrenia has not, in my own experience, been valuable, as patients seem to have a normal amount of libido but direct it in ways which contravene social norms. This may be the case across a wide range of behaviour problems: the patient may have a vague awareness that their behaviour is undesirable, but does not understand that this matters in terms of its effects on other people.

Behavioural management

Behavioural treatment is apposite for the majority of patients. An assessment is made of the antecedents and consequences, which may be modified to make the behaviour less likely (Box 3). The reinforcements most valued by the individual patient are identified: these may be withdrawn for unacceptable behaviour, or the patient may earn extra reinforcements by refraining from the behaviour. Social disapproval by staff whom the patient respects may be a powerful means of modifying behaviour, but it is important that the patient must understand what are the alternatives to the behaviour that is being criticised. Formal behaviour programmes should be discussed with and understood by the patient, and must be structured so that the patient is not set up for demoralising failure. The value of

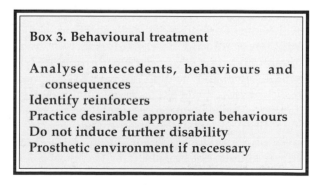

Box 3. Behavioural treatment

Analyse antecedents, behaviours and
 consequences
Identify reinforcers
Practice desirable appropriate behaviours
Do not induce further disability
Prosthetic environment if necessary

unexpected kindness, in the form of occasionally bending the rules in the patient's favour, is much underestimated.

Loss of personal function

Rehabilitation

Loss of self-care, communication and community skills is germane to loss of independence and increased resource uptake in schizophrenia. Overall, such deficits may reflect severity and chronicity of the disease, and be accompanied by negative symptoms and cognitive impairment. Positive symptoms may not be as relevant, but when the disorganisation syndrome is present or the patient is largely preoccupied with abnormal experiences, it may not be possible to engage them: the patient has no 'well part' which can be worked with.

Rehabilitation has much to offer once symptom management is optimised, and should be available in community settings. Skills which are lacking are identified and attempts made to teach the patient through repeated practice. Patients may need extra aids to do this, such as printed instructions about the stages of cooking a meal or using a washing machine. It is important that the patient appreciates why such activities are useful, and receives verbal and social reinforcement for improved performance. A behaviour programme may be set up in which the patient is rewarded for getting up, having a bath, doing laundry, etc. Social skills training, the use of role play, and opportunities to interact with the community outside the hospital are all useful ways of helping both the patient to function better and the team to monitor progress. Outside contacts with family, friends or volunteers should be encouraged. Sheltered work may help patients raise their self-esteem by achieving something, but exploitation should always be guarded against. As an overall aim, the patient should spend more time doing things which 'normal' people do, and less time doing nothing or 'mental patient-type' activities.

For patients unwilling to learn necessary skills, alternatives should be considered. Our own attitudes and values may not be appropriate. For instance, a patient who does not wish to cook may be housed close to an inexpensive cafe. If lack of function is consequent on cognitive compromise, rehabilitation may prove impossible and a prosthetic environment supplied. However, patients should not be subject to over-provision, which may induce further disability.

Cognitive impairment

Nature and importance of cognitive impairment

There is now virtually irrefutable evidence that schizophrenia is characterised by a compromise of intellectual function, ranging through specific deficits to frank dementia. Evidence of independent dementia pathology from post-mortem brain samples is, however, conspicuous by its absence, suggesting that the process is potentially reversible.

Memory and executive (frontal) functions are frequently impaired in patients with schizophrenia even when there is no significant general cognitive dysfunction. Such specific cognitive deficits are substantial correlates of psychiatric disability: a recent review (Green, 1996) found that verbal memory and certain aspects of executive performance were associated with outcome in terms of community functioning, social problem-solving and skills acquisition. By contrast, psychotic symptoms were not correlated with functional outcome in any study. Remediation of memory and executive deficits thus has the potential to overcome consequential rate-limiting steps in rehabilitation and to improve outcome. This is especially important given the enormous costs of long-term support for chronic dependent patients.

Neuroleptics and cognition

Any drug which could remediate cognitive deficit – a 'smart drug' for schizophrenia – would have major advantages. Unfortunately, there is little evidence that conventional neuroleptics have any therapeutic effect on cognition (Mortimer, 1997). Atypical neuroleptics have not been adequately tested to date. Several studies on clozapine suggest that it may improve memory and frontal function (Mortimer, 1997). It has been suggested that dopaminergic and cholinergic agonists should be investigated as possible specific remedies for cognitive impairment, although this would risk antagonism of antipsychotic effects of neuroleptics and worsening of Parkinsonism.

Direct cognitive remediation

Attempts have been made to correct specific cognitive abnormalities through practice at tasks or tests which employ the intellectual skills found to be lacking. It has been shown that test performance can be improved, but unfortunately these new skills do not generalise to everyday behaviour, and symptoms do not seem to benefit either (Liberman *et al*, 1995). Social skills training, role play and similar rehabilitation strategies are perhaps more valid in terms of the relevant executive and memory abilities required by patients.

Care programmes and management of the stable patient

The CPA is the recommended model for management of psychiatric patients. It formalises good professional practice (Kingdon, 1998) (Box 4). The CPA has the potential to assess patients' needs comprehensively, to improve communication between professions and to match patient requirements with appropriate interventions and facilities.

Patients who are stable and whose problems are largely resolved may no longer require the CPA. Such patients should still be reviewed at least annually by a mental health care professional, preferably working in primary care. The review should include a general health care check, assessment of mental state, compliance and side-effects, personal function and cognition, with the views of an informant if possible (Box 5).

The future

Clozapine has been joined by a choice of alternative atypical neuroleptics. Long-term studies of relapse rates, quality of life and economic benefits are favourable (e.g. Guest *et al*, 1996). Family intervention and CBT have gained a foothold. The importance of investing resources in the psycho-education of first-episode patients and families, and of compliance counselling, is slowly becoming established. Despite these hopeful advances, for

---

Box 4. Care Programme Approach

Multi-disciplinary assessment of health and social needs
Named keyworker
Written care plan
Regular reviews of needs and progress

Box 5. Essentials of long-term treatment

Maximise compliance to prevent relapse
Address unresolved positive symptoms
Manage unacceptable negative symptoms
Deal with behaviour problems
Assess cognitive status
Evaluate rehabilitation needs

---

many patients their benefits appear to be as far away as ever. Regarding drugs, the situation has been termed "a revolution waiting to be prescribed" (Kerwin, 1995).

The demand for psychological interventions may rise if treatment of new patients with atypical drugs creates a cohort who have milder symptoms and who are eminently suitable for such input. Trusts should be encouraged to invest in appropriate training of nurses, for instance for the Thorne diploma.

There is perhaps more potential now than at any time since the introduction of conventional neuroleptics for psychiatrists to make a real difference to the outcome of patients with long-term schizophrenia. These patients should not continue to suffer from the low expectations of their doctors, as well as from their illness.

References

Anonymous (1994) Long-term management of people with psychotic disorders in the community. *Drugs and Therapeutics Bulletin*, **32**, 73–77.

Chadwick, P. & Birchwood, M. (1994) The omnipotence of voices. A cognitive approach to auditory hallucinations. *British Journal of Psychiatry*, **164**, 190–201.

Christison, G. W., Kirch, D. G. & Wyatt, R. J. (1991) When symptoms persist: choosing among alternative somatic treatments for schizophrenia. *Schizophrenia Bulletin*, **17**, 217–245.

Crow, T. J., MacMillan, J. F., Johnson, A. L., *et al* (1986) A randomised controlled trial of prophylactic neuroleptic treatment. *British Journal of Psychiatry*, **148**, 120–127.

Davis, J. M. (1975) Overview: maintenance therapy in psychiatry. 1: Schizophrenia. *American Journal of Psychiatry*, **132**, 1237–1245.

——, Metalon, L., Watanabe, M. D., *et al* (1994) Depot anti-psychotic drugs. Place in therapy. *Drugs*, **47**, 741–773.

Dye, S. M., Mortimer, A. M. & Lock, M. (1996) Clozapine versus treatment as usual in schizophrenia. *Schizophrenia Research*, **18**, 126.

Gerlach, J. & Peacock, L. (1995) New antipsychotics: the present status. *International Clinical Psychopharmacology*, **10**, 39–48.

Green, M. F. (1996) What are the functional consequences of neurocognitive deficits in schizophrenia? *American Journal of Psychiatry*, **153**, 321–330.

Guest, J. F., Hart, W. M., Cookson, R. F., *et al* (1996) Pharmaco-economic evaluation of long-term treatment with risperidone for patients with chronic schizophrenia. *British Journal of Medical Economics*, **10**, 59–67.

Kavanagh, D. J. (1992) Recent developments in expressed emotion and schizophrenia. *British Journal of Psychiatry*, **160**, 601–620.

Kemp, R., Hayward, P., Applewhaite, G., *et al* (1996) Compliance therapy in psychotic patients: a randomised controlled trial. *British Medical Journal*, **312**, 345–349.

Kerwin, R. (1995) Editorial: A revolution waiting to be prescribed. *Hospital Update*, June, 263–264.

—, Mortimer, A. M. & Lynch, K. (1998) Antipsychotic treatment of severely ill patients with schizophrenia. In *Understanding Psychiatric Treatment of Mental Health Disorders* (eds G. O'Mahony & J. Lucey), pp. 133–148. Chichester: John Wiley.

Kingdon, D. (1998) Making care programming work. In *Acute Psychosis, Schizophrenia and Comorbid Disorders. Recent Topics from Advances in Psychiatric Treatment*, vol. 1 (ed. A.S. Lee), pp. 73–77. London: Gaskell.

Kissling, W. (1994) Compliance, quality assurance and standards for relapse prevention in schizophrenia. *Acta Psychiatrica Scandinavica*, **89** (suppl. 32), 16–24.

Liberman, R. P., Spaulding, W. D. & Corrigan, P. W. (1995) Cognitive–behavioural therapies in psychiatric rehabilitation. In *Schizophrenia* (ed. D. R. Weinberger), pp. 605–625. Oxford: Blackwell Science.

McKenna, P. J. (1994) The natural history of schizophrenia. In *Schizophrenia and Related Syndromes*, pp. 52–72. Oxford: Oxford University Press.

Mortimer, A. M. (1994) Newer and older antipsychotics. A comparative review of appropriate use. *CNS Drugs*, **2**, 381–396.

— (1997) Cognitive deficit in schizophrenia – do neuroleptics make a difference? *Pharmacology, Biochemistry and Behaviour*, **56**, 789–795.

Siris, S. G. (1993) Adjunctive medication in the maintenance treatment of schizophrenia and its conceptual implications. *British Journal of Psychiatry*, **163**, 66–78.

Turkington, D. (1996) Cognitive therapy in schizophrenia. *Schizophrenia Monitor*, **6**, 1–3.

— & Kingdon, D. G. (1994) *Cognitive Therapy of Schizophrenia*. New York: Guilford Press.

Wing, J. K. & Brown, G. W. (1970) *Institutionalism and Schizophrenia: A Comparative Study of Three Mental Hospitals, 1960–1968*. Cambridge: Cambridge University Press.

Cognitive–behavioural treatments in schizophrenia

Gillian Haddock & Shôn Lewis

The first-line of treatment for patients with psychotic disorders such as schizophrenia is neuroleptic medication. Neuroleptics have provided substantial benefits to patients with this type of severe mental illness since their discovery as a treatment for psychosis in the 1950s. Despite this, there is still a large number of patients who do not respond fully to neuroleptic medication or who are not able to tolerate it. For example, although as many as 70% of patients are substantially improved following drug treatment, a considerable proportion continue to experience persistent, distressing and recurrent symptoms. In a survey of patients in a London psychiatric hospital, Curson et al (1988) found that just under half of the patients continued to experience hallucinations and delusions despite the prescription of medication. In addition, many patients experience intolerable side-effects or do not wish to comply with neuroleptic medication, yet look for some effective alternative. Depression, anxiety and a high rate of suicide are additional problems faced by patients with schizophrenia.

As a result of this, psychological treatments for schizophrenia and other psychotic disorders have been developing over the last decade, particularly in the area of cognitive–behavioural interventions. Recent research has focused on the following areas: (a) family interventions aimed at improving patient and carer functioning and reducing relapse; (b) individual cognitive–behavioural interventions aimed at reducing the severity of drug-resistant psychotic symptoms; (c) attempting to teach patients and their carers to monitor prodromal signs to facilitate early intervention; and (d) strategies aimed at increasing compliance with medication. This chapter will briefly review each of these areas and the implications for training and service provision will be discussed. It will not attempt to cover more traditional psychological approaches such as social skills training or token economy approaches for negative symptoms (see Kavanagh, 1992a for a review of these areas).

Family interventions

Following the observations of George Brown in the 1950s, that some patients with schizophrenia discharged to certain environments were more likely to relapse than others, much research has focused on the family environment as a predictor of relapse. Brown & Rutter (1966) introduced the concept of 'expressed emotion' (EE) to describe those environments which most contributed to relapse. A high-EE environment (as measured by the Camberwell Family Interview; Vaughn & Leff, 1976a) consists of relatives who demonstrate high levels of criticism, hostility and emotional over-involvement towards their relative with schizophrenia. Patients living in high-EE environments have been shown to have a significantly higher relapse rate than those living in low-EE environments (see Kavanagh, 1992b for a review).

Vaughn & Leff (1976b) observed that the amount of contact with high-EE relatives and whether the patient was taking medication were factors which interacted with high EE and predicted relapse. Patients who were not taking medication and who spent more than 35 hours per week with their high-EE relative had a high relapse rate over nine months (92%). Those who had similar contact but who were taking medication showed an intermediate relapse rate over a similar period (53%), as did those with less contact but who were not taking medication (42%). Those with less contact and who were taking medication showed a low relapse rate (15%), as did patients who were living in low-EE environments. In low-EE environments, the relapse rate was relatively unrelated to whether the patient was taking medication or not (12 and 15%, respectively).

Following these observations, many researchers have examined whether family interventions could reduce the EE status of relatives and whether this has a consequential effect on relapse rates. A number of studies (e.g. Tarrier et al, 1988) have shown that family interventions for patients with a diagnosis of schizophrenia and their families, in addition to treatment as usual, could reduce the relapse rate of the patients, increase their social functioning and reduce subjective burden in their families. The benefits of these approaches have been shown to be apparent up to eight years after the intervention (Tarrier *et al*, 1994). In a meta-analysis of the best six published studies (involving a total of 350 patients, 181 controls and 169 experimental subjects), De Jesus Mari & Streiner (1994) showed that nine months following implementation of a family intervention there was a marginally significant superior effect for family interventions over controls on patient relapse rates. Patients receiving family intervention also showed increased drug compliance and lower overall hospitalisation than controls, and families of patients receiving a family intervention were more likely to become low-EE over nine months of treatment compared with the families of control patients.

The family interventions differed slightly in each of the published studies but all have a number of common components. The interventions have usually been behavioural or cognitive–behavioural in orientation (a psychoanalytically oriented approach carried out by Kottgen *et al* (1984) in Hamburg failed to demonstrate that the family intervention had any benefit over routine treatment in terms of subsequent relapse rates). Most interventions have consisted of education regarding the nature of the illness, its treatment, management and prognosis, together with strategies to reduce stress in the family, increase independence and to solve problems generated during day-to-day life. Most interventions have taken place over nine months and some have provided booster sessions for families and patients which increased the benefits over longer periods (Falloon *et al*, 1985).

Despite the research findings, the integration of family interventions into routine services for patients has not occurred. Why is this? It may be due to a lack of training in family interventions or a view that these types of intensive treatments are more expensive than conventional ones. Although it is true that family interventions require trained professionals who will provide intensive input, this is generally over a relatively short period of time in the career of a person with schizophrenia and their family. Therefore, the economic savings made by reducing future relapse rates can easily justify any initial costs. With regard to training the appropriate staff to deliver these interventions, recent research has demonstrated that community psychiatric nurses (CPNs) are in a good position to deliver the interventions and can be trained to do so, resulting in improved patient and carer out-comes. In a study by Brooker *et al* (1992), two groups of CPNs were taught assessment techniques and trained to deliver family interventions. Improvements were found in positive and negative psychotic symptoms and in social functioning of patients. Relatives' satisfaction with services and reports of their own minor psychiatric morbidity improved.

Individual psychological management of psychotic symptoms

Many people with a diagnosis of schizophrenia continue to have residual positive and negative symptoms which have not responded to medication, and which can contribute to continued distress, reduced social functioning and may increase the risk of self-harm (Falloon & Talbot, 1981). Traditionally the medical model in psychiatry has stressed the Jasperian notion of the 'non-understandability' of symptoms in schizophrenia (Jaspers, 1963). This has carried the implication that psychological treatments will, by definition, not work. For some psychological treatments this may well be the case: for example, psychoanalytically oriented psychotherapy has not been shown to be effective in people with schizophrenia (Meuser & Berenbaum, 1990).

None the less, studies examining the efficacy of cognitive–behavioural approaches in the management of drug-resistant symptoms have shown that these can be successful at reducing the occurrence of symptoms and the distress associated with them. The majority of early studies were individual case studies or case series (reviewed by Haddock *et al*, 1994). The approaches described are varied: operant procedures designed to provide reinforcement when the patient is engaged in non-psychotic behaviour or speech (Wincze *et al*, 1972); distraction techniques designed to reduce auditory hallucinations (Margo *et al*, 1981); belief modification approaches designed to alter the characteristics of delusions (Chadwick & Lowe, 1990); and systematic desensitisation to the factors which contribute to the occurrence of symptoms (Slade, 1972).

Until recently, many authors have focused on single behavioural or cognitive techniques in order to reduce the severity of the psychotic symptoms. Researchers have now begun to see the need for controlled studies with larger numbers of subjects (Tarrier *et al*, 1998) in order to demonstrate the efficacy of psychological approaches. Two recent randomised controlled trials have evaluated the effectiveness of cognitive–behavioural therapy for patients with chronic neuroleptic-resistant psychosis (Kuipers *et al*, 1997; Tarrier *et al*, 1998) and shown that cognitive–behavioural treatment is significantly superior to routine treatment, both after therapy and at 18-month follow-up (Kuipers *et al*, 1998). These studies utilised cognitive–behavioural therapy directed at individual symptoms of psychosis, but also adopted a comprehensive approach which addressed the multiple needs of patients with psychosis. This included strategies to manage depression, low self-esteem, social functioning anxiety, side-effects of medication, and negative symptoms.

Monitoring of prodromal signs and early intervention

The natural history of schizophrenia is typically one of repeated relapse of acute psychosis. Birchwood *et al* (1989) showed that it is possible to train patients and their carers to identify early signs which may herald a relapse in order to intervene to reduce the severity of the relapse. They observed that many patients have individually characteristic changes in affect and cognition which precede a full-blown relapse, although there is much variation in the characteristics of these prodromes between patients. The term 'relapse signature' describes this and demonstrates that through regular and frequent monitoring of symptoms and behaviours it is possible to identify the early signs which are likely to herald a relapse. Early intervention can then be directed at reducing the likelihood of relapse using increases in neuroleptic medication, support and cognitive–behavioural techniques.

There is a small amount of evidence that this type of early intervention can be effective, provided the monitoring process is frequent enough to identify the time window between 'well-being' and a subsequent relapse. For some patients this can be over a matter of days, whereas for others it can be over a number of months. Birchwood suggests that monitoring should occur at least fortnightly for the majority of patients, if the time window is unknown, as this has been shown to identify approximately 75% of patients who go on to a full-blown relapse.

Adherence to medication

Non-compliance with neuroleptic medication is an important contributory factor in prolonged psychosis and the occurrence of relapse. In the study by Vaughn & Leff (1976*b*) reported above, patients who refused medication for one month out of a nine-month follow-up period had approximately three times the relapse rate compared with those who remained fully compliant. Although it could be speculated that non-compliance in patients who are severely mentally ill is related to the nature of their illness, it has been shown that non-compliance is no more prevalent than in other illnesses which require long-term medication treatment, and can sometimes be viewed as a marker of health rather than illness (Ley, 1992). Factors identified as contributing to non-compliance include complex drug regimes, demographic factors (Sellwood & Tarrier, 1994), level of symptomatology (Bartko *et al*, 1988), insight (Bartko *et al*, 1987) and attitudinal factors (Ludwig *et al*, 1990). Poor compliance can be secondary to side-effects such as sedation, akathisia or insight gain. Seltzer *et al* (1980), have also found that fear of side-effects was associated with non-compliance, but that if patients were provided with education about the nature of side-effects, this reduced their fear without affecting compliance. Non-compliance is possible both with oral and depot drugs, but covert non-compliance is only possible with oral drugs.

Recent approaches to increase compliance have focused on providing education regarding the nature of side-effects and medication (Eckman & Liberman, 1990), establishing a collaborative approach (Corrigan *et al*, 1990) and attempts to teach patients the skills needed for compliance, for example memory aids (Eckman *et al*, 1990). More recently, Sellwood *et al* (1994) have been investigating the effectiveness of motivational interviewing with non-compliant patients. This is a collaborative approach which involves structured assessment and education about the nature of diagnosis, medication and its potential side-effects and an emphasis on helping the patient to review what they have to gain or lose by not accepting treatment and remaining ill. The therapist aims to help the patient to generate a range of possible options, of which taking medication or other treatment may be one, and examining the possible consequences of each. Kemp *et al* (1998) showed that this type of approach provided benefits on compliance, insight and attitudes to treatment for in-patients with acute psychosis 18 months following a four- to six-session therapeutic intervention.

Cognitive remediation of psychological deficits

Patients with schizophrenia show a range of information processing deficits. These are thought to reflect underlying cognitive deficits implicated in schizophrenia, although the large number of information processing deficits which have been identified have not led to a clear understanding of the core deficits which are shown by all patients (Hemsley, 1993). This area is further complicated by the difficulty in distinguishing whether a particular deficit is a feature of the illness itself or whether it is a secondary consequence of other factors, such as coping with distressing symptoms. Despite this, a number of authors have attempted to identify the frequent psychological deficits found in patients with schizophrenia and develop training packages specifically to remedy the deficits and ultimately lessen their impact on behaviour and symptoms. Early advocates of this approach were Meichenbaum & Cameron (1973) who developed an intensive programme which assumed that the attentional deficits of patients with schizophrenia arise from a failure in verbal self-regulation. They attempted to train patients to overcome this difficulty by using self-instructional training, where patients are helped to complete puzzles using self-directed verbal instructions. The authors reported that improvements were found over a range of intellectual tasks and resulted in reductions in disordered speech in the patients. Despite these findings, there have been problems in completely replicating the findings, particularly in relation to the generalisability of improvements (Bentall *et al*, 1987). More recently, other authors have also demonstrated improved performance of patients trained on specific cognitive tasks (e.g. Bellack *et al*, 1990). Despite this, these studies have shown little or no evidence that these changes generalise to any other area of functioning.

Using a slightly different therapeutic approach, Brenner *et al* (1990, 1992) developed integrated psychological therapy (IPT) which combines cognitive therapy with forms of interpersonal skills training in a modular group training programme comprising five sub-programmes. The sub-programmes are arranged so that the first interventions target basic cognitive skills whereas later ones target complex interpersonal problems. The IPT intervention has been evaluated and compared with a placebo activity control and routine treatment, and results indicated that the IPT group scored significantly higher on tests of attention than either of the two control groups and overall psychopathology decreased significantly for the IPT groups but not for the control groups. These results were maintained at 18-month follow-up, which also revealed a lower hospitalisation rate for the IPT group.

Despite these recent developments in combining cognitive therapies with social performance training and the observation that patients can be trained to improve on specific tasks, there is still a long way to go before it becomes a viable approach to treatment. First, there is no consensus among researchers as to the nature of a deficit which is common to all patients who have a diagnosis of schizophrenia, and second, as a result of this there is no consensus as to which of the range of deficits demonstrated by patients should be targeted for treatment.

Interventions with acute patients

Most of the interventions described above have been delivered to patients experiencing chronic psychotic symptoms, rather than patients who are experiencing a recent-onset acute episode. It could be hypothesised that if patients can be targeted in the early stages of their illness, long-term gains may be even greater. Indeed, there is some support for this. A recent study by Drury *et al* (1996*a,b*) has shown that a comprehensive psychological treatment approach can also be appropriate for acute in-patients with a short illness history as well as patients with more chronic problems. An intensive ward-based individual cognitive–behavioural intervention together with family sessions and an eight-week education programme was compared with an equal contact recreational activity control group. Results indicated that the time to operationally defined recovery was reduced by 25–50% in the experimental group as compared to the control group. Mean time to discharge from hospital was also approximately halved in the experimental group. The present authors are currently engaged in a study to replicate these findings and to demonstrate the effectiveness of cognitive–behavioural therapy solely with acute in-patients with less than a two-year history of schizophrenia (further details available from the first author upon request).

Implications for training

There is little doubt that cognitive–behavioural interventions for patients with severe mental health problems can have a large impact, not only on relapse rates, but on the severity of psychotic symptoms, length of hospital stay, affective symptoms and social functioning of carer and patient. Yet their dissemination into routine services is sadly lacking.

Recent work at the University of Manchester and the Institute of Psychiatry, London (funded by the Sir Jules Thorn trust) attempts to provide mental health professionals with the additional skills necessary to carry out these types of psychosocial interventions. A three-module diploma programme (the Thorn psychosocial intervention training) has been developed and, so far, CPNs have been taught to deliver problem-oriented case management, family management and individual psychological management to individuals and their families.

Preliminary findings from students in Manchester have proved encouraging (Lancashire *et al*, 1996). Nurses were trained in the reliable assessment of mental state using an extended version of the KGV Symptom Scale (Krawiecka *et al*, 1977) and in the assessment of social functioning using the Social Functioning Scale (Birchwood *et al*, 1990); these were administered to all patients prior to Thorn psychosocial intervention and 12 months later. Pilot data from 27 patients show a significant reduction in positive, negative and affective symptoms, together with a significant improvement in social functioning (Lancashire *et al*, 1996). These results compare favourably with those from initial pilot studies reported by Brooker *et al* (1994), which assessed patient outcome in a similar way. The control sample of patients in Brooker *et al*'s study showed no significant changes in symptoms or social functioning following 12 months of standard psychiatric nursing care.

Clinical implications

The main types of psychological interventions shown to be effective for patients with schizophrenia involve individual work to reduce the impact of symptoms, increase compliance with medication and improve patients' ability to detect and alert services to the start of an acute relapse, and family work aimed towards reducing the risk of relapse and increasing patients' and relatives' social functioning (Box 1). Even though these are specialist types of interventions which usually require the services of a clinical psychologist, it is possible to train other mental health professionals, such as CPNs, to deliver the interventions, providing they receive appropriate guidance and supervision. As a result of this, as well as the current development of new antipsychotic drugs, there can now be fresh optimism for the future of services for individuals with schizophrenia. Policy makers and purchasers of mental health care need to be assertively educated about the unmet needs arising

---

> **Box 1. Key points**
>
> Although drug treatments remain the mainstay of acute treatment, many patients continue to experience psychotic symptoms
>
> Family interventions can significantly reduce patient relapse rates
>
> Persistent positive symptoms are often amenable to cognitive–behavioural interventions
>
> Detection of prodromal signs is possible in individual patients and may be useful to aid early intervention prior to acute relapse
>
> Poor compliance is multi-factorial but can often be improved with education and psychological techniques
>
> Neuropsychological deficits in chronic schizophrenia are identifiable and may be remediable by intensive cognitive approaches
>
> Despite good evidence for their efficacy, many psychological interventions have yet to be implemented into routine services
>
> A variety of mental health professionals are able to provide the approaches as long as they have appropriate training and supervision
>
> Despite research findings supporting the efficacy of psychological approaches they have not become routine in clinical practice

---

out of these new technologies. Psychological treatments can offer an adjunct or even an alternative to conventional drug treatments. It is likely that any progress made could be considerably enhanced by the increasing interest in the viability of these approaches and the amount to which this interest is carried from researchers and clinicians to fundholders and policy makers, who will ultimately be responsible for determining the future of services to individuals experiencing psychotic symptoms.

References

Bartko, G., Maylath, E. & Herczeg, I. (1987) Comparative study of schizophrenic patients relapsed on and off medication. *Psychiatry Research*, **22**, 221–227.

—, Herczeg, I. & Zador, G. (1988) Clinical symptomatology and drug compliance in schizophrenic patients. *Acta Psychiatrica Scandinavica*, **77**, 74–76.

Bellack, A. S., Meuser, K., Morrison, R. L., *et al* (1990) Remediation of cognitive deficits in schizophrenia. *American Journal of Psychiatry*, **147**, 1650–1655.

Bentall, R. P., Higson, P. J. & Lowe, C. F. (1987) Teaching self-instructions to chronic schizophrenic patients: efficacy and generalisation. *Behavioural Psychotherapy*, **15**, 58–76.

Birchwood, M., Smith, J., Macmillan, F., *et al* (1989) Predicting relapse in schizophrenia: the development and implementation of an early signs monitoring system using patients and families as observers. *Psychological Medicine*, **19**, 649–656.

—, —, Cochrane, R., *et al* (1990) The development and validation of a new scale of social adjustment for use in family intervention programmes with schizophrenic patients. *British Journal of Psychiatry*, **157**, 853–859.

Brenner, H. D., Kraemer, S., Hermanutz, M.,*et al* (1990) Cognitive treatments in schizophrenia. In *Schizophrenia: Concepts, Vulnerability and Intervention* (eds E. R. Straube & K. Hahlweg). Berlin: Springer-Verlag.

—, Hodel, B., Roder, V., *et al* (1992) Treatment of cognitive dysfunctions and behavioural deficits in schizophrenia: integrated psychological therapy. *Schizophrenia Bulletin*, **18**, 21–26.

Brooker, C., Tarrier, N., Barrowclough, C., *et al* (1992) Training community psychiatric nurses for psychosocial intervention. Report of a pilot study. *British Journal of Psychiatry*, **160**, 834–844.

—, Falloon, I. R. H., Butterworth, A., *et al* (1994) The outcome of training community psychiatric nurses to deliver psychosocial intervention. *British Journal of Psychiatry*, **165**, 222–230.

Brown, G. W. & Rutter, M. (1966) The measurement of family activities and relationships: a methodological study. *Human Relations*, **19**, 241–263.

Chadwick, P. & Lowe, C. F. (1990) The measurement and modification of delusional beliefs. *Journal of Consulting and Clinical Psychology*, **58**, 225–232.

Corrigan, P. W., Liberman, R. P. & Engel, J. D. (1990) From noncompliance to collaboration in the treatment of schizophrenia. *Hospital and Community Psychiatry*, **41**, 1203–1211.

Curson, D. A., Patel, M., Liddle, P. F., *et al* (1988) Psychiatric morbidity of a long-stay hospital population with chronic schizophrenia and implications for future community care. *British Medical Journal*, **297**, 819–822.

De Jesus Mari, J. & Streiner, D. L. (1994) An overview of family interventions and relapse in schizophrenia: meta-analysis of research findings. *Psychological Medicine*, **24**, 565–578.

Drury, V., Birchwood, M., Cochrane, R., *et al* (1996a) Cognitive therapy and reovery from acute psychosis: a controlled trial. I. Impact on psychotic symptoms. *British Journal of Psychiatry*, **169**, 593–601.

—, —, —, *et al* (1996b) Cognitive therapy and recovery from acute psychosis: a controlled trial. II. Impact on recovery time. *British Journal of Psychiatry*, **169**, 602–607.

Eckman, T. A. & Liberman, R. P. (1990) A large scale field test of a medication management program for people with schizophrenia. *Psychosocial Rehabilitation Journal*, **13**, 31–35.

—, —, Phipps, C. C., *et al* (1990) Teaching medication management skills to schizophrenic patients. *Journal of Clinical Psychopharmacology*, **10**, 33–38.

Falloon, I. R. H. & Talbot, R. E. (1981) Persistent auditory hallucinations: coping mechanisms and implications for management. *Psychological Medicine*, **11**, 329–339.

—, Boyd, J. L. & McGill, C. W. (1985) Family management in the prevention of morbidity in schizophrenia: Clinical outcome of a two year longitudinal follow-up. *Archives of General Psychiatry*, **42**, 887–896.

Haddock, G., Sellwood, W., Yusupoff, L., *et al* (1994) Developments in cognitive–behaviour therapy for persistent psychotic symptoms, *Behaviour Change*, **11**, 1–16.

Hemsley, D. R. (1993) A simple (or simplistic?) cognitive model for schizophrenia. *Behaviour, Research and Therapy*, **31**, 633–645.

Jaspers, K. (1963) *General Psychopathology* (translated by J. Hoenig & M. W. Hamilton). Manchester: Manchester University Press.

Kavanagh, D. (ed.) (1992a) *Schizophrenia: An Overview and Practical Handbook*. London: Chapman & Hall.

— (1992b) Recent developments in expressed emotion and schizophrenia. *British Journal of Psychiatry*, **160**, 601–620.

Kemp, R., Kirov, G., Everitt, B., *et al* (1998) Randomised controlled trial of compliance therapy. 18-month follow-up. *British Journal of Psychiatry*, **172**, 413–419.

Kottgen, C., Soinnichesen, I., Mollenhauer, K., *et al* (1984) Results of the Camberwell Family Interview study, I–III. *International Journal of Family Psychiatry*, **5**, 61–94.

Krawiecka, M., Goldberg, D. & Vaughan, M. (1977) A standardised psychiatric assessment scale for chronic psychiatric patients. *Acta Psychiatrica Scandinavica*, **55**, 299–308.

Kuipers, E., Garety, P., Fowler, D., *et al* (1997) London–East Anglia randomised controlled trial of cognitive–behavioural therapy for psychosis. I: Effects of the treatment phase. *British Journal of Psychiatry*, **171**, 319–327.

—, Fowler, D., Garety, P., *et al* (1998) London–East Anglia randomised controlled trial of cognitive–behavioural therapy for psychosis. III: Follow-up and economic evaluation at 18 months. *British Journal of Psychiatry*, **173**, 61–68.

Lancashire, S., Haddock, G., Tarrier, N., *et al* (1996) The impact of training community psychiatric nurses to use psychosocial interventions with people who have severe mental health problems. *Psychiatric Services*, **48**, 39–41.

Ley, P. (1992) *Improving Communication, Satisfaction and Compliance*. London: Chapman & Hall.

Ludwig, W., Huber, D., Schmidt, S., *et al* (1990) Assessment of compliance related attitudes in psychiatry. A comparison of two questionnaires based on the health belief model. *Social Psychiatry and Psychiatric Epidemiology*, **25**, 298–303.

Margo, A., Hemsley, D. R. & Slade, P. D. (1981) The effects of varying auditory input on schizophrenic hallucinations. *British Journal of Psychiatry*, **139**, 122–127.

Meichenbaum, D. & Cameron, R. (1973) Training schizophrenics to talk to themselves: a means of developing attentional control. *Behaviour Therapy*, **4**, 515–534.

Meuser, K. T. & Berenbaum, H. (1990) Psychodynamic treatment of schizophrenia. Is there a future? *Psychological Medicine*, **20**, 253–262.

Miller, W. R. & Rollnick, S. (1991) *Motivational Interviewing: Preparing People to Change Addictive Behaviour*. New York: Guilford Press.

Sellwood, W., Haddock, G. & Tarrier, N., *et al* (1994) Advances in the psychological management of positive symptoms of schizophrenia. *International Review of Psychiatry*, **6**, 201–215.

— & Tarrier, N. (1994) Demographic factors associated with extreme noncompliance in schizophrenia. *Social Psychiatry and Psychiatric Epidemiology*, **20**, 172–177.

Seltzer, A., Roncari, I. & Garfinkel, P. (1980) Effect of patient education on medication compliance. *Canadian Journal of Psychiatry*, **25**, 638–645.

Slade, P. D. (1972) The effects of systematic desensitisation on auditory hallucinations. *Behaviour, Research and Therapy*, **10**, 85–91.

Tarrier, N., Barrowclough, C., Vaughn, C., *et al* (1988) The community management of schizophrenia: A controlled trial of behavioural intervention with families to reduce relapse. *British Journal of Psychiatry*, **153**, 532–542.

—, Barrowclough, C., Porceddu, K.,*et al* (1994) The Salford family intervention project: relapse rates of schizophrenia at five and eight years. *British Journal of Psychiatry*, **165**, 829–832.

—, Yusupoff, L., Kinney, C.,*et al* (1998) A randomised controlled trial of intensive cognitive–behaviour therapy for chronic schizophrenia. *British Medical Journal*, in press.

Vaughn, C. E. & Leff, J. P. (1976a) The measurement of expressed emotion in families of psychiatric patients. *British Journal of Social and Clinical Psychology*, **15**, 157–165.

— & — (1976b) The influence of family life and social factors on the course of psychiatric illness. *British Journal of Psychiatry*, **129**, 125–137.

Wincze, J. P., Leitenberg, H. & Agras, W. S. (1972) The effects of token reinforcement on the delusional verbal behaviour of chronic paranoid schizophrenics. *Journal of Applied Behaviour Analysis*, **5**, 247–262.

Deploying a community mental health team for the effective care of individuals with schizophrenia

Geraldine Strathdee

Community mental health teams (CMHTs) have their origin in the American Community Mental Health Centre programme of the 1960s. The teams were mandated to provide services with an emphasis on the needs of people with severe mental illness. However, over time the focus of work shifted towards those with more common mental health problems, to the neglect of those with severe mental illness. Community mental health teams are now a firm feature of British psychiatry. Onyett *et al* (1994) identified over 300 CMHTs across England, defining themselves as comprising at least four members, from two or more disciplines, with a case load of individuals with mental health disorders, largely residing in the community.

In 1994 the focus of work, organisation, approach to service development and styles of management of British CMHTs were the subject of intensive study by over 14 national reviews. One of the most common findings was the variability of targeting of people with severe mental illness. In particular, the Audit Commission (1994) and Mental Health Foundation (1994) reports made recommendations for achieving more focused and effective team development.

This chapter is based on the experience of clinicians involved in the planning and development of two CMHTs in urban areas which focused on those with severe mental illness and incorporates some of the main recommendations of the national reviews.

Service development approach

A strategic service development approach to the planning and implementation of services and working practices is essential if a CMHT is to be effective in treating people with severe mental illness, including those with schizophrenia. The strategy should be informed by an understanding of the theoretical and research bases of community care programmes and, equally importantly, a knowledge of where this has been translated into good practice, not just in well-funded 'model' programmes but also in pragmatic working practices in the UK (Test & Scott, 1990; Wood, 1995/6).

Box 1 outlines the key elements that such a service development approach should include. First, recognition of the range of needs of patients with schizophrenia. Second, the establishment of the components of a system of service structures between the disciplines and agencies involved in the care of people with mental illness. Third, the use of a range of effective therapeutic interventions which address the wider needs of people with severe mental illness and which have been demonstrated to result in improved health, social and other outcomes. Fourth, the use of explicit and effective organisation and management techniques within the CMHT and the service system. Finally, it should include an analysis of the current and required skill mix of the team members, a plan for continuing development through training, and establishment of mechanisms of support for staff.

Understanding the needs of people with schizophrenia

The development of community services has had two consistent themes: that the traditional inherited service systems, dominated by large institutions, should be replaced with a more

> **Box 1. Strategic development of services for individuals with severe mental illness**
>
> Recognition of the needs of individuals with severe mental illness
> Establishment of the structural components of a comprehensive community mental health service system
> Use of effective interventions
> Effective organisation and management of the community mental health team
> Planning of staff skill mix, training and support

> **Box 2. Components of a comprehensive mental health service**
>
> Indentification and needs assessment systems
> Care Programme Approach integrated with care management
> Range of hospital and community beds and effective bed management strategy
> Case management and assertive outreach
> Day care, rehabilitiation, education and work
> Crisis response
> Assessment and consultation
> Carer and community education and support
> Primary care liaison
> User advocacy and community alliances

balanced and flexible range of alternative services; and that services should be directed to meeting individual needs. Individuals with both severe and the more common mental health disorders have a wide range of social and health needs. They include the need for: appropriate housing; welfare benefits; a meaningful day, leisure or working life; social and support networks; physical and dental care; medication and psychoeducation; psychological treatments; work and rehabilitation (Strathdee & Sutherby 1995).

Components of a comprehensive community mental health service system

One of the most positive aspects of British psychiatry in recent years has been the emergence of a consensus of the components of a comprehensive community mental health service system (Box 2). These have been articulated by policy makers (Department of Health, 1994*b*), clinicians (Royal College of Psychiatrists, 1995) and by user groups such as Mind (1983). The role of CMHTs in assessing the need for, and planning and development of, some of these components will be discussed in detail below.

Epidemiological and local planning information

To plan strategically, a community team must first assess the full extent of the service needed. The starting point for any CMHT must be to develop, over a one- to three-year timetable, a detailed

knowledge of the number and needs of individuals with schizophrenia and other severe mental disorders in its locality. By using epidemiological techniques teams can estimate the expected number of individuals with schizophrenia for their locality. The Office of Population Censuses and Surveys national morbidity survey (Meltzer *et al*, 1995) has produced surprising findings of wider variation in the prevalence of psychosis in England than has previously been identified, from 0.2% in affluent areas to 0.9% in more deprived areas.

Of those with psychiatric morbidity, it is likely that only a proportion will be in contact with specialist services. Between 25 and 40% may be in contact only with their general practitioner (GP), social services, the housing agencies, police, local churches or user groups. A fundamental building block in establishing an effective team is to develop an identification component of the service, developing regular liaison with all other agencies who may be serving the needs of the severely mentally ill in the community. Box 3 indicates the likely contact points of people with schizophrenia. In many services nationally the implementation of the Care Programme Approach (CPA) has been used as the vehicle to audit the number of people with severe mental illness in contact with the service compared with that expected from the epidemiological data.

Needs assessment for rational service planning

Having identified individuals with schizophrenia in the CMHT locality, the next step is the introduction of a system of needs assessment. The

---

Box 3. Identification of people with schizophrenia

Mental health service contacts
Out-patients
Domiciliary visit records
Care Programme Approach, supervision register and Section 117 records
Community psychiatric nurse case loads
Depot clinic patients
Mental Health Act
In-patient audit data
Crisis attenders (e.g. accident and emergency attenders)
Residents of long-stay institutions

Primary care team contacts
Practice register diagnosis of psychosis
Repeat psychotropic drug prescriptions
Frequent emergency and other consultations
Hostel/group home/sheltered residence populations
Community psychiatric nurse attenders and health visitor contacts

Social service contacts
Area social worker case loads
Care management recipients
Housing department clients causing concern

Voluntary sector and other agency contacts
Residents of sheltered accommodation
Individuals presenting to churches in distress
Imprisoned and homeless people
Probation officer case loads
Drop-in and other casual facility users

---

routine collection of clinical data and care planning assessment and review are vital, facilitating the development of services based on the aggregated needs of patients, informing the case for resources, and facilitating multi-agency coordination of service planning and delivery; also, this process is vital at a national level for the mental health agenda (Kingdon, 1998).

Despite the many standardised assessment instruments in mental health, remarkably few are used in routine clinical practice. This discrepancy may arise because, although many instruments are helpful in monitoring symptoms, they do not lead directly to the informed decision-making of management plans. In general, any innovation which is seen as a time-consuming addition to,

rather than an integral part of, routine clinical practice is unlikely to succeed. Newer instruments are a first stage in combining research validity with practical application. These include the Health of the Nation Outcome Scales (Department of Health, 1994*a*) and the Camberwell Assessment of Need (Phelan *et al*, 1995).

In many areas the CPA documentation is evolving to combine several functions and to avoid time-consuming duplication for clinicians. Efficiently implemented by clinicians, it serves as the accurate record of the met and unmet needs of the service user, the agreed interventions with time scales for implementation and responsibilities and roles of team members, and highlights risk and relapse prevention strategies. It replaces the time-consuming lengthy letters to GPs and other agencies and can easily be faxed or communicated to users, carers and GPs and other involved agencies in line with confidentiality policies.

Case management and assertive outreach services

To meet the complex needs of people with schizophrenia, case management as a service or at least a technique is essential in drawing together all the necessary services into one coherent package of care. Studies have compared a number of models of case management which offer acute home-based care with hospital care (Stein & Test, 1980; Hoult *et al*, 1984; Muijen *et al*, 1992). Despite differences in the models and evaluative methodologies used, these and several other studies confirm changes in clinical and social outcomes and the patterns of service utilisation and greater patient satisfaction from acute home-orientated care. However, CMHTs cannot regard case management as a panacea. It is only effective where those practising case management are trained in, and employ, effective intervention techniques and where it is supported by an adequate infrastructure of resources. One of the biggest dilemmas faced by those involved in service development is how to ensure that the most vulnerable individuals receive case management services. Local service configuration needs to take account of local morbidity, primary care infrastructure, existing service strengths in rehabilitation, crisis and other services.

Hospital and community beds

People with schizophrenia account for 60% of all in-patient bed use in mental health units. It is essential that a CMHT's use of hospital beds, the most expensive resource, is necessary and based on sound therapeutic reasons. A great deal of controversy has surrounded the number, use and management of acute mental health beds. The evidence points to the complexity of the problems and the need to develop a broad range of services to resolve them. Some services have required additional acute beds to deliver safe care (Department of Health, 1994b). Lelliott & Wing's (1994) study of new long-stay patients found that 61% were considered to be inappropriately placed in hospital beds, 47% required a community-based residential setting, and of these over half were in hospital because no suitable community placement was available. Several analyses of acute bed unit use indicate that: 30–70% of those in the beds are 'revolving door regulars', well known to services; and a significant proportion had been readmitted within three months of discharge, due to a lack of provision of high-support community accommodation and effective discharge planning mechanisms.

The success of community-based services is crucially related to the nature and availability of accommodation with appropriate levels of support. Community mental health teams must have a wide range of hospital and community beds available to them. These should range from responsive and community-sensitive secure facilities for mentally disordered offenders, through to acute hospital beds, 24-hour staffed units in hospital hostels and community places for the 'new long stay', especially those with mild to moderate challenging behaviours, and a range of community beds for crisis diversion, quarter- and half-way hostel purposes, respite facilities, and residential and permanent accommodation. Community mental health teams are ideally placed to play a leadership role in ensuring the planning of such facilities if they have concrete local data to present on the numbers of their patients with schizophrenia and the number and range of bed provision needed.

Community mental health teams and bed management

In addition to planning and ensuring the development of an adequate number and range of beds, community teams have been shown to be effective in preventing unnecessary and inappropriate acute bed use by a range of bed management strategies (Box 4). These illustrate the need for a system approach to include needs assessment, admission prevention, increasing throughput, discharge planning and development of both residential and non-residential alternatives.

Examples of such strategies include a study where the CMHTs' senior and experienced clinicians did initial home-based assessments, rather than using the hospital out-patient clinic site, and admission was reduced by 50–70% (Burns *et al*, 1993). Gate-keeping, with senior doctors and nurses becoming involved in any decision to admit a patient, can support junior staff, who are less experienced in assessment of risk and safe alternatives to admission.

Box 4. Effective use of beds and bed management strategies for CMHTs

Needs assessment
Routine audit of bed occupancy and length of stay
Audit of pathways into care
Audit of delayed discharges and reasons
Audit of local supported sheltered housing

Admission prevention strategies
Accident and emergency triage
Senior gate-keeping and supervision for juniors
Induction for all staff
Home-based assessments where feasible
Relapse prevention plans for all patients with severe mental illness
Availability of flexible home support systems

Increasing throughput strategies
Pro formas to communicate reasons for admission to in-patient staff
Agreed outcomes and time scales at onset of admission
Bed manager with proper job description
Frequent, well-chaired care planning meetings (e.g. ward rounds)
Therapeutic environments on wards
Well-trained staff with optimal face-to-face time with patients

Discharge planning
Maximal support in the first six weeks after discharge
'Surgeries' by special needs housing workers on wards

Safe alternatives (residential and non-residential)
Home assertive treatment teams
Adequate crisis intervention services
Family placements
Well-supported housing

As research has repeatedly shown, continuity of care is important. The most likely time of readmission and suicide attempts is in the first 4–12 weeks after discharge. Support by keyworkers is more likely to be successful if it is intense in this vulnerable period. Another of the most consistent findings is that integrated hospital and community services are essential to maximise the use of resources. Unless community teams have control over their own hospital beds, both bed use and length of stay are significantly increased.

Crisis response services

Individuals with schizophrenia are vulnerable to environmental stressors which may result in exacerbation of symptoms and relapse, and episodes of acute illness. Successful CMHTs must aim to provide support and help for the client, family members, and others to cope with the emergency while maintaining to the greatest extent the client's status as a functioning community member. Studies of users, carers and GPs (Beeforth *et al*, 1994; Strathdee & Sutherby, 1995) produce almost interchangeable findings. All want crisis services to be available at a single point of telephone or face-to-face contact. They would value services on an extended basis, manned by experienced and known mental health professionals and providing crisis diversion facilities as a viable alternative to hospitalisation. Nationally this type of service is provided by a limited number of teams. Even when individuals with severe mental illness are in contact with a CMHT, it is often the GP or casualty staff with limited training who provide the majority of crisis care. There is growing evidence that where the core basic services for the most vulnerable people with schizophrenia and other disorders are comprehensive and effective during office hours, there is less demand for out-of-hours and crisis services. Indeed, it could be argued that where patients known to the service with longer-term schizophrenia have to wait until they are in crisis to access the service, there is a problem with the service model and delivery.

Day care and rehabilitation

The role of day hospital and partial hospitalisation programmes has undergone radical review in recent years. Holloway (1988) defined four possible functions of the day hospital for those with a mental disorder: as an alternative to hospital admission when acutely ill (for provision of

support, supervision and monitoring in the transition between hospital and home); as a source of long-term structure and support for those with chronic disabilities; as a site for brief intensive therapy for those who require short-term focused rehabilitation; and as an information, training and communication resource.

Creed *et al* (1990, 1991, 1997) and Harrison & Marshall (1997) describe services which are effective in admission prevention, but which need to evolve both in terms of the hours of functioning and the provision of home-based outreach services. In a service committed to community integration and normalisation, Wood (1995/6) and Foulds *et al* (1998) as the occupational therapists responsible for the development of day care services for a CMHT stress the importance of user consultation and the formation of formal liaison and networks with other local providers of work, education and day care.

Assessment and consultation services

Like the role of day hospitals, the role of out-patient clinics is under review in many services. The decreasing availability of medical time for clinical care and the multi-disciplinary nature of CPA implementation has led to a review of the value and outcomes of out-patient clinics.

Until the past few decades the majority of consultation services were conducted in hospital out-patient settings. Evaluation of these services indicates dissatisfaction with communication patterns, clinical and referral outcomes and up to 45% non-attendance. The response of clinicians, uninformed by policy or research considerations, was to work on a sessional basis in primary care centres. Early criticisms of these primary care-based clinics was that they would result in psychiatrists serving only the 'worried well'. The evidence refutes this. They provide a service to groups of people with severe mental disorders who previously dropped out of contact with the specialist services (i.e. women with long-term disorders, young men with schizophrenia, the homeless with psychoses, and those with paranoid disorders who felt stigmatised by attendance at a hospital site (Tyrer, 1984)).

In many community services community psychiatric nurses were the first to develop attachments to particular general practices. Where the nurses have been hospital based and work as members of the secondary care team, 80% of their referrals are from psychiatrists, and individuals with severe mental illness form a considerable proportion of their workload. In other organisations where nurses, although employed by secondary care services, are attached to particular general practices, the referral pattern shifts with 80% of their referrals coming directly from GPs. Case loads tend to be large, composed of patients with neurotic and adjustment disorders. Although the case loads of both the hospital-based and primary-care-based community psychiatric nurses remain similar in terms of the numbers of individuals with schizophrenia, the mean time in contact with patients with psychosis is a third of the time spent with those with non-psychotic disorders and is almost entirely limited to the administration of injections.

Primary care liaison

One of the great strengths of the British health care system is its primary care infrastructure. To a large extent its significant involvement with people with schizophrenia goes unrecognised. Although the numbers of such patients are small (about 4–7 per GP with an average list size of around 2000), their use of primary care services is high where they are not well supported by the CMHT. Based on research findings in the primary care area and the implementation of a successful shared care model for diabetes and asthma (also longer-term conditions), a range of initiatives to improve joint working between the primary health care teams and the CMHT can be proposed (Box 5).

Effective interventions for schizophrenia

However well a CMHT has developed the service structures, outcomes for their patients with schizophrenia will only improve where there is an analysis of the skills of the team, funding dedicated for training in acquiring new skills and the routine use of effective interventions (Conway *et al*, 1994). Box 6 is not comprehensive but outlines some of the most important interventions.

Psychosocial interventions

In a comprehensive review Slade *et al* (1995) found that up to 45% of the severely mentally ill do not apply for or receive their entitlement to welfare benefits. The provision of welfare benefits to provide an adequate standard of living is a major

---

Box 5. Primary care liaison in the care of individuals with schizophrenia

Communication strategy
Provide directory of street boundaries, sector team names, roles and contact numbers
Information booklets of therapies available
Named contacts to advise on appropriate referrals

Crisis services
Well-publicised single telephone contact access point
Agreed crisis response service

Assessment and out-patient services
Agreed referral–appointment point intervals
Stated referral criteria for CMHT members
Clear communication with stated objectives of management, predicted response, complications and side-effects
Six-monthly review plans for longer-term patients
Clearly stated role of GP and specialist in treatment
Clarification of prescribing responsibilities

Shared care for people with schizophrenia
Set up a joint case register similar to that for diabetes
Negotiate link worker job description; negotiate priority of severe mental illness
Agree annual physical care reviews
Ensure GP has verbal/physical/fax input into CPA care planning reviews
Identify GP/practice nurse involved in development of relapse prevention plan and crisis contracts
Agree protocols for group homes/hostels
Discuss consequences of expensive new psychotropic drugs and extra-contractual referrals
Obtain support for appropriate range of beds and community alternatives to hospital admission

---

priority for service users. Motivation to attend day care programmes is likely to increase if buying the bus fare no longer conflicts with buying food. Likewise, having permanent, affordable, comfortable housing is important in achieving a stable mental state, free of worries about rent, damp, harassing neighbours and so forth. Craig *et al*'s

> **Box 6. Range of effective interventions for people with schizophrenia**
>
> Housing with adequate support
> Welfare benefits and financial advice
> Physical and dental care
> Medication and psychoeducational programmes
> Cognitive–behavioural therapy for psychotic symptoms
> Identification and development of coping strategies
> Crisis prevention and relapse prevention
> Family problem-solving therapy
> Rehabilitation, practical skills and support
> Work and education

(1995) studies of the homeless have shown that outcomes are improved when care programmes include interventions which address housing needs.

Physical and dental care

Coexisting physical morbidity is common in patients with longer-term schizophrenia. In a study of long-term day centre attendees, Brugha *et al* (1989) found that 41% suffered medical problems potentially requiring care. Annual physical review as a minimum should be arranged with the GP by the patient's keyworker.

Medication and psychoeducational programmes

Medication is an important element in the management of many people with schizophrenia in the acute and longer-term phases of their illness. It is important that members of community teams familiarise themselves with good practices in medication prescribing (Thompson, 1994). An understanding of the need for regular review, monitoring of side-effects and tailoring medication type and dosage to individual needs, both in the acute and continuing care phases, is basic good practice.

Where easily accessible psychoeducational packages of information on conditions and treatments (preferably developed jointly with users and carers) are used, colloboration with treatment is enhanced and relapse prevention increased.

Family and carer education, support and therapies

Adequate early treatment, associated with client, family and staff education and training, can prevent the onset of many crises (Birchwood *et al*, 1989). Falloon *et al* (1993) showed reductions in family disruption, physical and mental disorders, and perceived burden after structured family interventions. Because of the episodic nature of the illness, however, there will be instances that require acute care and rapid response crisis stabilisation services. The need to see the individual in the context of his or her family environment is well understood. Controlled studies (Falloon *et al*, 1985; Smith & Birchwood, 1990; Kuipers *et al*, 1992))have illustrated the impact of wider intervention packages on relapse rates in households with high expressed emotion. Successful programmes contain the following features: a problem-focused approach to reduce expressed emotion and stress in the home environment; an educational component; long-term application for six to nine months; involvement of the patient in the family treatment; well-trained intervention staff; and close liaison with members of the clinical team and other agencies (Kuipers & Bebbington, 1991)

Effective organisation of CMHTs

The effective care of people with schizophrenia requires the skills of nurses, occupational therapists, psychologists, social workers and psychiatrists. No one discipline working autonomously has the range of skills required if clinical and social outcomes are to be improved. Therefore, there are a number of key organisational questions for CMHTs to consider.

First, how can the team develop, not as a set of independent and autonomous practitioners, but with multi-disciplinary and, preferably, inter-agency integrated working. Both the Audit Commission(1994) and the Mental Health Task-force London (Department of Health, 1995) studies found that the development of community services which targeted those with severe mental illness was most advanced in those areas where there were integrated health and social CMHTs with clear management structures.

Second, how should the team organise to protect people with severe mental illness. In the majority of services CMHTs are generic, that is they provide care to both new referrals requiring acute care and also those with severe mental illness. Unless effective management systems are in place to ensure a continuing prioritisation of the most needy and vulnerable, the drift away from individuals with severe mental illness is well described. Services have developed a number of organisational formats to prevent this trend. First, in some areas a separate rehabilitation service exists where a dedicated case management and assertive outreach team serves a limited number of those with severe mental illness across several sectors. Second, within generic sector teams two strategies are especially common: agreed case loads and case mix are regularly monitored to ensure that the proportion of those with severe mental illness remains high and/or specialist case managers or rehabilitation experts are appointed within the generic team. They develop or retain specialist expertise by having dual membership of both their generic sector team and a district-wide rehabilitation service. In areas where the prevalence of severe mental illness is high, sectors have divided their total pool of staff resource to form two sector teams, one providing acute care while the other provides case management and specialist rehabilitation services which emphasise normalisation and community integration.

Whatever the arrangement, case loads must be realistic, with one case manager for 10–15 patients requiring assertive outreach and high levels of input. The ratio can extend to 1 : 30–40 where the individuals in the case load have had comprehensive assessments, well-developed care plans, are stable, engaged and trusting of services offered, have rehearsed relapse prevention and crisis contracts, and are well supported by a range of community agencies.

Management of CMHT

The development of an operational policy is a prerequisite for the effective working of any CMHT. Box 7 serves as a useful basis for both team building and service development.

In British psychiatry we have a consensus about the range of services we need to offer, the interventions we recognise as effective and the outcomes we hope to achieve. Effective organisation and management of CMHTs is an essential building block to the future. There is no standard blueprint to guide individual teams. Success depends on a shared vision at local level, alliances forged between community agencies and solutions developed based on local strengths and resources. As Tansella (1991) concludes "Only the past can be copied, the future must be created".

> **Box 7. Issues in development of an operational policy for management of a community mental health team**
>
> **Team aims and client groups served**
> **Catchment area and local needs assessment**
> **Team functions**
> **Referrals to and from the team: criteria for acceptance and discharge**
> **Team membership**
> **Team relationships and accountability mechanisms**
> **Team meetings: conduct, agenda, decision-making procedures**
> **Case allocation and management**
> **Team member's role: all members, key-workers, team manager/coordinator**
> **Systems and procedures: health care records (format, access and confidentiality), budget formulation and monitoring, evaluation of service and of individual members**
> **Staff development, support and training**
> **Details of service provided**
> **Team plan (six-month, one-year and three-year plans, with costs)**
> **Appendices: reports of workload, services provided, grants obtained**

References

Audit Commission (1994) *Finding a Place: A Review of Mental Health Services for Adults.* London: HMSO.

Beeforth, M., Conlan, E. & Graley, R. (1994) *Have We Got Views for You.* London: The Sainsbury Centre for Mental Health.

Birchwood, M., Smith, J., MacMillan, F., *et al* (1989) Predicting relapse in schizophrenia: the development and implementation of an early signs monitoring system using patients and families as observers. *Psychological Medicine*, **19**, 649–656.

Brugha,T., Wing, J. & Smith, B. (1989) Physical ill-health of the long-term mentally ill in the community. Is there an unmet need? *British Journal of Psychiatry*, **155**, 777–782.

Burns, T., Deadsmore, A., Bhat, A., *et al* (1993) A controlled trial of home based acute psychiatric services. *British Journal of Psychiatry*, **163**, 49–61.

Conway, M., Melzer, D., Shepherd, G., *et al* (1994) *A Companion to Purchasing Adult Mental Health Services.* London: Sainsbury Centre for Mental Health.

Craig, T., Bayliss, E., Klein, O., *et al* (1995) *The Homeless Mentally Ill Initiative.* London: Department of Health.

Creed, F. H., Black, D., Anthony, P., *et al* (1990) Randomised controlled trial comparing day and in-patient psychiatric treatment. *British Medical Journal*, **300**, 1033–1037.

——, ——, ——, *et al* (1991) Randomised controlled trial of day and in-patient psychiatric treatment. 2: Comparison of two hospitals. *British Journal of Psychiatry*, **158**, 183–189.

——, Mbaya, P., Lancashire, S, *et al* (1997) Cost effectiveness of day and in-patient psychiatric treatment: results of a randomised controlled trial. *British Medical Journal*, **314**, 1381–1385.

Department of Health (1994*a*) *The Health of the Nation: Key Area Handbook, Mental Illness* (2nd edn). London: HMSO.

—— (1994*b*) *Mental Health in London: Priorities for Action*. London: Mental Health Task Force.

—— (1995) *Mental Health Taskforce London Project Report*. London: NHS Executive.

Falloon, I. M., LaPorta, M., Fadden, G., *et al* (1993) *Managing Stess in Families. Cogitive and Behavioural Strategies for Enhancing Coping Skills*. London: Routledge.

Falloon, J. R. H., *et al* (1985) Family management in the prevention of morbidity in schizophrenia. *Archives of General Psychiatry*, **42**, 887–896.

Foulds, G., Wood, H. & Bhui, K. (1998) Quality day care services for people with severe mental health problems. *Psychiatric Bulletin*, **22**, 144–147.

Harrison, J. & Marshall, J. (1997) Psychiatric day hospitals. In *The London Bed Management Learning Set Manual*. London: The Sainsbury Centre for Mental Health.

Holloway, F. (1988) Day care and community support. In *Community Care in Practice* (eds A. Lavender & F. Holloway). Chichester: Wiley.

Hoult, J., Rosen, A. & Reynolds, I. (1984) Community orientated treatment compared to psychiatric hospital orientated treatment. *Social Sciences and Medicine*, **18**, 1005–1010.

Kingdon, D. (1998) Making care programming work. In *Acute Psychosis, Schizophrenia and Comorbid Disorders*. Recent Topics from Advances in Psychiatric Treatment, vol. 1 (ed. A.S. Lee), pp. 73–77. London: Gaskell.

Kuipers, L. & Bebbington, P. (1991) *Working in Partnership: Clinicians and Carers in the Management of Long Term Illness*. London: Heinemann.

——, Leff, J. & Lam, D. (eds) (1992) *Family Work for Schizophrenia: A Practical Guide*. London: Gaskell.

Lelliot, P. & Wing, J. (1994) A national audit of new long-stay psychiatric patients. II. Impact on services. *British Journal of Psychiatry*, **165**, 170–178.

Meltzer, H., Gill, B., Petticrew, M., *et al* (1995) *OPCS Surveys of Psychiatric Morbidity in Great Britain: The Prevalence of Psychiatic Morbidity among Adults Living in Private Households*. London: I IMSO.

Mental Health Foundation (1994) *Creating Community Care*. London: Mental Health Foundation.

Mind (1983) *Common Concerns*. London: Mind.

Muijen, M., Marks, I., Connolly, J., *et al* (1992) Home-based care and standard hospital care for patients with severe mental illness: a randomised controlled trial. *British Medical Journal*, **304**, 749–754.

Onyett, S., *et al* (1994) *The Organisation and Operation of Community Mental Health Teams in England: A National Survey*. London: The Sainsbury Centre for Mental Health.

Phelan, M., Slade, M., Thornicroft, G., *et al* (1995) The Camberwell Assessment of Need: the validity and reliability of an instrument to assess the needs of people with severe mental illness. *British Journal of Psychiatry*, **167**, 589–595.

Royal College of Psychiatrists (1995) *Caring for a Community*. Council Report CR36. London: Royal College of Psychiatrists.

Slade, M., McCrone, P. & Thornicroft, G. (1995) Uptake of welfare benefits by psychiatric patients. *Psychiatric Bulletin*, **19**, 411–413.

Smith, J. & Birchwood, M. (1990) Relatives and patients as partners in the management of schizophrenia. The development of a service model. *British Journal of Psychiatry*, **156**, 654–660.

Stein, L. & Test, M. (1980) Alternative to mental hospital treatment.I.Conceptual model, treatment programme and clinical evaluation. *Archives of General Psychiatry*, **37**, 392–397.

Strathdee, G. & Jenkins, R. (1995) Contracting for primary care mental health services. In *Purchasing Mental Health Services* (eds G. Thornicroft & G. Strathdee). London: HMSO.

—— & Sutherby, K. (1995) Liaison psychiatry and primary health care settings. In *Multi-Professional Cooperation in Community Care* (eds S. Ritter, N. Watkins, N. Hervey, *et al*). London: Edward Arnold.

Tansella, M. (1991) Community care without mental hospitals – ten years experience. *Psychological Medicine*, **suppl. 19**, 47–48.

Test, T. M. & Scott, R. (1990) Theoretical and research bases of community care programmes. In *Mental Health Care Delivery: Innovations, Impediments & Implementation* (eds I. Marks & Scott). Cambridge: Cambridge University Press.

Thompson, C. (1994) The use of high-dose antipsychotic medication. *British Journal of Psychiatry*, **164**, 448–458.

Thornicroft, G. (1990) Case management for the severely mentally ill. *Social Psychiatry and Psychiatric Epidemiology*, **25**, 141–143.

Tyrer, P. (1984) Psychiatric clinics in general practice: an extension of community care. *British Journal of Psychiatry*, **145**, 571–575.

Wood, H. (1995/6) *The Community Mental Health Team Manager Series*. London: Mental Health Foundation.

Setting up an assertive community treatment service

Andrew Kent & Tom Burns

The past 20 years have witnessed a surge of interest in assertive community treatment (ACT) for the severely mentally ill (Drake & Burns, 1995). Assertive community treatment aims to help people who would otherwise be in and out of hospital on a 'revolving door' basis to live in the community and enjoy the best possible quality of life. Services based on the ACT model seek to replace the total support of the hospital with comprehensive, intensive and flexible support in the community, delivered by an individual key-worker or core services team. They are organised in a way that optimises continuity of care across different functional areas and across time.

Assertive community treatment has been most extensively deployed in the USA, where various developments have culminated in the Programs in Assertive Community Treatment (PACT) model. The origins of PACT lie with the innovative and highly successful Training in Community Living (TCL) programme developed during the 1970s at the Mendota Mental Health Institute in Madison, Wisconsin (Marx et al, 1973). The TCL programme sprang from a recognition that contemporaneous community treatments did little more than maintain the chronically disabled patient in "a tenuous community adjustment on the brink of rehospitalisation" (Stein & Test, 1980).

The concepts underpinning TCL were simple, yet revolutionary. Its architects, Arnold Marx, Leonard Stein and Mary Ann Test, realised that an effective community treatment programme must assume responsibility for helping the patient meet all of his or her needs. They argued that these needs include: the material essentials of life, such as food, clothing and shelter; coping skills necessary to meet the demands of community living; motivation to persevere in the face of life's adversity; freedom from pathologically dependent relationships; and support and education of 'significant others' involved with the patient in the community.

The expectation that the socially disabled patient would come to the clinician was replaced with the expectation that the clinician would be assertive in delivering care and go to the patient. The assumption that the patient would negotiate the difficult pathways between different caring agencies was replaced with the assumption that the clinician is responsible for ensuring coordination of inter-agency care. The role of the keyworker became pre-eminent, assuming responsibility for delivering a greater proportion of direct care to a much smaller number of allocated patients. Care became needs-led, and care programmes were designed for each individual.

The results of Stein and Test's original, randomised, controlled study of TCL retain their power to impress. Over the first year of the programme, 58% of the patients randomised to progressive, standard care were readmitted to a psychiatric hospital compared with 6% of patients receiving TCL. Not only were people on the TCL programme more likely to live independently in the community, but their clinical state improved, together with their social functioning, likelihood of employment, compliance with medication and, most importantly of all, their quality of life. These gains were achieved without additional burden on families or other informal carers, and (despite the intensity of intervention) at no extra cost because of the saving on beds (Test & Stein, 1980; Weisbrod et al, 1980). These results have been interpreted to suggest that TCL was significantly less expensive than standard, progressive care. When funding for the programme was withdrawn, all of the gains were lost: ACT needs to be offered to patients over the longer term.

The enormous influence of the TCL model can be attributed to the rigour with which the original programme was evaluated. Many other studies have followed (Olfson, 1990; Burns & Santos, 1995). One of the most influential of these was an early replication of the TCL model in Sydney, Australia (Hoult *et al*, 1983). To date there have been over 20 randomised controlled trials of ACT, making it the most extensively researched service development in community psychiatry. In spite of this, we still do not know exactly which components of ACT are critical for outcome.

In Britain, the largest ACT study to date is that of the Daily Living Programme (DLP; Marks *et al*, 1994). The results of this were a significant reduction in duration of hospitalisation, although not in its frequency. There were modest clinical gains at 18 months and considerable improvement in patient satisfaction. Like TCL, the DLP demonstrated a rapid loss of gains when the service was withdrawn. Unlike TCL, however, the investigators found no financial advantage – probably because of the major start-up costs of the scheme and a focus on a more acutely ill patient group. The study was also compromised by a number of extraneous factors – a highly publicised homicide and shifts in clinical control of in-patient services.

Key elements of assertive community treatment

The TCL/PACT approach has been very well described (Test, 1992). A multi-disciplinary core services team (continuous treatment team) is responsible for helping its patients meet all of their needs, and does so by being the primary provider of relevant services wherever possible. The team offers continuity of care over time and across traditional service boundaries 24 hours a day, seven days a week. Patients are engaged and followed-up assertively, and treatment is offered in the community rather than at traditional service settings. The emphasis is on helping patients to function as independently as possible, by teaching and enhancing skills in the environment where they will be needed, rather than in day hospitals and sheltered workshops. Individuals are assisted in meeting basic needs, such as housing, food and work, and the development of a supportive social and family environment. Care plans are individualised and adaptable to changing needs over time. Goals, such as reduced symptom severity, increased community tenure and improved instrumental functioning, are explicit. A keyworker from the team is responsible for providing and coordinating the care of each individual, and helps in the management of his or her symptoms on a day-to-day basis, including overseeing medication (see Box 1).

Box 1. Key elements of the PACT model (adapted from Test, 1992)

Core services team is responsible for helping the patient meet all of his or her needs and provides the bulk of clinical care

Improved patient functioning (in employment, social relations and activities of daily living) is a primary goal

The patient is directly assisted in symptom management

One team member acts as a patient's keyworker and coordinates all of the patient's care

Individual keyworkers have small case loads (10–15 patients)

Treatment is individualised between patients and over time

Patients are engaged and followed-up in an assertive manner

Treatment is provided *in vivo*, in community settings – skills learnt in the community can be better applied in the community

Care is continuous both over time and across functional areas

---

Assertive community treatment is, therefore, a pure form of clinical case management (Kanter, 1989) and lies at the opposite end of the case management continuum to the earlier 'brokerage' model (Thornicroft, 1991). Many of its underlying concepts have become emblematic of good clinical practice. Individualised, needs-led care planning coordinated by a keyworker is the cornerstone of the Care Programme Approach (Department of Health, 1990).

A few authors have attempted to tease out those components of PACT which are critical for its success (McGrew *et al*, 1994; Teague *et al*, 1995). A better understanding of the critical components will facilitate precise application of the model in a greater variety of circumstances. Although there is widespread consensus on the likely components, prospective studies of programme fidelity are urgently required (Taube *et al*, 1990).

What does an assertive community treatment team do?

Assertive community treatment has traditionally been delivered by discrete clinical teams operating alongside generic, locally based mental health services. An individual team member acts as an intensive case manager (ICM) to a small group of patients (no more than 15, and usually fewer than 12) to help each patient meet all of his or her needs. Before these needs can be identified, the keyworker must engage the patient in a therapeutic relationship. It is difficult to overstate the importance, and all too often the difficulty, of this task. One of the obvious strengths of the ACT model is that keyworker time is protected and available for such fundamental work.

The core task of engagement is to build and foster a positive attitude on the part of the patient to both the keyworker and to treatment. The process of engagement pervades many other tasks, but in its purest form involves general problem-solving, joint recreational activity (e.g. going to see a film together) and befriending. These are generally not activities afforded high status in mental health work, often being delegated to voluntary organisations. The need for the keyworker to foster a close therapeutic relationship that in all probability will last for many years lends them a new, and appropriate, priority.

Case 1

N.H. is a 53-year-old isolated Irish man with a 30-year history of schizophrenia who despite several admissions has always resisted follow-up. When he had been admitted to hospital, it was always in a severely neglected state, usually under a section of the Mental Health Act. His previous compliance with medication had been very poor and he had consistently refused follow-up from a community psychiatric nurse (CPN). His ICM was initially subject to the same resistance. He noted amid the general squalor of N.H.'s small flat that the toilet did not flush and found out that it had not for over two years. N.H. had regularly filled a bucket of water to flush it. It took the case manager 40 minutes and £3.60 of petty cash to fix it. N.H. (who had previously insisted that he did not mind the problem) was clearly delighted and allowed the case manager to visit more regularly and start to take him shopping (an activity previously inhibited by a complex set of delusions). As a consequence, he began to eat a more adequate diet.

In the midst of this, he allows his medication to be monitored and has no great opposition to taking it. There remains much to be done – he is still refusing to seek his benefits, get a check up from his general practitioner or improve his hygiene. He has, however, remained in contact for 15 months, which for him is a record.

Case 2

G.H. is a 32-year-old man of West African descent who has suffered from schizophrenia for nine years, with a history of multiple admissions under the Mental Health Act. His family are concerned and support him when he is well, but are excluded when he deteriorates. Despite his severe disability, he regularly seeks open employment and becomes threatening and hostile when rejected. Previous follow-up has usually been restricted to depot phenothiazines and is often characterised by suspicion and rejection of his community psychiatric nurse.

In the early stages of engagement, he regularly 'sacked' his ICM. The ICM found that if he went back a few days later and did not mention the 'sacking', it was not brought up by the patient. The ICM has found that periods of resistance and hostility are best managed simply by changing the focus of the interview, and this is possible because they are engaged in a number of ventures – redecorating the flat and pursuing a place on a motor mechanic training course. Medication has been maintained for over one year and regular family meetings have helped the patient's mother to understand his illness better. She has successfully adopted some of the conflict avoidance techniques she has seen the ICM use.

At an early stage, the ICM works collaboratively with the patient to identify his or her needs. This process must be systematic, and may be facilitated by the use of a standard instrument such as the Camberwell Assessment of Need (Phelan *et al*, 1995). The ICM activity with individual patients can be grouped in the following broad categories: help with housing, finance, medication, occupation and leisure, daily living skills, the criminal justice system and physical health. Clear and explicit goals, derived from identified needs, strengthen collaboration between the ICM and patient on a day-to-day basis. For example, the task of getting up at a reasonable hour can be linked with the goal of getting a job and earning money. American ACT services place a high emphasis on occupational rehabilitation. The motivation to earn money and be identified with a more normal role in society can be harnessed to powerful effect by a keyworker who has intensive contact (at least twice a week) with the patient over many years.

Setting up a local assertive community treatment service

Establishing the local need

Assertive community treatment has been shown to benefit those patients trying to live in the community who have the highest degree of social disablement. Such patients are not necessarily those who have the highest level of contact with community mental health teams (CMHTs); many actively avoid contact. Our own experience has also taught us that while CMHTs readily identify the small group of patients who require a disproportionate amount of care, they tend to overestimate the number of severely mentally ill patients with whom they have regular contact. This reflects the absence of a consensus on the definition of severe mental illness. Diagnosis alone is clearly a poor indicator, but a rigidly formulaic approach to definition is impractical. We have found Bachrach's (1988) characterisation most useful, using diagnosis, duration and disability.

Team structure

Assertive community treatment appears to work best when the ACT team has overall clinical responsibility for all aspects of patient care – including in-patient care. The DLP study demonstrated the problems which may arise with divided consultant responsibility. The easiest, and arguably the neatest, system is for the ACT team to be self-contained, retaining consultant medical responsibility for care of the patients at all times and exercising control over a small in-patient facility. There are potential problems with this approach in the UK, where over 80% of mental health services are sectorised (Johnson & Thornicroft, 1993). The creation of additional teams may fragment the existing comprehensive service. There is a danger, too, of blunting the commitment of CMHTs to work with the severely mentally ill, by removing responsibility for the care of the most disabled. Our approach has been to integrate ACT keyworkers into existing CMHTs. In addition to avoiding service fragmentation, this model utilises existing patterns of vertical (primary–secondary–tertiary) and horizontal (health–local authority) service integration. A potential problem with this approach is the dilution of programme fidelity and diminished influence on in-patient care (see Table 1).

Surprisingly little is known about the ideal size of a mental health team in the UK (Onyett *et al*, 1994). We suggest a minimum of five ICMs to allow leave to be covered internally. More than eight begins to become unwieldy, making regular review, and familiarity of all case managers with all patients, difficult. Services in the USA have successfully used both skilled mental health professionals and 'fresh' staff with non-vocational qualifications as case managers. Skilled staff with an accredited training in mental health work are significantly more expensive to employ, and many

Table 1 Integrating assertive community treatment keyworkers into existing community mental health teams	
Potential advantages	Potential disadvantages
Full multi-disciplinary support	Loss of programme fidelity
Vertical and horizontal service integration	Secondment of key-workers to other (non-ACT) tasks
Avoids fragmentation of sectorised community mental health services	Inefficient use of time (e.g. multiple meetings)
Retains CMHT focus on the severely mentally ill	Professional isolation
Skill sharing	Reduced control of in-patient stays

of the core tasks of ACT appear relatively straightforward and simple. Their skill, however, lies in achieving them with people who are profoundly disabled by severe mental illness and in maintaining a longer-term relationship. Fresh staff, on the other hand, may be unburdened by inappropriate professional attitudes, and better able to adapt to the role of ICM. Arguments for and against the employment of highly skilled staff remain unresolved, although available evidence suggests that they may achieve better outcomes.

There is no evidence to indicate that any one group of mental health professionals is better equipped to act as case managers than any other. Assertive community treatment is holistic in its attention to patients' needs, and ICMs must adopt a generic approach, whatever their professional backgrounds. Nevertheless, in the absence of hard data it seems logical to recommend that ACT teams retain a multi-disciplinary skills mix. Community psychiatric nurses have a particularly valuable role with respect to medication, and perhaps of all mental health professionals are the most skilled at promoting compliance with medication – an important vector of good outcome in ACT. Occupational therapists and social workers also have highly relevant skills, and if they can be recruited to the ACT team, this is to be particularly recommended. Clinical psychologists have been more prominent in some of the American ACT teams than they have in the UK. If it is not possible to recruit a psychologist to the team, then access to psychological skills outside the team is essential. We suggest that a team which mixes nurses and non-nurses in equal proportion is optimal.

Team meetings

In the USA, most ACT teams meet briefly every day. A team should certainly meet at least twice a week. We suggest at least three times a week in the first year to build cohesiveness and strengthen the new professional identity. Each meeting should include hand-over information about all patients, and a review of two or three patients in-depth each week to update individual care programmes. Time needs to be devoted on a regular basis to professional development and discussion of the new and challenging role of being an ICM.

Cross cover

Keyworkers should not just cover each other for holidays and absences. Patient involvement with other ICMs is essential to avoid the development of pathological and over-dependent relationships. Individual case managers can then discuss their patients with colleagues who have first-hand knowledge of them. Although the concept of 'team responsibility' for all patients has been advocated by some services (Witheridge, 1991; Haringey Mental Health Group, 1994), we see a major benefit in having a clearly identified individual responsible for the care of the patient. The likelihood of confusion is decreased, and the essential benefits of case management (i.e. a clear focus for the planning, coordination and delivery of care) are protected. In our opinion, a team model undervalues the essential importance of the individual therapeutic relationship in supporting the patient.

Extent of service

Services adhering fully to the PACT model offer access to a keyworker from the team 24 hours a day. It is not apparent, however, that there are substantial advantages to 24-hour access to an ACT service in the UK, where primary care and out-of-hours emergency mental health services are highly developed and accessible. The tasks of case management are usually most efficiently conducted during office hours, when liaison with other key agencies (e.g. social services, housing, social security) is possible. As few of the patients using the service are employed, most will be able to meet with their keyworkers between 9 a.m. and 5 p.m. Keyworkers will, however, need to be regularly available outside of these times – particularly when engaging a patient, supporting leisure activities or working with carers. Our own review of the literature indicates that 24-hour services in the UK may add little to an 'extended hours' service at a considerably greater cost. We piloted an extended hours ACT service (until 10 p.m.) in our district and found it very little used, and have subsequently disbanded it.

Supervision and leadership

As we gain clearer understanding of the critical components of ACT, the importance of programme fidelity is increasingly apparent. An ACT team needs to be led by someone with previous experience of the model, who can provide regular supervision and support to other keyworkers. Staff burnout has been perceived as a potential problem with ACT, but ICMs typically report high job satisfaction. None the less, long-term, intensive work with a small number of seriously ill patients brings its own unique stresses.

Team model and operational policy

Identifying a model and drawing up an operational policy should logically come first, but experience has taught us otherwise. Although a team model has to be identified before staff are recruited, the operational policy is best evolved and regularly reviewed with the team members themselves. This leads to a greater sense of ownership and commitment.

A well-written operational policy will become an invaluable document which will both guide subsequent development and implementation of the service, and also serve as a reference once the service is up and running. It needs to be written in clear and simple language and should describe the definition, philosophy and aims of the service, together with operational details such as staff skills mix, training and deployment, together with a brief, operationalised definition of patients who will be accepted by the service and broad practice guidelines. The components of the PACT model identified in this paper could usefully be used as a starting point (see Box 2).

Resistance and problems

Setting up a new, innovative service may generate major resistance. This has been repeatedly reported by investigators of such services in the UK and needs to be approached philosophically. The source of resistance is both external and internal.

External resistance

The major external resistance is professional anxiety about change. The new service may be perceived as a threat to the position and status of the various mental health professions. We experienced initial resistance from psychiatry, nursing, clinical psychology and occupational therapy, and much later on from social work. Many psychiatrists felt that the proposal for a new ACT service described nothing new, and that intensive case management was already being provided as required by CMHTs. There was also a concern that the new service could lead to confusion regarding clinical responsibility for individual patients.

Community psychiatric nurses were worried that their jobs might be threatened. For occupational therapists and clinical psychologists it appeared that the high profile of a major service development which relied heavily on their skills, but which was not under their control, contributed to their fears. Resistance from social workers developed more slowly, reflecting their generally positive view of generic functioning. The clarity of definitions in such a service (e.g. patient characteristics, case load size, regularity of contact) is unusual in National Health Service mental health services and can be perceived as implied criticism of the imprecision that is traditionally accepted. For example, rigorously established case loads can highlight uncertainty about workloads and skills mixes elsewhere in the system. Tight control over such a service also evokes fears of a rigid 'medical model'.

Internal resistance

Within the new team there will be anxiety about the new keyworker role, particularly with regard to tasks outside traditional professional boundaries. Concerns about over-dependency on the part of the patient partly derive from the increased level of self-disclosure that is inevitable in such an extended keyworker role. The ethics of pursuing reluctant patients was regularly debated by members of our service. This is a real issue but often served as a platform for the expression of external resistance. There is a fine line between assertiveness and harassment. Such judgements have to be made in most clinical situations, but are particularly prominent in ACT services.

Summary

Our service is only in its fourth year and is subject to an extensive evaluation. Informed judgements about its value will have to await that analysis. Some early differences can, however, be observed. After an initial period of finding the new role difficult and feeling 'uncontained', case managers report high levels of job satisfaction from their limited case loads and extended remit. Keeping patients engaged has undoubtedly been improved by the new approach and the sense of freedom to do what is needed to make the patient feel better (rather than to focus too narrowly on 'illness issues') has resulted in an improved therapeutic alliance. Medication compliance may have improved because it is no longer such an issue – just one part of a complex and generally rewarding relationship. One gratifying result has been a markedly improved uptake of benefits by the patients and an overall impression of improved material conditions. The relationship between ICMs and other disciplines has steadily improved. It has been helped along by shared experience of admissions of case manager clients and a recognition that this approach is not a 'cure-all'. Nothing succeeds like failure.

In spite of all of the potential problems that may be encountered in setting up an ACT service, the benefits are considerable. Benefits to the patients include obvious improvement in quality of life and, for many, the avoidance of episodic crises resulting in major emotional and social upheaval. There are also benefits to other users of the mental health service – as a consequence of the more efficient use of expensive in-patient services and the liberation of these resources for CMHTs.

The gap between the outcome for patients of ACT and standard community mental health services may continue to close as the latter adopt more of the principles of the former (Burns & Santos, 1995). If so, then the pioneers of ACT have a great deal to be thanked for. There are certainly potential benefits for CMHTs in the UK in terms of new learning and new practice. Greater clarity and definition of target populations and openness about activities are attributes that all teams facing the demands and challenges of the 'new' National Health Service would be served by. Such clarity is rapidly developed in ACT teams.

References

Bachrach, L. L. (1988) Defining chronic mental illness: a concept paper. *Hospital and Community Psychiatry*, **39**, 383–388.

Burns, B. J. & Santos, A. B. (1995) Assertive community treatment: an update of randomised trials. *Psychiatric Services*, **46**, 669–675.

Department of Health (1990) *The Care Programme Approach for People with a Mental Illness Referred to the Specialist Psychiatric Services* (HC(90)23/LASSL(90)11). London: Department of Health.

Drake, R. E. & Burns, B. J. (1995) Special section on assertive community treatment: an introduction. *Psychiatric Services*, **46**, 667–668.

Haringey Mental Health Group (1994) Tulip. *Annual Report 1993/1994*. London: Haringey Mental Health Group.

Hoult, J., Reynolds, I., Charbonneau-Powis, M., *et al* (1983) Psychiatric hospital versus community treatment: the results of a randomised trial. *Australian and New Zealand Journal of Psychiatry*, **17**, 160–167.

Johnson, S. & Thornicroft, G. (1993) The sectorisation of psychiatric services in England and Wales. *Social Psychiatry and Psychiatric Epidemiology*, **28**, 45–47.

Kanter, J. (1989) Clinical case management: definition, principles, components. *Hospital and Community Psychiatry*, **40**, 361–368.

Marks, I. M., Connolly, J., Muijen, M., *et al* (1994) Home-based versus hospital based care for people with serious mental illness. *British Journal of Psychiatry*, **165**, 179–194.

Marx, A. J., Test, M. A. & Stein, L. I. (1973) Extrahospital management of severe mental illness. *Archives of General Psychiatry*, **29**, 505–511.

McGrew, J. H., Bond, G. R. & Dietzen, L. L. (1994) Measuring the fidelity of implementation of a mental health program model. *Journal of Consulting and Clinical Psychology*, **62**, 670–678.

Olfson, M. (1990) Assertive community treatment: an evaluation of the experimental evidence. *Hospital and Community Psychiatry*, **41**, 634–641.

Onyett, S., Heppleston, T. & Bushnell, D. (1994) *The Organisation and Operation of Community Mental Health Teams in England: A National Survey*. London: The Sainsbury Centre for Mental Health.

Phelan, M., Slade, M., Thornicroft, G., *et al* (1995) The Camberwell Assessment of Need: the validity and reliability of an instrument to assess the needs of people with severe mental illness. *British Journal of Psychiatry*, **167**, 589–595.

Stein, L. I. & Test, M. A. (1980) Alternative to mental hospital treatment. I. Conceptual model, treatment program and clinical evaluation. *Archives of General Psychiatry*, **37**, 392–397.

Taube, C. A., Morlock, L., Burns, B. J., *et al* (1990) New directions in research on assertive community treatment. *Psychiatric Services*, **41**, 643–647.

Teague, G. B., Drake, R. E. & Ackerson, T. H. (1995) Evaluating use of continuous treatment teams for persons with mental illness and substance abuse. *Psychiatric Services*, **46**, 689–695.

Test, M. A. (1992) Training in community living. In *Handbook of Psychiatric Rehabilitation* (ed. R. P. Liberman), pp. 153–170. New York: Macmillan.

——& Stein, L. I. (1980) Alternative to mental hospital treatment. III. Social cost. *Archives of General Psychiatry*, **37**, 409–412.

Thornicroft, G. (1991) Concept of case management for long-term mental illness. *International Review of Psychiatry*, **3**, 125–132.

Weisbrod, B. A., Test, M. A. & Stein, L. I. (1980) Alternative to mental hospital treatment. II. Economic benefit-cost analysis. *Archives of General Psychiatry*, **37**, 400–405.

Witheridge, T. F. (1991) The 'active ingredients' of assertive outreach. In *Psychiatric Outreach to the Mentally Ill* (ed. N. L. Cohen), pp. 47–64. San Francisco, CA: Jossey-Bass.

Commentary

Steven R. Hirsch

It is difficult not to be won over by the description of assertive community treatment that promises nearly total caring for the most chronically disabled mentally ill, including "the material essentials of life such as food, clothing and shelter, coping skills necessary to meet the demands of community living and motivation to persevere in the face of life's adversity". If we keep in mind that this approach is for patients who in previous decades would have spent their life in a mental institution, one can readily justify the transfer of expense and resources to this hopefully more humane form of treatment which allows patients to live within the context of open society, a preference they inevitably opt for when surveyed after a move from hospitalisation to community care.

Unfortunately there are serious questions as to what extent this model can meet the shortcomings of community care in modern Britain. Even 18 years after Stein & Test's (1980) original article there does not seem to be a description in the literature of any service which has been tested over a sustained period, say five years. The authors of this article are only in their fourth year of providing such a service and they report that the Stein and Test service, and Hoult *et al*'s (1983) service in Australia, were both closed down with a loss of patients' previous benefits. Nor is it clear to me whether the division between social security, social services, housing and health in the UK allows for the type of total combined approach which ACT seems to require. Care management should offer such an opportunity by providing a single total budget for patients selected for such treatment so perhaps this should be combined with ACT.

It would appear that ACT should improve the quality of life and level of functioning of some patients with chronic mental illness. There is a problem in identifying which patients should receive this type of care as opposed to alternative approaches, such as the provision of a haven of supervised residential homes for patients who cannot function even when offered ACT. There are also the groups who are violent, misuse drugs, or remain resistant to assertive outreach because of their own peculiar psychopathology. These limitations should be given recognition by advocates of any single approach so that a

comprehensive mental health system can be provided to replace institutional.

Purchasers and providers should keep a reasonable balance between the resources invested into the most severely mentally ill and the resources required by the rest of the population, so that they too can have decent and respectable facilities when they require acute treatment in hospital, and have access to psychologists, psychiatrists and community psychiatric nurses even when they do not fall into the most severely disabled group. Advocates for mental health services should approach ACT with some caution until knowledge of the costs and benefits and the ability to sustain such a service on a long-term basis has been well established.

References

Hoult, J., Reynolds, I., Charbonneau-Powis, M., *et al* (1983) Psychiatric hospital versus community treatment: the results of a randomised trial. *Australian and New Zealand Journal of Psychiatry*, **17**, 160–167.

Stein, L. I. & Test, M. A. (1980) Alternative to mental hospital treatment. I. Conceptual model, treatment program and clinical evaluation. *Archives of General Psychiatry*, **37**, 392–397.

Mental health nursing: issues and roles

Kevin Gournay

In 1994 the report of the Mental Health Nursing Review Team was published (Department of Health, 1994). This report signified the end of a three-year process in which mental health nursing was examined from the perspectives of practice, education, research and management. The last review of mental health nursing took place in 1968, but since that time there have been enormous changes in our thinking about mental illness, in the delivery of services and a number of very exciting developments in treatment. The review process included the widest possible consultation with other professionals, user organisations, patients, relatives and carers. It also co-opted expert advisers and took written and oral evidence, and visited clinical services across England. There were altogether 42 recommendations and throughout this chapter reference will be made to a number of the most important of these.

Before a detailed examination of the issues, it is worth commencing with the 10th recommendation of the Review, that is that the title Mental Health Nurse (MHN) be used both for nurses who work in the community and for those who work in hospital and day services. Although there are those who would prefer to use the more descriptive term, psychiatric nurse, using one term to cover all nurses is now much more appropriate. Mental Health Nurses should be using the same core skills regardless of the setting in which they practice. Current thinking about continuity of care reinforces the view that the continued separation of care and treatment between community and in-patient settings is counter-productive.

Serious mental illness

One of the most important recommendations of the Review was that nurses focus their efforts on those with serious and enduring mental illnesses. This recommendation is in accord with more general public policy and is supported by specific findings. For example, White (1990), in his quinquennial review of community psychiatric nursing in the UK, highlighted the scandalous situation where 80% of people with schizophrenia in the community had no services whatsoever from an MHN. Only 27.2% of clients of community psychiatric nurse (CPN) case loads had a principal diagnosis of schizophrenia and a quarter of CPNs in the UK had no people with schizophrenia on their case loads. At the same time, this survey showed that nurses were increasingly working with populations with depression, anxiety and non-psychotic problems in primary health care, taking their referrals directly from a general practitioner (GP). Gournay & Brooking (1994, 1995) showed, in a large randomised controlled trial, that CPN interventions with these populations were both ineffective and very expensive.

Thus, at present, the emphasis for MHNs must be with those people with the most serious illnesses, although (as will be discussed below) there are limited opportunities for nursing to develop with other populations. Unfortunately, the national survey of community mental health teams (Onyett *et al*, 1995) and the Clinical Standards Advisory Group report (Department of Health, 1995) showed that CPNs still have a long way to go in meeting the recommendations of the Mental Health Nursing Review and that case loads still include many with less serious mental illnesses.

Contemporary services and nursing roles

Following 40 years of de-institutionalisation we are now in an era where the unit of delivery of mental health care is increasingly the community mental health team. In turn, the mode of delivery is of case management. This was developed from the work of Test & Stein (1980). The case manager provides a range of interventions, including the brokering of services, establishing networks with community agencies, acting as a client advocate, supervising medication, training the patient in community living skills and using various psychotherapeutic and family interventions. Case management should also include the important principle of actively seeking out people who drop-out of services. The problem-orientated model of case management has been gradually developed in the UK, Australia and the USA (e.g. Hoult, 1991; Marks *et al*, 1994) and will become much more central to the role of nurses working within community teams.

However, there are two issues which need to be considered further. First, it has become clear that nurses are not the only professionals who will adopt the role of case manager and it may be that in the future this role will also be occupied by occupational therapists, social workers or indeed non-professionals. This was confirmed by Ford *et al* (1993) in a study of the original case management development sites in the UK. Second, there is often confusion regarding the approach described above, which is predominantly a clinical method, with 'care management', a term describing what is essentially an over-arching system. To complicate matters further, clinical case management has been developed in different ways with different theoretical underpinnings. For example, the 'strengths' model of case management (Rapp & Winterstein, 1989) concentrates on building on client strengths rather than targeting deficits. Conversely there are models of case management based on the opposite approach of targeting deficits: for example, using social skills training as a central intervention. Detailed discussion of the various models of case management is out of place here but research has begun to identify which approaches are more effective (see Andrews & Teesson, 1994; Muijen, 1994; Santos *et al*, 1995).

In summary, the research findings so far indicate that clinically focused approaches are the most effective and that the brokerage models favoured by many social services departments may actually lead to negative outcomes (Curtis *et al*, 1992; Rossler *et al*, 1992). Although case management has become more widespread it is in itself not a panacea and certainly demands that staff are appropriately trained. For example, Muijen (1994) showed that merely reconfiguring nursing teams within case management arrangements conferred no additional benefit over nurses working in their usual generic fashion.

Dual diagnosis populations

Nurses in contemporary services are increasingly working with new populations, which will demand changes in approach. For example, the dual diagnosis of substance misuse and serious mental illness is now a growing and substantial problem. A range of work from the USA (Bartels *et al*, 1995; Teague *et al*, 1995) shows that an integrated approach to both serious mental illness and substance misuse and/or dependence is necessary for a positive outcome.

Although the majority of people with serious mental illness are no more dangerous than the general population, violence is an increasing problem in services. Work from the USA (e.g. Torrey, 1994) shows that violence is particularly linked to patients who misuse substances and those who are non-compliant with medication. Although some research (Dvoskin & Steadman, 1994) has shown that intensive case management can reduce it, violence places increasing stress on mental health team workers and makes conditions of work that much harder.

Neglected nursing roles

Physical health

There are two areas traditionally associated with nursing which have been gradually neglected over the years. The physical health of people with long-term mental illness is an important area for attention, particularly as we know that standardised mortality rates in schizophrenia are 2.5 times those of the rest of the population and 45% of people with long-term mental illness also have substantial physical illnesses, particularly those of the cardiovascular and respiratory variety (Allbeck, 1989; Department of Health, 1995). Furthermore, we also know that this population is at considerable risk from infection with HIV (Sacks *et al*, 1990). Medical care is the responsibility of both the patient's GP and the responsible medical officer of the mental health team. However, as recent work (Department of Health, 1995) shows, patients do not always receive appropriate physical monitoring. This may be for many reasons: for example, not registering with a GP, or the GP assuming that the mental health service is attending to these needs. Mental Health Nurses are ideally placed to ensure that patients are properly registered with a GP and that any clearly defined problems receive appropriate attention. Further, nurses can monitor weight, blood pressure and also provide health education and interventions in areas such as diet, smoking and sexual behaviour.

Box 1. **Important roles in serious mental illness**

Case management
Psychosocial interventions
Physical health – monitoring and education
Medication management
Working with dual diagnosis patients
Behavioural therapy

Medication management

Mental Health Nurses have a natural central role in ensuring that medication is managed effectively. The importance of this cannot be overstated, particularly as there is a wide array of evidence (McCreadie *et al*, 1992) which shows that the majority of people with schizophrenia being treated with psychotropic medication suffer significant side-effects. Unfortunately, medication management has not been high on the list of priorities for practice or education (White, 1990), and research (e.g. Bennett *et al*, 1995*a,b*) shows that nurses are often not sufficiently skilled to detect even the most serious side-effects of neuroleptic medication. There have been some commendable initiatives recently such as the guidance document issued jointly by the Department of Health and the Royal College of Nursing (1995). However, educators and managers in mental health nursing need to place more emphasis on this important area, particularly as a new generation of drugs are gradually coming on to the market, each of these compounds having their own profile of actions and side-effects.

Nurse behaviour therapists

While there is a clear case for focusing on serious mental illness, we have known for many years that severe phobic and obsessional states can cause tremendous disability. However, the majority of sufferers can be helped dramatically by brief behavioural psychotherapy (Marks, 1987). The recognition that adequate numbers of sufferers could not be treated by psychiatrists or clinical psychologists alone, led to the setting up of the first Nurse Therapy Training Programme at the Maudsley Hospital in 1972 (Marks *et al*, 1977). Several studies have shown that nurse therapists produce excellent results in terms of both clinical and economic outcomes (Ginsberg *et al*, 1984).

However, despite strong evidence, only about 200 nurse therapists have been trained since 1972 and therefore their impact on the health care system has been very limited. There is no reason why we should not develop new nurse therapy training programmes. Experienced nurse therapists could also provide support and supervision for more numerous groups, such as practice nurses and non-professionals, to deliver simple exposure-based programmes. These skills could probably be taught in a relatively short space of time to these personnel.

Education and training

Psychosocial interventions – the Thorn Programme

The UK is currently leading the world in the development of comprehensive training initiatives. The Sainsbury Centre in London has developed case management in various demonstration sites throughout the UK and their training division assists many local services. Furthermore, Masters programmes in problem-orientated case management and psychosocial interventions are gradually developing in universities. For example, the author developed a multi-disciplinary programme in 1992, and Brooker commenced a similar programme in Sheffield in 1995. However, the most important development is the Thorn Nurse Initiative. This is based at the Institute of Psychiatry in London and at Manchester University, and was set up by a generous grant from the Sir Jules Thorn Trust. The first programme was developed by a team of influential psychiatrists, nurses and psychologists, including Dr Jim Birley, Professors Isaac Marks, Tom Craig, Julian Leff, Nick Tarrier, Tony Butterworth, and other colleagues. The year-long course sets out to produce a specialist nurse dedicated to work with patients with schizophrenia, analogous to the Macmillan nurse for cancer. Training is skills-based and focuses on a clinical and problem-orientated method of case management. There is also training in the various contemporary psychosocial methods, including family management, cognitive–behavioural interventions with positive and negative symptoms, and prodrome and relapse strategies.

By the end of 1997 this programme had produced about 200 graduates and the plan is for satellite centres to be set up throughout the UK over the next couple of years. The programme has attempted to ensure rigorous adherence to training principles and the use of clinical supervision, as research shows that at follow-up, after training in psychosocial interventions, both of these issues seemed problematic (Kavanagh *et al*, 1993; McFarlane *et al*, 1993). Initially it was envisaged that the Thorn programme would be confined to nurses, but by late 1995 the Manchester programme had begun to admit others and the Institute of Psychiatry programme has opened its doors to psychologists, occupational therapists and social workers.

There is a need to evaluate the work of Thorn nurses in some detail, particularly as case management outcome is still far from clear (e.g. Andrews & Teesson, 1994; Muijen, 1994; Santos *et al*, 1995). The Thorn programme has an integral evaluation of clinical outcomes of patients treated by students. However, full-scale studies with randomised controlled trials are still some way off. On a positive note, Brooker *et al* (1992, 1994) have already demonstrated that CPNs can be trained, using relatively brief programmes, to become effective deliverers of family interventions.

Undergraduate nurse education

The education and training of nurses is now the responsibility of universities, the framework being Project 2000. Essentially, this means that nurse training has become much more theory-based, with a move away from apprenticeship. All nurses now receive a basic education within a common foundation programme for 18 months and after that they spend another 18 months studying either general nursing, mental health nursing, learning disabilities nursing or child nursing. It is likely that nursing will soon become an all-graduate profession and that specialisms such as mental health will only be available at Masters level. This development is much against the recommendations of the Mental Health Nursing Review, which drew attention to the problems associated with genericism in social work and recommended unequivocally that mental health nursing be retained in its present form (Box 2). Should nursing become an all-graduate and generic profession, it seems likely that none of the nurses of the future will want to attend to basic nursing care tasks for the mentally ill, and instead of receiving attention from a skilled registered nurse, patients will receive direct care from health care assistants, with a nurse acting as a supervisor.

There are three other major difficulties associated with nurse education. First, the Mental Health Nursing Review recognised that nurse tutors are very often removed from the realities of clinical practice and recommends that they spend at least a day a week in a clinical area. However, this recommendation does not go far enough: the optimum arrangement is that of a lecturer–practitioner with a 50–50 split. The second problem is that the current mental health nursing curriculum contains a great deal of arguably redundant theory which is often underpinned by an anti-psychiatric philosophy. On the other hand, there seems to be very little information regarding the biological aspects of mental illness or indeed little skills training in important areas such as medication management.

The final area of education which is of paramount importance concerns the large numbers of nurses who were trained in and have spent all of their working lives working in large institutions. It is completely unreasonable to expect these nurses to make the transition to community mental health teams without training. However, this is happening all over the country. Once more, we are drawn to the issue of investment in training and it is arguable that this represents, alongside the provision of sufficient residential facilities, the biggest priority for future action.

Management

The Review was particularly concerned that the standards of management and leadership in

---

Box 2. Recommendations of the Mental Health Nursing Review

(6) "The essential focus lies in working with people with serious or enduring mental illness"

(10) "The title Mental Health Nurse be used for nurses who work in the community and for those who work in hospital and day services"

(12) "Action is taken to improve the standards of management and leadership"

(19) "The collective and individual needs of nurses presently working in large mental hospitals should be identified and met"

(32) "Teachers of mental health nursing should spend the equivalent of at least one day per week in practice"

mental health nursing needed strengthening and consequently the Department of Health has set up a programme to develop the leadership potential of small numbers of mental health nurses. The Review also recommended that nursing managers develop strategies with particular emphasis on use of standards protocols. Thus the recent Clinical Standards Project on schizophrenia provides nurses with a framework for action. Finally, the Review recognised that nurse managers need to adapt to the contemporary demands of multi-disciplinary/inter-agency working and recommended greater collaboration with other social and health care providers.

Research

The Review recognised that research in mental health nursing needs strengthening and made several recommendations to assist with the development of an appropriate infrastructure. These include the setting up of information systems and targeting central research and development resources on mental health nursing activity. It also seems essential that research in mental health nursing be much better integrated with the efforts of other disciplines. Furthermore, nursing interventions should be subjected to the tests of randomised controlled trials and economic analysis. Unfortunately, such methods have rarely been used by nursing researchers who have generally concentrated on qualitative methods. Hopefully, the establishment of mental health nursing departments within our medical schools and universities, which is now taking place, will lead to researchers being able to benefit from the collaboration and supervision of more established groups.

Conclusion

Mental health nursing, like the rest of mental health care, is in a state of rapid transition. There are many opportunities for the development of mental health nursing skills and these can only be beneficial for the sufferers of mental illness. However, there are also many challenges for the future. Fortunately we can be guided by important work such as the Mental Health Nursing Review and the Clinical Standards Advisory Group on Schizophrenia, and these provide the basis for future action and improvement in what mental health nursing has to offer.

References

Allbeck, P. (1989) Schizophrenia: a life shortening illness. *Schizophrenia Bulletin*, **15**, 81–89.

Andrews, G. & Teesson, M. (1994) Smart versus dumb treatment: services for mental disorder. *Current Opinion in Psychiatry*, **7**, 181–185.

Bartels, S., Drake, R. & Wallach, M. (1995) Long-term course of substance use disorders among persons with severe mental illness. *Psychiatric Services*, **46**, 248–251.

Bennett, J., Done, J., Harrison-Read, P., *et al* (1995a) Development of a rating scale – check list to assess the side-effects of antipsychotics by Community Psychiatric Nurses. In *Community Psychiatric Nursing: A Research Perspective*, Vol. 3 (ed by C. Brooker & E. White), pp. 1–19. London: Chapman & Hall.

—, — & Hunt, B. (1995b) Assessing the side-effects of antipsychotic drugs: a survey of CPN practice. *Journal of Psychiatric Mental Health Nursing*, **2**, 177–182.

Brooker, C., Tarrier, N., Barrowclough, C., *et al* (1992) Training community psychiatric nurses for psychosocial intervention: report of a pilot study. *British Journal of Psychiatry*, **160**, 836–844.

—, Falloon, I., Butterworth, A., *et al* (1994) The outcome of training psychiatric nurses to deliver psychosocial intervention. *British Journal of Psychiatry*, **165**, 222–230.

Curtis, J., Millman, E., Struening, E., *et al* (1992) Effect of case management on rehospitalisation and neutralisation of ambulatory case services. *Hospital and Community Psychiatry*, **43**, 895–899.

Department of Health (1994) *The Report of the Reveiw of Mental Health Nursing*. London: HMSO.

— (1995) *Report of the Schizophrenia Committee of the Clinical Standards Advisory Group*. London: HMSO.

— & Royal College of Nursing (1995) *Good Practice in the Administration of Depot Neuroleptic Drugs; A Guidance Document for Mental Health & Practice Nurses*. Manchester: BAPS, Health Publication Unit.

Dvoskin, J. & Steadman, H. (1994) Using intensive case management to reduce violence by mentally ill persons in the community. *Hospital and Community Psychiatry*, **45**, 679–684.

Ford, R., Beadsmoore, A., Norton, P., *et al* (1993) Developing case management of the long term mentally ill. *Psychiatric Bulletin*, **17**, 409–411.

Ginsberg, G., Marks, I. M. & Walters, H. (1984) Cost benefits in a controlled trial of nurse therapy for neuroses in primary care. *Psychological Medicine*, **14**, 683–690.

Gournay, K. J. M. & Brooking, J. I. (1994) The community psychiatric nursing primary care: an outcome study. *British Journal of Psychiatry*, **165**, 231–238.

— & — (1995) The community psychiatric nursing primary care: an economic analysis. *Journal of Advanced Nursing*, **22**, 169–178.

Hoult, J. (1991) Home treatments in New South Wales. In *The Closure of Mental Hospitals* (eds P. Hall & I. F. Brockington), pp. 107–114. London: Gaskell.

Kavanagh, D., Clark, D., Piat Kowska, O., *et al* (1993) Application of cognitive behavioural family interventions for schizophrenia: what can the matter be? *Australian Psychologist*, **28**, 1–8.

McCreadie, R. G., Robertson, L. J. & Wiles, D. H. (1992) The Nithsdale schizophrenia survey: akathisia, Parkinsonism, tardive dyskinesia and plasma neuroleptic levels. *British Journal of Psychiatry*, **160**, 793–799.

McFarlane, W., Dunne, E., Lukens, E., *et al* (1993) From research to clinical practice: dissemination of New York State's family psychoeducation project. *Hospital and Community Psychiatry*, **44**, 265–270.

Marks, I. M. (1987) *Fears, Phobias and Rituals*. Oxford: Oxford Medical.

—, Connerly, J., Hallam, R., *et al* (1977) *Nursing in Behavioural Psychotherapy*. London: RCN Publications.

—, —, Muijen, M., *et al* (1994) Home based versus hospital based care for people with serious mental illness. *British Journal of Psychiatry*, **165**, 179–194.

Muijen, M. (1994) Rehabilitation in the care of the mentally ill. *Current Opinion in Psychiatry*, **7**, 202–206.

Onyett, S., Pillinger, T. & Muijen, M. (1995) *Making Community Mental Health Teams Work*. London: Sainsbury Centre.

Rapp, C. & Winterstein, R. (1989) The strengths model of case management: results from 12 demonstrations. *Psychosocial Rehabilitation Journal*, **13**, 23–32.

Rossler, W., Loffler, W., Fatkenheuer, B., *et al* (1992) Docs case management reduce the rehospitalisation rate? *Acta Psychiatrica Scandinavica*, **86**, 445–449.

Santos, A., Henggeler, S., Burns, B., *et al* (1995) Research on field based services: models for reform in the delivery of mental health care to populations with complex clinical problems. *American Journal of Psychiatry*, **152**, 1111–1123.

Sacks, N., Terry, F. & Braver, R. (1990) Self-reported HIV related risk behaviours in acute psychiatric out-patients. *Hospital and Community Psychiatry*, **41**, 1253–1255.

Teague, G., Drake, R. & Ackerson, T. (1995) Evaluating use of continuous treatment teams for persons with mental illness and substance abuse. *Psychiatric Services*, **46**, 689–695.

Test, M. A. & Stein, L. (1980) Alternative to mental hospital treatment. III. Social cost. *Archives of General Psychiatry*, **37**, 409–412.

Torrey, E. (1994) Violent behaviour by individuals with serious mental illness. *Hospital and Community Psychiatry*, **45**, 653–662.

White, E. (1990) *A Quinquennial Survey of Community Psychiatric Nursing*. University of Manchester: Department of Nursing.

Commentary

Richard Lingham

Professor Gournay's chapter on the issues and roles in mental health nursing could alternatively have been titled: situation and process, skills and experience, generic and specialist, clinical and eclectic, or proactive and preventive. His research review supports a viewpoint at the structured/tested end of this spectrum, where he sees ready evidence that nurses now require clinically focused training and re-training if they are to provide care and treatment for patients with the most seriously disabling mental illnesses. This reinforces the Butterworth Report's conclusions (Department of Health, 1994), the *Health of the Nation*'s expectations and the specifications in *Building Bridges* (Department of Health, 1995*a*) and the *Spectrum of Care* (National Health Service Executive, 1996) relating to the Care Programme Approach.

However, the Clinical Standards Advisory Group on Schizophrenia (Department of Health, 1995*b*) found "little systematic assessment of mental health nurses' training needs in psychological/family interventions, case management approaches (including assertive outreach), and the assessment of the side-effects of medication". Also, "in some districts CPNs were unhappy about the stigmatising effects of 'labelling' and did not wish to use the term 'schizophrenia'. This led, on occasion, to a lack of co-ordination between the professions and deployment of their time away from the care of the severely mentally ill".

Professor Gournay recalls research findings from 1990 that only a small minority of patients with schizophrenia see CPNs. His own recent research concludes that their main work with primary health care patients who suffer from depression and anxiety states is "ineffective and very expensive". He identifies the need to improve standards of management to develop focused methods of work with patients and families, and to instil basic clinical knowledge and awareness.

Much of the nursing story mirrors the path trodden by social workers. In the 1970s, before all social work and training became generic, six universities provided postgraduate training in psychiatric social work. Only one does now, but specialism in mental health has mainly re-emerged by statutory accident since 1983, in the form of in-service training for approved social workers, which has gradually expanded from four weeks to six months. Since 1995, specialised post-qualifying training has taken more substantial form via the statement on competencies for forensic social work published by the Central Council for Education and Training in Social Work (1995).

Many CPNs and social workers would need comprehensive re-training and re-orientation to work competently as keyworkers within the sort of structured programmes operating in Wisconsin, Sydney, and increasingly evolving in this country. Successful assertive outreach work will demand that professional opinions, contributions to clinical judgement and decision-making are based on secure knowledge, sound professional philosophies and shared accountability. Patients and carers must be enabled to feel secure about treatment and care plans. Within their individual capacities, all members of the resultant team should recognise that the principal sources of understanding of mental illness stem from clinical psychiatry and psychology. The training and practice of those who earn their living in mental health care must acknowledge this reality. Apart from anything else, how can detractors of 'the medical model', when circumstances justify firm opposition to a doctor's views, hope to present a credible opinion if they cannot demonstrate that they know what they are talking about?

References

Central Council for Education and Training in Social Work (1995) *Achieving Competence in Forensic Social Work.* London: CCETSW.

Department of Health (1994) *The Report of the Review of Mental Health Nursing.* London: HMSO.

—— (1995a) *Building Bridges. A Guide to Arrangements for Inter-Agency Working for the Care and Protection of Severely Mentally Ill People.* London: HMSO.

—— (1995b) *Report of the Schizophrenia Committee of the Clinical Standards Advisory Group.* London: HMSO.

National Health Service Executive (1996) *The Spectrum of Care.* HSG(96)6. Leeds: NHSE.

Making care programming work

David Kingdon

It is hard to disagree with the principles of the Care Programme Approach (CPA) (Social & Community Planning Research, 1993; Kingdon, 1994) but it has been much harder to agree how to put them into practice. What should be 'just good practice' becomes more complex the more it is discussed by clinical teams.

This is even more so where the experience and expertise of clinicians have not been made available or used by managers, who have then developed a system required by the Department of Health but not precisely defined by it. In these circumstances, inevitably some provider unit systems have become bureaucratic and over-inclusive. Every unit is different and so procedures for implementation need to be shaped to best fit the needs of the users, carers and others involved locally, and the ways of working of professional staff within services.

Pressures on services are such that the fewer the changes necessary to meet the objectives of the CPA, the more likely are the devised systems to be effective. Although there is no one correct way to implement the CPA, this chapter provides some suggestions on refining local implementation.

Local implementation

It is important to bear in mind that the CPA is primarily designed to ensure that severely mentally ill people do not fall through the 'safety-net of care'. It applies to all people accepted by mental health services or discharged from an in-patient setting. Only by including all patients in the approach can all patients with severe mental illness be identified. However, this may be a reason why so many districts have been over-prescriptive in the form-filling and review procedures required. Paradoxically, it may have slowed down implementation of the CPA and deterred targeting of severely mentally ill people. As it is to apply to all patients and consequently applied by all staff receiving direct referrals or involved in discharge of patients, the CPA needs to be integrated as far as possible with present practice, particularly in the absence of computerised systems in most units to support it. However, to introduce the CPA, many districts have commenced by identifying patients with severe mental illness currently in contact with services and applying the CPA to them before extending it to the service as a whole (see Boxes 1 and 2).

Collaboration

The CPA also involves inter-professional collaboration which should occur within teams (Kingdon, 1992). But this does not mean that everyone, or even the majority, needs a multi-disciplinary review – clearly that would be impractical as thousands of patients are seen by individual sector teams annually.

The care plan should always be drawn up in consultation with the user/patient. Unless it is understood and agreed, a care plan is unlikely to be followed. This means discussion, understanding and agreement of the different components of the plan as it is developed. Exceptionally, there may be necessary components which are not agreed despite full discussion, for example placement on a supervision register or taking of medication while on leave under a section of the Mental Health Act, but these will occur rarely.

The care plan should also include the views of carer, general practitioner (GP) and any other involved professional. Sometimes patients do not want their carer involved and difficult issues of confidentiality can arise. While information about

---

Box 1. The care programme approach should ensure that mentally ill people have:

Their health and social care needs assessed
A named keyworker
An identifiable care plan
A date when their care is to be reviewed

Box 2. Patient, carer, GP and others involved should be aware of:

The next care plan review date
The name of the keyworker
How and where to contact the keyworker or deputy
Information about risk to self or others
What to do if the patient fails to follow the care plan

---

the patient can be disclosed against their will only in exceptional circumstances, patients are often prepared to allow limited information to be given and this should be negotiated with them.

Needs assessment

As part of good practice, assessment should be of both health and social needs, whoever carries it out, for example as part of a psychiatric interview or social work assessment. For psychiatrists, the CPA was intended to draw particular attention to the social care needs of patients, the importance of which may have been neglected previously. Where specific needs are noted, it may be appropriate to refer to the relevant professional for further, more detailed or specialised assessment, for example a social worker for social care needs or a doctor or nurse for health care needs.

In most services, this does not involve a radical change in practice, although it may be an improvement in it, and, under the CPA, it does not need duplication of documentation. Inter-professional collaboration means that the results of assessments will be discussed (such as at ward rounds and reviews), written in case notes, mental health nursing records, and so forth, and sent in referral letters/forms or other letters to GPs and to others when they are also involved in the person's care.

Keyworkers

Basic personal details are collected as part of the initial referral process and so it is difficult to conceive of a reason why they should need to be repeated in CPA documentation. However, they may need to be supplemented and one way of doing this would be to include a sheet attached to the inside of the medical and other clinical notes to include (a) the name and full address details of the current CPA keyworker, and (b) any other relevant information (regarding inclusion on supervision registers, whether the person is subject to care under Section 117, and care management details).

This could be completed on initial assessment, even if it has only the name of the person making that assessment prior to another keyworker being appointed, and then kept up-to-date. Labels with the names, addresses and telephone numbers of all potential keyworkers can be produced by most patient administration systems and can be circulated so that everybody has a stock of their own to use. If someone is appointed as a keyworker, they should agree to this – which, unfortunately, has not always been the case, as detailed in the Ritchie Report (North East Thames & South East Thames Regional Health Authorities, 1994).

Care Programme Approach keyworkers can come from any discipline, including psychiatry, psychology, social work, occupational therapy, art therapy and mental health nursing. Their major responsibilities are to be a specific contact point for users/patients, carers, GPs and others, and to ensure that reviews occur where needed. Such reviews may be made regularly, usually every three to six months or even annually where someone's needs are not changing, or urgently where concern arises.

Keyworkers cannot be responsible for all the care of any individual but they can ensure that if problems do arise they are brought to the attention of those others caring for the person (or rarely, where there is concern about an individual professional's performance, the relevant manager).

Flexibility

One of the key principles of the CPA is that of flexibility in response to people with severe mental illness, so that where one aspect of a care programme is unacceptable to a patient, alternatives are offered as far as is practical. For example, a patient may refuse depot medication but accept oral or an alternative type of neuroleptic or even day care, and while this may be medically less appropriate, it may be worth offering as an alternative.

While the patient may then fail to comply with the alternative, the use of a negotiating approach in the longer term is likely to improve compliance and is certainly what patient groups are asking for. (Kemp *et al*, 1996). 'All or nothing' approaches, in which the response where the patient does not accept the 'package' on offer has been that 'there's nothing we can do', cannot be acceptable any longer.

Keeping in contact

If the patient will not take medication or accept a rehabilitation programme or offer of supported accommodation, they may nevertheless agree to continuing contact. They may change their mind about treatment or deteriorate to an extent when intervention under the Mental Health Act is appropriate. But at least continuing contact means that this occurs early rather than later, before the secondary impairments caused by the illness (damage to relationships, loss of job or accommodation) can occur.

It may be that the only continuing contact possible is with the carer, who then can be offered continuing support and access to services if the patient deteriorates. Although, occasionally, the patient may object to such continuing contact with carers, carers also have rights to support which can not be overridden by patient's demands as long as confidentiality boundaries are maintained.

Ensuring continuity

Inter-professional collaboration is integral to the provision of continuing care. When interruptions to care occur, for example when patients fail to attend appointments or they discharge themselves from hospital, follow-up by a social work or mental health nurse to re-engage them with services may be the most cost-effective strategy. It may be more appropriate for the GP or psychiatrist to make contact by telephone or by visiting. This would be the case where contact by a nurse or social worker has failed, or where specific medical issues or reassessment mean that a medical opinion is necessary. It would be appropriate where the relationship between the patient and GP or psychiatrist has been good, and is especially likely to result in successful re-engagement.

The organisation of continuing care and supervision for individuals with severe mental illness outside hospital is best done by a combination of community team members, usually a nurse, social worker and doctor, although only one of the group may be required to be in contact at any one time. Continuity can be a problem where out-patient settings are relied upon, unless the consultant ensures continuing personal contact with patients. Patients commonly complain that each time they come to out-patient departments they see a different doctor. This reduces the potential for early intervention.

Prioritisation

Associate specialists, staff grade and clinical assistants as well as consultants can assist in improving continuity of care although their workloads may need re-prioritising.

Expressed need for mental health care is constantly increasing and case loads cannot be expanded infinitely. Prioritisation of new referrals and continuing cases according to need is fundamentally important. Consultants and nurse, social work and psychology managers acting together can produce manageable and equitable systems for allocating work which are defensible to GPs and health authority purchasers, but too often this is still dependent on goodwill and hard bargaining rather than rational criteria.

Prioritisation may mean that examination of referrals together with current case loads leads to increased waiting times or briefer interventions for those with less severe mental health problems. The introduction of the Health of the Nation Outcome Scales (Department of Health, 1994) may assist in the future by giving some quantification of need and outcome on which to base prioritisation. It may be easier to 'sell' prioritisation to regional health authority and GP purchasers, other GPs and also psychiatric and community team colleagues if the evidence for the comparative effectiveness of treatments for severe and less severe mental illnesses is cited (Conway *et al*, 1994; Department of Health, 1994).

Counsellors

In this context, while the rapid growth of counsellors in general practice has mixed blessings, they are likely to be most effective and of greatest assistance to community and primary care teams if integration or at least good communication with them occurs. Counsellors are expected to develop their own support and supervision frameworks, and participation in these by community teams can maximise their effectiveness and allow community teams to concentrate their efforts on those with greatest need. Self-help techniques and voluntary groups also have a major part to play, being as effective in management of minor neurotic disorders as trained nursing staff (Tyrer *et al*, 1988).

Individual care plans

Written care plans should be completed at initial assessments and updated at reviews. This simply means that the care plan, which would normally be completed at the end of an assessment and re-assessment, for example in an out-patient clinic or at a review meeting, should be written in clinical notes.

A care plan needs to be clearly identifiable (i.e. on a separate sheet or under a separate heading). It is important that a current care plan does not get lost within clinical records, and that it can be located rapidly by medical colleagues or locums who may be looking after a patient temporarily.

For most individuals with severe mental illness, a care plan would contain specific actions involving more than one professional. For example:

(a) continue medical review in out-patients
(b) continue administration of depot medication
(c) encourage attendance at a day centre
(d) assist in claiming Disability Living Allowance
(e) start behavioural family therapy.

A review date and location would be set such that reviews occur regularly and as frequently as the team providing care for them decide.

A copy of this plan may be given to patients/ users, carers, GPs and other professionals. For in-patients being discharged and patients who are reviewed by the multi-disciplinary team, this can be a way of improving compliance with management regimes and is worth considering in all instances. On the reverse of the plan, spaces for labels giving names and contact points of key-workers and others can ensure that the patient, carer and GP know who is involved in care.

Case studies

B., aged 20 and unemployed, was being seen in an out-patient department and by a community psychiatric nurse (CPN). She had been distressed with suicidal ideas over the past year and had frequently taken to her bed after minor disagreements with her parents. Work was under way with her parents and herself independently and jointly. Reviews were programmed with the patient and her mother, and also occurred between psychiatrist and CPN at their regular meetings to discuss patients with whom they were both involved. Her care plan involved:

(a) continue individual counselling at home ...SE
(b) continue family work with B. and mother ...DK/ SE
(c) medication: fluoxetine 20 mg (mornings) ...DK
(d) review in one month in out-patients ...DK
Keyworker: SE .... (Tel. No.)

M., aged 39, has a 20-year history of schizophrenia. He lives in a council flat and his parents remain in regular contact with him but find this stressful. He will not attend the local day centre but he accepts visits from a social work assistant and attends an out-patient department every six weeks for medication. A domiciliary care assistant was withdrawn after she became concerned about her safety.

A care manager coordinates his care. He has been considered for inclusion on the local supervision register but after analysis of the evidence of risk to others (from the care assistant and her supervisor)

and to self (as he had made a serious suicidal attempt five years previously), and consultation with the team involved, the consultant psychiatrist decided not to seek his inclusion as he was complying with care and not at risk of 'falling through the net'. This would, however, be reviewed at his regular six-monthly review meetings which usually last between 30 and 45 minutes. His care plan was:

(a) medication monitored in out-patients ...DK
(b) bi-weekly visits from social work assistant ...GD
(c) re-negotiate domiciliary services assistance ...BH
(d) parents contact DK/BH if concerns arise
(e) next review meeting – 23 April 1998 at 11.30
Keyworker: BH .... (Tel. No.)

Care management, after-care and supervision registers

The CPA and care management involve very similar processes – assessment, review and coordination of care. The differences are primarily theoretical. The CPA is led by health services, and care management by social services; the former applies to people referred to specialist psychiatric services, the latter to other client groups, such as old people and people with physical and learning disabilities. Care management applies to many people with severe mental illness as most have social care needs to be met.

When patients with mental illness are allocated a care manager by social services, it should usually make sense for that manager to be the nominated CPA keyworker if they are a mental health worker. Likewise, procedures for the CPA and care management assessments need not duplicate each other and there is much to be said for using the same core procedures to avoid repetition for patients.

The Mental Health Act

Section 117 of the Mental Health Act places legal obligations on health and social services to provide after-care for patients detained under certain sections of the Act (e.g. Sections 3 and 37). The CPA places precisely the same obligations on health and social services for all patients accepted by mental health services, but does so in guidance. Thus, using the same core procedures and documentation can avoid repetition.

The procedures for assessing whether someone should go on a supervision register require a multi-disciplinary review and, as the guidance describes, this can be usefully combined with a general care programme review (Kingdon, 1996). This will be a small group of patients whose risk to themselves and others is greatest.

Conclusions

The CPA does mean modifying the way in which many services have delivered care, allowing the needs of individuals with severe mental illness to be prioritised, but it is not designed to bureaucratise it. It is essential that systems are: comprehensive and comprehensible but not over-inclusive; integrated with procedures for Section 117 after-care, care management and supervision registers; easy to audit; and, above all, workable and cost-effective in terms of time expended.

Systems usually have teething problems and so need to be formally reviewed at intervals in the relevant forums, including medical staff meetings. The evidence from evaluations of the CPA (Tyrer *et al*, 1995) is now confirming its effectiveness in improving the delivery of care to people suffering from severe mental illness.

References

Conway, A. S., Melzer, D. & Hale, A. S. (1994) The outcome of targeting community mental health services: evidence from the West Lambeth schizophrenia cohort. *British Medical Journal*, **308**, 627–630.

Department of Health (1994) *Health of the Nation. Key Area Handbook: Mental Illness* (2nd edn). London: HMSO.

Kemp, R., Heyward, P., Applewhaite, G., *et al* (1996) Compliance therapy in psychotic patients: a randomised controlled trial. *British Medical Journal*, **312**, 345–349.

Kingdon, D. G. (1992) Interprofessional collaboration in mental health. *Journal of Interprofessional Care*, **6**, 141–148.

—— (1994) The care programme approach. *Psychiatric Bulletin*, **18**, 68–70.

—— (1996) Supervision registers: care or control? *British Journal of Hospital Medicine*, **56**, 461–464.

North East Thames & South East Thames Regional Health Authorities (1994) *The Report of the Inquiry into the Care and Treatment of Christopher Clunis*. London: HMSO.

Social & Community Planning Research (1993) *Factors Influencing the Implementation of the Care Programme Approach*. London: HMSO.

Tyrer, P., Sievewright, N., Kingdon, D., *et al*. (1988) The Nottingham study of neurotic disorder: comparison of drug and psychological treatments. *Lancet*, **ii**, 235–240.

——, Morgan, J., Van Horn, E., *et al* (1995) A randomised control study of close monitoring of vulnerable psychiatric patients. *Lancet*, **345**, 756–759.

Appendix: Brief guide to supervision registers

(1) Aim: to ensure that those patients who are most at risk to themselves or others receive adequate care, support and supervision in the community.

(2) The decision about inclusion rests with the consultant psychiatrist responsible for care, in consultation with a multi-disciplinary team.

(3) Evidence on which judgement of risk is made must be recorded in written form and made available to the relevant professionals for the review meeting.

(4) Categories of inclusion:

(a) significant risk of suicide

(b) significant risk of serious violence to others

(c) significant risk of severe self-neglect.

This applies to those outside hospital – if they are immediately admitted to hospital, registration may not be necessary unless they are already on the register. But they should not be removed during the period of admission while significant risk persists.

(5) Method of including a patient on the register:

(a) All patients should be assessed for above categories of risk, at assessments (e.g. in out-patients) and at review meetings.

(b) If they may qualify, a review meeting should be set up with relevant team members, the person and their carer to consider whether the person should be included on the register.

(c) If they are included, a register form should be completed and conveyed to the register manager.

(d) If they are included, the patient must be informed orally and in writing of: (i) when and broadly why they have been included, (ii) to whom the registration details may be disclosed, and (iii) mechanisms of review. Only in very exceptional circumstances can they not be informed and such a decision would need to be taken by the team and psychiatrist. The GP should always be informed.

(e) Review of inclusion should occur at least every six months and the patient taken off the register if risk no longer exists.

(6) If the patient appeals against being on the register, the consultant psychiatrist needs to consider this in consultation with other members involved in the person's care. If the patient remains dissatisfied, the normal routes for complaint and right to a second opinion apply.

(7) If someone on the register is transferred to another provider unit, a copy of their record should be urgently transferred with them.

(8) An executive member of the trust, preferably with a clinical background, should be identified to oversee the management of the register.

(Note: this guide is not a substitute for reading the full guidance)

Management aspects of care for homeless people with mental illness

P. Timms

People with mental illness have always been marginalised and economically disadvantaged. Warner (1987) has shown that this is particularly true in times of high unemployment. Poor inner-city areas have excessive rates of severe mental illness, usually without the health, housing and social service provisions necessary to deal with them (Faris & Dunham, 1959). The majority of those who suffer major mental illness live in impoverished circumstances somewhere along the continuum of poverty. Homelessness, however defined, is the extreme and most marginalised end of this continuum, and it is here that we find disproportionate numbers of individuals with mental illness.

Reliable estimates of the numbers of homeless people are difficult to come by, although the last UK census (Office of Population Censuses and Surveys, 1992) enumerated around 3000 people sleeping out and 50 000 people living in homelessness hostels of some sort. Although the absolute numbers are small, homeless people suffer high rates of physical and psychiatric morbidity and place disproportionately large demands on service providers. Compared with the general population, at least twice as many homeless people have some kind of significant mental health problem and in hostel populations major psychotic illnesses are over-represented by a factor of 20 or 30.

There is no evidence that substantial numbers of homeless people with mental illness have been discharged from long-stay beds in mental hospitals. They will, however, often have had multiple, brief admissions to psychiatric units. Associated drug and alcohol problems are common, as is a reluctance to engage with mainstream psychiatric services.

Although homelessness is often perceived as a London problem, levels of homelessness are significant across other areas of the country (Randall, 1992). On taking a wider perspective, concentrations of homeless people are found in the centres of most major European cities, where there are similar concerns about their high levels of psychiatric morbidity.

Definition of 'homelessness'

The stereotype of the homeless person is the man or woman who sleeps out on the street. However, people who sleep out constitute a small portion of those who are homeless. There is a range of unsatisfactory types of accommodation in which people find themselves (see Box 1).

In these milieux are found such disparate groups as the unemployed, middle-aged drinking men, teenage drug misusers, individuals with schizophrenia and homeless families with children. Quite clearly these different groups have very different needs. However, the group which has elicited particular concern has been that of people who live in 'traditional' homeless settings. They might be sleeping on the streets, sleeping in night shelters or direct-access hostels, or using other services targeted at homeless people such as day centres or soup runs.

It may be asked, if someone is not actually roofless, why should they be considered homeless? In terms of providing psychiatric services, the main factor to be considered is whether a person's housing status prevents them from gaining access

---

Box 1. Accommodation for homeless people

Open-air sleeping ('rough sleepers')
Abandoned buildings ('skippering')
Night shelters
Direct-access hostels
Referral-only hostels
Bed-and-breakfast hotels
Sleeping on a friend's floor
Prison (if no address prior to release)

to both psychiatric and general health care. Although a person may have accomodation of a sort, their situation may effectively exclude them from the services and opportunities that are used by most people. They may thus be viewed as 'socially marginalised'. This chapter will address the needs of this group of people, whatever the nature of their homelessness.

Nature of the problem

There are no psychiatric illnesses peculiar to homeless people. However, there are two main differences when compared with a typical inner-city general practice population:

(a) The distribution of psychiatric disorders is completely different, with psychosis predominating.
(b) A social substrate for health (housing, nutrition, clothing, social network, etc.) is normally assumed by doctors and other helpers. For homeless people this is usually absent, or certainly severely compromised.

The problem to be addressed is not one of a unique pathology, but one of a different pattern of pathology existing in the context of extreme deprivation, disability and social marginalisation. Homeless people with schizophrenia tend not to present for treatment (Priest, 1976) and this contributes to the high prevalence of psychotic illness in this population.

A complicating factor is the high level of chronic chest, skin and dental problems which are commonly untreated.

Support networks – existing caring agencies

A variety of statutory agencies are involved in providing for the multiple needs of homeless people. However, their involvement is often brief and unsatisfactory for both parties, and a plethora of voluntary agencies has sprung up to fill the gaps in provision. The result is a complicated patchwork of services. Although they would best function as a network, they often do not.

The list in Box 2 is not exhaustive and the most relevant agencies will differ according to local conditions. Those providers most consistently and intimately involved with the homeless have been voluntary agencies. Historically, their relationships with the statutory sector have generally been, at best, distant and, at worst, hostile. This has obscured their role as the primary source of social

support and care for homeless people with mental illness.

Barriers to care

Homeless people report that they have been unable to register with general practitioners (GPs), have been treated in an offhand manner in hospitals or have been given a hostile reception in accident & emergency departments (Shiner & Leddington, 1991). Agencies advocating on behalf of the homeless urge doctors, nurses and receptionists to behave better. However, little serious thought has been given to the reasons for this behaviour on the part of men and women who usually behave in a professional and caring manner.

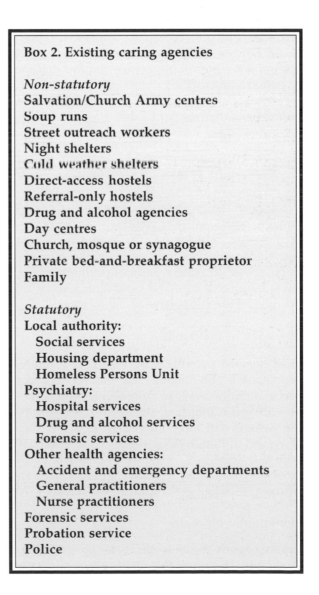

Box 2. Existing caring agencies

Non-statutory
Salvation/Church Army centres
Soup runs
Street outreach workers
Night shelters
Cold weather shelters
Direct-access hostels
Referral-only hostels
Drug and alcohol agencies
Day centres
Church, mosque or synagogue
Private bed-and-breakfast proprietor
Family

Statutory
Local authority:
    Social services
    Housing department
    Homeless Persons Unit
Psychiatry:
    Hospital services
    Drug and alcohol services
    Forensic services
Other health agencies:
    Accident and emergency departments
    General practitioners
    Nurse practitioners
Forensic services
Probation service
Police

Professional attitudes

Stereotyping

Professionals hold many of the same stereotypes about the homeless as do other people. They often perceive the homeless as being alcoholic, personality disordered, feckless, as having chosen to live in an unsettled way and as not appreciating the help they are given (Jeffery, 1979). This in turn means that they have very low expectations of homeless clients and that they may well not do as much for them as they would if they had an address. However, Morse & Calsyn's (1986) work suggests that, in spite of the fact that they may not be currently receiving them, homeless people are often willing users of psychiatric services.

Multiplicity of needs

Most professionals do not work in a truly multi-disciplinary environment. When they are confronted with a client who is both homeless and mentally ill, they are presented with an array of problems, most of which they do not have the skills to deal with. They may therefore experience profound feelings of impotence and feel that they have nothing to offer.

Lack of a 'substrate for health'

Most medical and psychiatric staff are trained to examine fairly circumscribed areas of pathology. Their repertoire of interventions tends to assume the presence of an array of social factors (housing, adequate nutrition and a social network) that make possible both health and treatment. In the absence of this substrate for health, purely medical or psychiatric interventions may well be perceived as pointless. Treating a depressive illness may be felt to be futile if a person's situation is so lacking in any of these supportive social factors.

The myth of the tramp

Most service providers believe that homeless people are highly mobile. This perception breeds a lack of enthusiasm, as there seems little point in providing a committed, sustained intervention if the patient will have moved on in a few days. However, although 'long-distance patients' have been identified in the USA by Chmiel *et al* (1979), most homeless people move infrequently and within a restricted geographical area (Priest, 1970).

Therapeutic nihilism

Taken together, these factors can produce a therapeutic nihilism that may not only prevent professionals from doing what they can, but may even serve as a conscious, or unconscious, justification for neglect. "Staff tend to view these patients as adversaries, thus avoiding the guilt of recognising how little they can in fact offer them" (Breakey, 1987).

Organisation of services

Inter-agency working

Homeless persons with mental illness have multiple needs requiring the involvement of multiple agencies – health, social and housing, in addition to any specific psychiatric input. In spite of community care legislation, inter-agency working is still limited in many places. Joint funding, and hence joint responsibility for projects, may better promote joint working where other approaches have failed (Farr, 1985).

No fixed abode (NFA) rotas

Many psychiatric units, especially in large cities, have an NFA rota, allotting to a duty consultant any homeless patients. Unfortunately, allocation in this way may not ensure continuity of care for the patient. If they present on a future occasion, they may be allocated to a different duty consultant and their care unnecessarily fragmented. If a patient is frequently mobile within a relatively small area, allocation of a client via the NFA rota should confer continuing responsibility for them. Very few people labelled as NFA are truly rootless and footloose – ideally they should be taken on by the catchment area team for the geographical area they frequent. This would obviously result in some services being unfairly burdened, but proper recording of such admissions could enable some re-allocation of resources to such services.

Philosophies of care

Different agencies have different philosophies of care. For instance, most mental health services consider that individuals are unable to make informed choices when in the throes of a severe psychosis. However, many housing organisations take the view that people are always fully responsible for their choices and actions, no matter how thought-disordered or deluded they may be. This attitude may precipitate inappropriate evictions, when a disturbed and often distressed client is deemed, by his or her difficult behaviour, to have made a rational choice. To be fair, the inaccessibility of psychiatric help has often made it difficult for housing agencies to respond in any other way.

Homeless lifestyles

Both physical and psychiatric care rank low in homeless people's hierarchies of needs. The demands of securing immediate survival needs (see Box 3) are often more pressing and more immediately rewarding than appointments with doctors, nurses or social workers.

Poor access to services

Although most surveys have suggested that the majority of homeless people are registered with a GP somewhere, it may not be locally. This may explain why, despite the relatively high rate of registration, actual use of primary care is often infrequent. Why does this matter? Someone with a home who wishes to make use of psychiatric services will have his or her GP as both a guide to those services and an advocate with them. For the homeless person with no regular GP this is not the case, and he or she will tend to approach services through accident and emergency departments. For obvious reasons, the activities of these departments are orientated towards brief intervention rather than continued involvement and advocacy.

Mobility

Mobility is as often forced upon the homeless as it is chosen. Even so, much of this mobility is relatively local. In spite of this, the consequent crossing of catchment area boundaries may lead to problems with services disclaiming responsibility.

Distrust of officialdom

To official helping agencies, homeless people mean trouble because their predicaments inevitably make demands that cannot be met. The resultant inadequate response is consequently disappointing for the client. Hospitals and GPs are reluctant to take them on. Benefit regulations often seem designed to penalise the homeless. Local authority housing departments are only interested in homeless families and the very vulnerable. The police are often involved in moving them on or arresting them for drunkenness. It is not surprising that homeless people are often suspicious and distrustful of services that regard themselves as caring and helping.

Service provision – strategies

Temporal access

The conventional system of organising access to a psychiatric service by means of GP referral and out-patient attendance does not work well for homeless people. It is often more effective to negotiate times to meet the homeless patient that fit in with their often irregular timetable, which may change from week to week. Even better is a drop-in service, where people can be seen quickly without any need to make an appointment (Segal & Baumohl, 1985).

Geographical access

Providing direct care in hostels has been shown to be more effective in maintaining contact with homeless men than encouraging them to use routine local services (Brent-Smith & Dean, 1990). Ferguson & Dixon (1992) suggested that regular sessions in hostels or day centres may be the best way of providing access to care where such facilities exist. For those with alcohol problems, in-hostel detoxification has been found to offer a relatively rapid response (within 24 hours) and to be preferred by users (Haig & Hibbert, 1990).

Access to community resources

Homeless people have problems in many areas of their lives, most of which are outside the expertise and resources of most doctors. Although in most cities there are extensive networks of voluntary agencies that do have these skills, professionals often find themselves hampered by their lack of knowledge of such agencies. These commonly include hostels, day centres, sources of cheap or free food and clothing, alcohol counselling services and advice centres. Each health authority or trust should obtain or create a directory of these services that is concise enough to be of use in a busy ward, general practice, or accident and emergency department (Anonymous, 1986).

Box 3. Priorities for homeless people, in rank order (Ball & Havassy, 1984)

Shelter
Money
Employment
Social activities
Food
Stopping drinking
Counselling
Help with managing money
Other (including health)

Finding a keyworker/advocate

When treatment plans are started with homeless clients, they may fall apart because it is automatically assumed that there is no carer outside hospital with whom contact can be maintained. For those with homes it would be a GP or relative, but homeless people often do not have a GP and are usually not in contact with family. However, there is nearly always a person or organisation in some sort of caring role with whom they maintain contact and who should be informed. This might be a hostel or day centre worker, an alcohol counsellor, a minister of religion, a social worker or a probation officer. Of course, they will usually not be medical personnel and so issues of confidentiality may arise. These can be overcome by obtaining the client's written permission and/or by producing an edited version of documents such as discharge summaries.

Access to housing and benefits

Homeless people are entitled to benefits like anyone else, although they often do not claim consistently or may not be aware of their entitlements, particularly with regard to incapacity benefit or disability living allowance. They are able to claim even when sleeping out, although the benefit will be at a lower level than if they are staying in a hostel. In large cities there may be a specific Benefits Agency office to deal with claims by homeless people.

Applications for housing may be made through the local authority homeless persons unit if the individual is accepted by them as being in priority need under the Housing Act 1985. Policies vary from place to place, but for most local authorities the presence of a significant mental illness is sufficient. Where foreign nationals are concerned, it has recently been established in law that unemployed, vulnerable European Union nationals have a right to be housed by a local authority.

For those with more complex needs, a community care act assessment may be the most effective way of unlocking the appropriate resources. These assessments often take time to arrange and so may never occur if a patient moves around. However, hospital admission may offer a window of opportunity. If at all possible, any such assessment should be carried out before discharge.

Enhancing communication and liaison

Increasing use of hostels by homeless people in Nottingham who were mentally ill prompted the establishment of a support team that encouraged liaison between the different agencies involved in patients' care (Pidgeon, 1991). Although this did not make any new resources available for direct care, it ensured the best use of existing services by making sure that they were properly coordinated.

Prescribing

Craig & Timms (1992) suggested that homeless facilities have been major providers of accommodation and care for people with chronic mental illness. Although hostels have always been meant to provide only temporary accommodation, they have become permanent homes for many people with chronic psychotic illnesses. This is presumably because they are environments where there is usually a low level of expressed emotion. Hostels tend to be tolerant of odd or bizarre behaviour and traditionally have placed very little 'rehabilitation' pressure on residents. These institutional and relatively tolerant milieux may create an opportunity for the introduction or re-introduction of antipsychotic medication.

Supervision and care is basic, but is still more than that received by patients living in independent accommodation. Issues of safety and self-neglect may therefore be less pressing, with less pressure to achieve quick results. In such settings it is often possible to start with low doses of neuroleptics, increasing slowly. This will usually avoid the problems with side-effects and the consequent resistance to treatment that is so common among people who have received large doses of these drugs in the course of an acute hospital admission. Most people living in hostels hold onto their own medication, although in some circumstances hostel staff may agree to look after it. Even if hostel staff do agree to do this, they should not be seen as dispensing medication, as they do not usually have the training or the procedures in place to do this safely.

It is generally best not to prescribe drugs that are liable to misuse. Although most homeless patients use their medication responsibly, drugs such as the benzodiazepines, chlormethiazole and procyclidine have a significant street value. In circumstances where it may be impossible to get hold of money any other way, it can be very tempting to sell a prescription.

Attitude

Various attitudes have been mentioned in the literature as being necessary for successful work with the homeless. Goldfinger & Chafetz (1984) recommended 'therapeutic nihilism', by which they seem to mean hoping for the best but expecting the worst. Breakey (1987) recommends patience, not so much with patients but with the workers in voluntary agencies who have often had bad relationships with psychiatric services in the past. They need to be convinced that the service has staying power and that it is not just a 'project' which is likely to disappear when a key member of staff moves on. It is also mutually beneficial for psychiatric workers to value the often extensive knowledge of hostel and day centre staff. Workers need to accommodate to a different set of expectations so that they are not perpetually disappointed and demoralised.

Joint working with the voluntary sector

Voluntary agencies are the front-line providers of care for homeless people, and so it is impossible to provide a good service to the homeless without a close working relationship with such hostels and day centres. However, this can be a difficult task for both partners, in spite of a mutual commitment to serve the interests of the clients. Their permanent staff, although usually highly experienced, will generally have little or no training in mental health. There is often a residue of resentment built up over years of receiving no acknowledgement or service from local psychiatric providers. A significant proportion of their workers will be volunteers, who will be young, will have had little or no training or experience and who will tend to change frequently. Shift systems may make it difficult to find a patient's keyworker quickly, and staff shortages may make effective keyworking systems impossible. The high levels of stress under which they are working may lead to an impatience with the more measured pace at which psychiatric services tend to work and may generate unrealistic demands. Workers may find it difficult to understand why psychiatrists will detain somebody with schizophrenia in hospital, but not individuals with personality disorders. Anti-psychiatric ideas are still prevalent and, even if not openly expressed, may sometimes sabotage psychiatric involvement. In spite of these problems, joint working can be extremely productive and the voluntary sector should be seen not as a liability, but as a collection of skilled, varied and committed resources. It is possible to improve both practice and relationships with such agencies by providing basic training in mental health issues for their staff. A regular psychiatric presence at staff meetings may also be found to be supportive.

Confidentiality

Confidentiality presents particular problems with voluntary agencies as policies regarding confidentiality within the organisations may not exist, or will certainly differ from agency to agency. There may be anxieties about how much information to release to people who are not part of statutory health or social services. It may be helpful to bear in mind that, as mentioned above, workers in voluntary agencies will often be the patient's main carer and may formally be registered as their next of kin. This should inform any decisions about release of information, as such workers may well need to know sensitive information so that they can carry out their work with the patient safely and effectively.

Problems for service providers

Surber *et al* (1987) developed a city-wide service for homeless people in San Francisco. They found that team members tended to have unrealistic expectations of each other and attributed to this their high turnover of staff. They also noted that making appropriate referrals was extremely difficult because the whole system of health and social care was functioning beyond capacity. As a result they shifted their focus from providing a directly clinical service to networking and training other care providers. Experience in services in this country has suggested that homeless agencies often have unrealistic expectations of statutory services and this may cause considerable tension between them.

Models of service provision

Over the past 15 years, and particularly in the USA, a considerable stock of expertise has developed in providing psychiatric services directly to disadvantaged and marginalised populations, including the homeless. A huge range of specialist psychiatric services has been developed in response to the large numbers of homeless mentally ill people. These may broadly be classified as:

(a) *Primary outreach*   where psychiatric staff make the first initial approach to potential patients.
(b) *Secondary outreach*   where the initial contact is made by a voluntary agency which initiates and/or provides the venue for subsequent contact with a psychiatric team.
(c) *Residential stabilisation*   special housing and support arrangements are made for homeless patients following episodes of hospital care.

Case management is the most common approach to individual casework, in the sense of having a particular worker taking responsibility for the coordination and delivery of care from several systems. Although commonly used with the people with severe and chronic mental illness in the general population, this approach makes particular sense for homeless people as their multiple needs will rarely, if ever, be met by one profession or worker.

Care Programme Approach

The Care Programme Approach (CPA) has two main arms:

(a) *Allocation of a named keyworker* This should facilitate the development of effective case management, and will be particularly valuable for homeless people whose tendency to be involved with multiple agencies may result in responsibility being taken by none.

(b) *Ensuring that comprehensive assessments, care plans and regular review meetings are carried out* The essential activity generated is communication between complex networks of caring agencies and consequent coordination of their activities. Homeless people tend to be more mobile, so their networks are often more complex and change more frequently

than do those for domiciled patients. They are consequently very difficult to maintain, particularly in terms of arranging regular review meetings. Voluntary agencies tend to be short-staffed and so may find it difficult to attend CPA meetings. Even so, it is essential to try to involve voluntary sector workers in any CPA planning meetings before discharge from hospital.

These new arrangements offer considerable scope for ensuring that vulnerable individuals receive the coordinated care they need. However, a considerable investment in time and resources is necessary to make them work in practice.

Supervision registers

All the above principles and problems apply to supervision registers, which can at their best ensure focused, multi-agency, consistent work with difficult or potentially dangerous individuals. An unforseen problem that has been encountered recently is that some hostels are now reluctant to accept or retain residents who have been placed on a supervision register.

Conclusions

In spite of the long association of homelessness with mental illness, the active provision of psychiatric services to homeless people is a relatively recent development. All effective treatment programmes have involved psychiatric provision as a coordinated part of more general provision of housing and social services. In many ways, they have anticipated the needs-led assessment, case management and coordination that have been specified as part of the CPA. Most of the characteristics of these services are really nothing more than the requirements for an effective, non-institutional community psychiatry, whether its users are domiciled or not.

> **Box 4. Desirable service characteristics (Breakey, 1987)**
>
> **Rapid response**
> **Willing and tolerant – informal and non-stigmatising**
> **Capable of linking mental health services and accommodation**
> **Flexible – in terms of sites of work, use of facilities, etc.**
> **Comprehensive – dealing with a range of social needs**
> **Continuous – good flow of information within and between services**
> **Individualised care planning and intervention**
> **Collaborative – part of a wider service network**
> **Meaningful – consonant with users' hierarchy of needs**
> **Responsive to changing circumstances**

References

Anonymous (1986) Gold Award: a network of services for the homeless chronic mentally ill: skid-row mental health service. *Hospital and Community Psychiatry*, **37**, 1148–1151.

Ball, J. & Havassy, E. H. (1984) A survey of the problems and needs of homeless consumers of acute psychiatric services. *Hospital and Community Psychiatry*, **35**, 917–921.

Breakey, W. R. (1987) Treating the homeless. *Alcohol Health and Research World*, **11**, 42–47.

Brent-Smith, H. & Dean, R. (1990) *Plugging the Gaps*. London: Lewisham and North Southwark Health Authority.

Chmiel, A. J., Akhtars, S. & Morris, J. (1979) The long-distance patient in the emergency room. *International Journal of Social Psychiatry*, **25**, 38–46.

Craig, T. & Timms, P. W. (1992) Out of the wards and onto the streets? Deinstitutionalisation and homelessness in Britain. *Journal of Mental Health*, **1**, 265–275.

Faris, R. E. & Dunham, H. W. (1959) *Mental Disorders in Urban Areas: An Ecological Study of Schizophrenia and Other Psychoses*. Chicago, IL: University of Chicago Press.

Farr, R. K. (1985) A programmatic view of the homeless mentally ill in Los Angeles County. *International Journal of Family Psychiatry*, **6**, 129–148.

Ferguson, B. & Dixon, R. (1992) Psychiatric clinics in homeless hostels – your flexible friend. *Psychiatric Bulletin*, **16**, 685–687.

Goldfinger, S. M. & Chafetz, L. (1984) Developing a better service delivery system for the homeless mentally ill. In *The Homeless Mentally Ill* (ed. R. H. Lamb), pp. 91–108. Washington, DC: APA.

Haig, R. & Hibbert, G. (1990) Where and when to detoxify single homeless drinkers. *British Medical Journal*, **301**, 848–849.

Jeffery, R. (1979) Normal rubbish: deviant patients in casualty departments. *Sociology of Health and Illness*, **1**, 91–107.

Morse, G. & Calsyn, R. J. (1986) Mentally disturbed homeless people in St Louis: needy, willing but underserved. *International Journal of Mental Health*, **14**, 74–94.

Office of Population Censuses and Surveys (1992) *Supplementary Monitor on People Sleeping Rough in 1991 Census – Preliminary Report for England and Wales*. London: OPCS.

Pidgeon, J. (1991) Unity in action. *Social Work Today*, January, 16–17.

Priest, R. G. (1970) Homeless men, a USA–UK comparison. *Proceedings of the Royal Society of Medicine*, **63**, 441–445.

—— (1976) The homeless person and the psychiatric services: an Edinburgh survey. *British Journal of Psychiatry*, **128**, 128–136.

Randall, G. (1992) *Counted Out*. London: CRISIS & CHAR.

Segal, S. P. & Baumohl, J. (1985) The community living room. *Social Casework: The Journal of Contemporary Social Work*, February, 111–116.

Shiner, P. & Leddington, S. (1991) Sometimes it makes you frightened to go to hospital ... they treat you like dirt. *Health Service Journal*, 7 November, 21–23.

Surber, R. W., Dwyer, E., Ryan, K. J., *et al* (1987) Medical and psychiatric needs of the homeless – a preliminary response. *Social Work*, March/April, 116–119.

Warner, D. (1987) *Recovery from Schizophrenia*. London: Routledge.

Substance misuse in severe mental illness

Roch Cantwell & Glynn Harrison

Comorbidity and dual diagnosis have a fashionable, and thus ephemeral, ring that belies their relevance to day-to-day practice. The topic has been increasingly addressed in North American literature where there is a recognition of the extent of substance misuse in those with severe mental illness, and of the need to find ways of managing its consequences effectively. Substance misuse may colour the diagnosis, management and prognosis of major mental illness and can adversely affect the relationship between staff and patients. Despite its common occurrence, it frequently remains undetected (Ananth *et al*, 1989). With burgeoning research interest, there is some consensus as to how to manage the problem, but, as yet, little agreement on the precise nature of causal relationships.

Links between substance misuse and psychosis

The role of some substances of abuse in precipitating psychotic symptoms, usually in the context of intoxication or withdrawal states, is undisputed. Hallucinogen intoxication, almost by definition, is manifested by sensory distortion, illusion and hallucination. Stimulant use is frequently accompanied by paranoid symptoms. Such symptoms may also accompany the acute use of cannabis, cocaine and methylenedioxymethamphetamine (MDMA, 'ecstasy'). Discontinuance syndromes are at their most dramatic in delirium tremens, but similar states can result from barbiturate and benzodiazepine withdrawal.

Drug-induced psychosis

The existence of prolonged or independent psychotic states triggered by substance use is more controversial. Alcoholic hallucinosis, while frequently described, remains perplexing (Glass, 1989). It may occur during heavy drinking and does not necessarily resolve on stopping, although abstinence is usually regarded as important in its management. The natural history is usually one of repeated relapses though these may take a variety of forms, including affective disorder, schizophrenia, and further episodes of hallucinosis, calling into question the nature of the initial illness. There may be evidence of cognitive impairment. The relationship to schizophrenia and delirium tremens is unclear, but treatment is conventionally with neuroleptics. Paranoid psychoses resulting from amphetamine use usually resolve within days to weeks of removal of the offending drug, often encouraged by antipsychotic medication. Cocaine psychoses appear to follow a similar path. Psychotic symptoms occurring in the course of prolonged hallucinogen use may also resolve over days to weeks, but, characteristically, acute and transient 'flashbacks' occur, sometimes years after drug use has ceased.

Cannabis and psychosis

The greatest controversy reigns over the relationship between cannabis use and psychosis. Acute psychotic reactions occur but, despite many reports, there appears little conclusive evidence for a prolonged 'cannabis psychosis', and no justification for its use as a diagnostic label. Cannabis has been cited as an independent risk factor in the development of schizophrenia, the strongest evidence coming from a prospective study of Swedish conscripts followed up over a 15-year period (Andreasson *et al*, 1987). The relative risk of developing schizophrenia was 2.4 for cannabis users, and 6.0 for heavy users, when compared with non-users at conscription. The study, and a further related paper, have been criticised on methodological grounds (Thomas, 1993), not least because of the difficulty in establishing causal relationships. Nevertheless, it has been reported that relatives of patients whose development of, or relapse into, schizophrenia is associated with cannabis use have themselves an increased risk of schizophrenia, suggesting a gene-to-environment (cannabis) effect in certain individuals (McGuire *et al*, 1995). While any aetiological links between cannabis and schizophrenia remain uncertain, the detrimental effects of cannabis use on the course of pre-existing illness are more clearly established.

Extent of dual diagnosis

Prevalence issues

The prevalence of comorbidity is not easy to assess. Rates quoted range from 15 to 65%. Accurate case definition is absent from earlier studies, and there is great variety in the choice of setting (in-patient, out-patient, general population) and in subjects (primary substance misusers, severely mentally ill). Extrapolating work carried out in North America to Europe is difficult given that substance misuse is greatly influenced by demographic factors and by temporal fluctuations. Finally, most studies have concentrated on patients with chronic illness, confounding any attempts to identify aetiological links between substance use and psychosis. The questions which need to be addressed by epidemiological studies, and which are important for clinical practice, include whether substance misuse is more common in people with severe mental illness than in the general population, whether rates of comorbidity differ between specific psychotic disorders, and whether certain substances are preferentially used over others.

The Epidemiological Catchment Area (ECA) study revealed a prevalence of 47% and 32% for substance misuse in schizophrenia and affective disorders, respectively (Regier *et al*, 1990). People with schizophrenia were 4.6 times more likely, and individuals with affective disorder 2.6 times more likely, to have drug or alcohol problems when compared with the general population. A further review of several studies suggests an increase over time in the prevalence of comorbidity (Cuffel, 1992). Recent UK findings suggest a one-year prevalence rate of 36.3% for substance-related problems in a London sample of people with psychosis (Menezes *et al*, 1996) and preliminary data from Nottingham suggest similarly high rates at onset of psychosis (Cantwell *et al*, 1996). Whether substance misuse is more common in certain types of severe mental illnesses is less easily determined.

An increase among patients with schizophrenia is strongly suggested by the ECA study, where only those with antisocial personality showed higher rates of substance use. There is a trend towards increased alcohol use in bipolar disorder, and recent evidence from studies of first-onset psychosis also found a raised prevalence in those with affective illness (e.g. Strakowski *et al*, 1993). Overall, however, those most at risk of drug and alcohol comorbidity are young men with chronic psychotic illness.

Preferential use

Those with chronic illness appear to preferentially use certain substances over others. Hallucinogens and stimulants are more often used, and central nervous system depressants such as alcohol, hypnotics and opiates less used, in schizophrenia (Schneier & Siris, 1987). Although this might be expected if a causal link between psychostimulants and psychosis is assumed, patients continue to use these drugs often in the clear knowledge, and experience, of the detrimental effect on their mental state.

Reasons for substance use

Individuals with psychosis may be at risk of substance misuse for a number of reasons. Downward social drift, associated especially with schizophrenia and the shift from institutional care, increase exposure of patients to drugs of abuse (Smith & Hucker, 1994). At the same time, there has been a growing acceptability and availability of drug use in society. Patients with severe mental illness may be least able to resist peer pressure toward drug use, and, as a result of their illness, they share many of the risk factors (negative affective states, poor self-esteem and role performance, impaired social skills and social isolation) associated with drug use in the general population (Lehman *et al*, 1989). The knowledge that psychotic symptoms can be reproduced by a drug may impart a sense of control to patients, increasing use despite their recognition of the adverse effects (Selzer & Lieberman, 1993). Reasons given by patients for their drug use, such as the relief of boredom, decrease in anxiety and improved socialisation, do not differ much from those of users with no psychosis, but those with mental illness often experience these difficulties more acutely than other drug users do (Box 1).

Premorbid functioning

An intriguing finding from several studies has been the evidence for better premorbid functioning in patients with schizophrenia and substance misuse (e.g. Arndt *et al*, 1992). It may be that those with greater social skills in the premorbid period are more likely to come in contact with drug and alcohol use, and that following the onset of illness are then at greater risk of escalating use. Paradoxically then, those patients who might be regarded as having the best prognosis may be most at risk of descending into drug use, with its attendant problems.

Self-medication

Patients may use alcohol and drugs to 'self-medicate' either their symptoms (whether positive, negative or dysphoric) or the side-effects of psychotropic medications. Alcohol and opiates can lessen the distress associated with positive psychotic symptoms, while psychostimulants such as amphetamines and cocaine are reported to counteract negative symptoms. Cannabis may also attenuate apathy and withdrawal – higher rates of negative symptoms are reported among non-users. The action of opiates in masking positive symptoms may delay the onset or diagnosis of psychosis, and it has been suggested that low rates of opiate misuse in schizophrenia could be explained by a powerful self-medicating action preventing presentation. It seems more likely, however, that the reduced co-occurrence relates to the socialisation and motivation often lacking in chronic patients, but which is essential to maintain an intravenous drug habit. Depressive symptoms have been found to be more prevalent in cocaine users, suggesting either that the drug worsens dysphoria or that it may be used as self-medication in those who show a more depressed clinical picture.

Box 1. Reasons for substance use in severe mental illness

Move from institutional to community care
Downward social drift
General increase in use and acceptability
Facilitate socialisation, relieve boredom
Self-medication of positive, negative or dysphoric symptoms
Self-medication of antipsychotic side-effects

Side-effects of neuroleptics can be particularly disturbing, and some have suggested that a rise in comorbidity has mirrored the introduction and increasing prescribing of these medications (Cuffel, 1992). In one in-patient sample, 15% of patients gave side-effects of medications as their reason for drug use (Dixon *et al*, 1991). Both alcohol and cannabis are cited as likely to ameliorate unwanted effects. Alcohol use has been related to subjective distress associated with akathisia, perhaps being used by patients to alleviate the accompanying agitation and dysphoria (Duke *et al*, 1994).

Comorbidity as a means of self-medication might be explained in terms of the neuro-pharmacological effects of drugs of abuse. Drugs with anticholinergic actions, such as cannabis, or dopaminergic effects, such as amphetamines, could be expected to ameliorate negative symptoms. Both cocaine and cannabis may exert their subjective beneficial effects by specifically antagonising the action of neuroleptics (Bowers *et al*, 1990).

Implications of dual diagnosis

Those who stand out as substance users among those with severe mental illness are young males. This is not surprising – it is also true in the general population. However, several studies suggest that substance users are not only younger but have an earlier age of onset of their psychosis. Breakey *el al* (1974) found an average difference of four years in onset of both symptoms and hospitalisation among their comorbid population when compared with subjects with uncomplicated schizophrenia. Earlier onset might suggest a role for drugs as precipitants of psychosis in vulnerable individuals, advancing the onset of the disorder by several years. Attempts to examine premorbid vulnerability have tended to reveal patients with a dual diagnosis to be a less impaired group when compared with subjects with schizophrenia who do not misuse drugs (Breakey *et al*, 1974; Arndt *et al*, 1992) and better premorbid functioning has also been used as evidence for a causal role for drugs in precipitating psychosis.

Good premorbid adjustment might suggest a better symptom profile and prognosis. Dixon *et al* (1991) found fewer positive and negative symptoms at discharge among a group of consecutively admitted patients with schizophrenia, schizo-affective disorder or schizophreniform disorder, and associated substance abuse or dependence. Other findings confirming this hypothesis include fewer hospitalisations among patients with major mental illness who use cocaine, less negative symptoms at onset of psychosis in those with a dual diagnosis, and better psychosocial functioning among a treatment-resistant comorbid group.

However, the overriding impression from studies examining psychopathology and prognosis in dually diagnosed subjects is that patients are adversely affected by their substance use (Box 2). Among those who use cannabis, use is associated with greater severity of psychotic symptoms, and earlier and more frequent relapses (Linszen *et al*, 1994; Martinez-Arevalo *et al*, 1994). Cocaine and alcohol, in turn, are associated with more affective symptoms, and alcohol misuse has been linked to the development of tardive dyskinesia (Duke *et al*, 1994). A less favourable outcome in comorbidity was also confirmed at two years in the World Health Organization Determinants of Outcome of Severe Mental Disorders study, although poorer compliance with medication was a confounding factor in those patients (Jablensky *et al*, 1992).

Allowing for the confounding effects of brief 'drug-induced' psychoses, the weight of evidence therefore points to poorer prognosis in those with established psychotic illness. This group is characterised by a greater frequency of hospitalisation and greater use of emergency services (Bartels *et al*, 1993). When not in hospital they are less able to cope with the rigors of daily life when compared with their non-misusing counterparts. They are more likely to be homeless and less effective in dealing with finances (Drake & Wallach, 1989). They show a greater propensity for violent behaviour, both current and future (Cuffel *et al*, 1994), and for suicidality (Drake & Wallach, 1989). Despite their increased hospitalisation, comorbid patients are more difficult to engage in treatment and comply poorly with medication. It is no surprise, then, that this group responds poorly to treatment, although this may be more than a function of their non-compliance. Bowers *et al* (1990) gave fixed doses of neuroleptics to subjects with psychosis in the early stages of illness and found that those with a history of psychoto-

genic drug use had a poorer response. They suggest that drug use may contribute to relative neuroleptic refractoriness. A similar lessening of effectiveness of drug treatment has been reported for lithium in dual diagnosis mania (Black *et al*, 1988).

In summary, substance misusers who develop psychosis may appear to be a better functioning group, and, in the short term, even show an improved outcome. Continued use, however, predicts greater symptomatology, higher rates of relapse, more social impairment and poorer compliance with management. A two-stage model has been suggested to explain this dichotomy (Arndt *et al*, 1992). Initially, good premorbid adjustment and sociability increase the likelihood of exposure to drugs and alcohol. Subsequently, the development of psychotic symptoms accelerates use in an attempt to cope with the stress of mental illness. However, it may also be possible that studies have examined two separate groups. Those in the acute stages of illness may indeed have a milder disorder which has been exacerbated by substance use. Discontinuation of drug use and adequate treatment would lead to rapid resolution of symptoms and better prognosis. Those with chronic mental illness, who drift into drug use because of social disadvantage and perhaps self-medication, are more disorganised by their use, and less equipped to escape from drug-using circles. Only longitudinal studies, following patients with dual diagnosis in inception cohorts, can identify which model is more accurate.

Management

Patients with dual diagnosis are often at a disadvantage even before treatment begins. Their substance use frequently remains undetected, and thus unaddressed. They are more likely to drop-out of management plans and comply poorly with medication. Management is not helped by the traditional structure of psychiatric services, which attempts to streamline patients along general or substance misuse pathways. Most clinicians will recognise the scenario where those presenting to one service with psychotic and substance misuse symptoms are redirected when treatment fails or the other aspect of their diagnosis is relabelled as 'primary', only to return again at a later date (the 'ping-pong effect'). Staff may feel de-skilled when only able to address one facet of the problem, and frustration with the almost inevitable lack of progress can lead to the rejection of a patient who is seen as 'attention-seeking and help-rejecting'. Patients' characteristics contribute to difficulties.

Box 2. Complications of substance misuse

Exacerbation of symptoms

Increased relapse and rehospitalisation

Homelessness and downward social drift

Violent and criminal behaviour

Poor compliance

Decreased response to medication

Poor prognosis and outcome in established
  psychotic illness

Their disruptive behaviour, poor compliance and greater propensity for violence may result in refusal of admission and premature discharge. Medication regimes may be compromised because of fears of drug interactions or self-harm, and Mental Health Act provisions underused when symptoms are judged to be induced by alcohol or drug-taking.

The first principle of effective management is a high index of suspicion (Box 3). Careful information gathering can be supplemented by laboratory screening, which should probably be routine in all cases of psychosis at first presentation and, where appropriate, in unexplained relapses in those with chronic illness. There is a danger, however, in over-reliance on urine samples and blood tests. Many drugs of abuse remain detectable for only brief periods of time, and the sensitivity of most readily available liver function tests is inferior to the simple 'CAGE' questionnaire (Chick *et al*, 1993). Highest levels of detection are achieved if several approaches are combined – including information from the patient and carers, and laboratory investigations.

Who should care for dual diagnosis patients?

An agreed policy on who should manage dual diagnosis patients will help to avoid the 'ping-pong effect', and develop skills and confidence among staff. Most comparative research in this area has been carried out in North America, where substance misuse services are often designed around the Minnesota or '12–step' Alcoholics Anonymous model of treatment, with its emphasis on abstinence and confrontational group work. Not surprisingly, this has several drawbacks for those with psychotic illness, and workers have tended to suggest that people with dual diagnosis are best managed within general psychiatry services (Selzer & Lieberman, 1993). The divisions are not so clear-cut in a UK setting, where substance misuse services are usually more eclectic. The best solution may well be a dedicated 'dual diagnosis service' but, at a minimum, close cooperation between substance misuse and general psychiatry, with policies on continuity of keyworkers and access to appropriate day and in-patient facilities if required, is essential.

Integrated treatments

Any management plan should be integrated, attempting to deal with both aspects of the

problem, although gaining control of the substance misuse will often result in a lessening of psychotic symptoms as well. Because of the higher drop-out rates from treatment in this group, the early stages of management should focus on engagement and building a therapeutic relationship. Insistence on abstinence at this stage is likely to result in drop-out. To date, studies have shown flexible approaches to be more successful at keeping patients in treatment. Even when abstinence is achieved, carers may need to be reminded that relapse is the norm rather than the exception, and will not lead to exclusion from treatment. Those who drop-out of treatment will need assertive follow-up in the community, and the relevant provisions of the Mental Health Act used where appropriate. Management must also take into account the slow nature of progress. In one study, those who achieved stable abstinence from alcohol did so after an average of two years' treatment (Drake *et al*, 1993). These patients are more socially disadvantaged. They tend to have few supports and are more likely to be homeless, unemployed, and to have poor control over their finances. Care plans which address social problems will be more successful in retaining patients in treatment.

Box 3. Good practice points

High index of suspicion – substance misuse is frequently denied, and often not assessed. Use screening devices such as urinalysis routinely

Integrated treatment – treat both aspects of the problem and avoid the 'ping-pong' effect

Social support – patients often require help with housing and finances. Addressing social problems may improve compliance

Education – about detrimental effects of alcohol and drugs, relapse prevention and harm reduction

Long-term focus – change is slow and relapse usual rather than exceptional. It should not lead to discharge from care

Optimistic approach – patients need continued encouragement, especially during crises or relapse

Team support – these are difficult patients to manage. Staff need to acquire appropriate skills and confidence

In common with most substance misuse programmes, regular monitoring of drug and alcohol use is important, though the approach is less confrontational or challenging. Patients need education in relapse prevention and in relapse management. This can take the form of discussions on triggers to relapse, rehearsing how to deal with potentially difficult social situations, and altering daily routines to reduce risk. Because of more chaotic lifestyles, patients with comorbid illness may be at greater risk of complications of drug misuse, including HIV and other infections, and particular attention should be paid to harm reduction strategies. Often the greatest difficulty workers face is in balancing a quick response to patients' problems as they arise, with the development of a care plan which focuses on long-term goals and recognises the slow rate of progress. Good peer support and supervision are essential for staff. Continued encouragement and an optimistic approach by staff are essential for patients.

Pharmacological management

The choice of medication for patients with dual diagnosis can cause anxiety. In treating any acute episode, it is important to attempt to delineate intoxication or withdrawal syndromes from exacerbation of the underlying psychosis. Neuroleptics are effective in treating psychotic reactions following drug use in patients without schizophrenia, so their use is justified in dual diagnosis patients, where the genesis of psychotic symptoms is seldom clear. Where drug use has contributed to acute relapse, it has been suggested that high-potency neuroleptics may be more advisable, given their lower risk in exacerbating substance-induced hypotension, tachycardia and anticholinergic effects (Siris, 1990).

Even more care than usual may be needed in guarding against side-effects, as substance misuse may increase in order to self-medicate unwanted symptoms, such as neuroleptic-induced akathisia and akinesia. Anti-Parkinsonian drugs should not be withheld if side-effects require treatment, but their potential for misuse must be borne in mind. Depot neuroleptic preparations are sensible given the risk of poor compliance. Establishing a stable dose regime may not be easy. Chronic alcohol use, for example, causes hepatic enzyme induction, thus reducing neuroleptic bioavailability. Acute alcohol binges, however, may impair drug metabolism, resulting in increased drug effects (Salloum *et al*, 1991). The best compromise may be the use of depot preparations, with 'top-up' oral

medications adjusted according to severity of symptoms and current substance use. Obviously, a good therapeutic relationship will make this easier. The role of newer antipsychotic medications is largely untested, but at least one report suggests that they are no less effective in people with dual diagnosis than in uncomplicated schizophrenia (Buckley *et al*, 1994).

Depressive syndromes are common in schizophrenia and in many substance use disorders. If antidepressants are indicated, selective serotonin reuptake inhibitors may be more appropriate than tricyclic drugs, given the risk of overdose and interactions associated with the latter. However, apart from their relative safety in association with alcohol, little is known about interactions between selective serotonin reuptake inhibitors and other drugs of abuse. Monoamine oxidase inhibitors should be avoided because of the risk of hypertensive crises. Lithium can be used if clinically indicated, but is limited by the need for good compliance. Cases should be judged individually. Benzodiazepines are clearly appropriate in some withdrawal syndromes, but their use in managing insomnia or anxiety symptoms should be time-limited and cautious. They are prone to misuse and may also exacerbate behavioural disinhibition, increasing aggression and self-harm. Because of the fashion for intravenous misuse of temazepam, sometimes resulting in serious medical complications such as peripheral vascular occlusion and gangrene, this drug is best avoided.

It is worth keeping in mind that many psychotropic medications, including antipsychotics and antidepressants, can lower seizure thresholds. While this is unlikely to be a reason for avoiding their use in patients with dual diagnosis, extra caution may need to be exercised in alcohol, barbiturate and benzodiazepine withdrawal states. Often, an upward adjustment or slower reduction in benzodiazepine treatment regimes will suffice.

Pharmacological treatments for substance misuse may also have potential for interactions. Disulfiram, through its inhibition of dopamine beta-hydroxylase, has been reported to cause exacerbation of psychosis, and may also interact with antipsychotic and antidepressant medications. However, other workers have reported its use without problem, and to good effect (Kofoed *et al*, 1986). When used, it is probably best to maintain dose levels below 500 mg daily. Methadone maintenance or reduction programmes may be appropriate for opiate-dependent patients – indeed, claims have been made for an antipsychotic potential for opiates – but its use may alter neuroleptic dose requirements (Siris, 1990).

Conclusions

Substance misuse among people with severe mental illness is a common and probably increasing problem. Whether drugs can cause prolonged and independent psychotic states, or whether they precipitate psychosis in vulnerable individuals, is perhaps less important in clinical practice than their clearly detrimental effect on the course and prognosis of mental illness. These individuals are often on the margins of psychiatric services, alienated by their poor compliance, social instability and behavioural problems, and by the inflexibility of service structures to accommodate them. Their care demands an integration of skills, and a recognition of the slow time scale necessary for change. The greatest impediment to care, however, is often the lack of awareness of substance misuse and its under-diagnosis.

References

Ananth, J., Vandewater, S., Kamal, M., *et al* (1989) Missed diagnosis of substance abuse in psychiatric patients. *Hospital and Community Psychiatry*, **40**, 297–299.

Andreasson, S., Allebeck, P., Engstrom, A., *et al* (1987) Cannabis and schizophrenia: a longitudinal study of Swedish conscripts. *Lancet*, **ii**, 1483–1486.

Arndt, S., Tyrrell, G., Flaum, M., *et al* (1992) Comorbidity of substance abuse and schizophrenia: the role of pre-morbid adjustment. *Psychological Medicine*, **22**, 379–388.

Bartels, S. J., Teague, G. B., Drake, R. E., *et al* (1993) Substance abuse in schizophrenia: service utilization and costs. *Journal of Nervous and Mental Diseases*, **181**, 227–232.

Black, D. W., Winokur, G., Bell, S., *et al* (1988) Complicated mania: comorbidity and immediate outcome in the treatment of mania. *Archives of General Psychiatry*, **45**, 232–236.

Bowers, M. B., Mazure, C. M., Nelson, J. C., *et al* (1990) Psychotogenic drug use and neuroleptic response. *Schizophrenia Bulletin*, **16**, 81–85.

Breakey, W. R., Goodell, H., Lorenz, P. C., *et al* (1974) Hallucinogenic drugs as precipitants of schizophrenia. *Psychological Medicine*, **4**, 255–261.

Buckley, P., Thompson, P., Way, L., *et al* (1994) Substance abuse among patients with treatment-resistant schizophrenia: characteristics and implications for clozapine therapy. *American Journal of Psychiatry*, **151**, 385–389.

Cantwell, R., Brewin, J., Dalkin, T., *et al* (1996) Schizophrenia in Nottingham: alcohol and drug misuse comorbidity. *Schizophrenia Research*, **18**, 108.

Chick, J., Badawy, A. & Borg, S. (1993) Identification of excessive drinking and alcohol problems. *Alcohol and Alcoholism*, **suppl. 2**, 121–125.

Cuffel, B. J. (1992) Prevalence estimates of substance abuse in schizophrenia and their correlates. *Journal of Nervous and Mental Diseases*, **180**, 589–592.

——, Shumway, M., Chouljian, T. L., *et al* (1994) A longitudinal study of substance use and community violence in schizophrenia. *Journal of Nervous and Mental Diseases*, **182**, 704–708.

Dixon, L., Haas, G., Weiden, P. J., *et al* (1991) Drug abuse in schizophrenic patients: clinical correlates and reasons for use. *American Journal of Psychiatry*, **148**, 224–230.

Drake, R. E. & Wallach, M. A. (1989) Substance abuse among the chronic mentally ill. *Hospital and Community Psychiatry*, **40**, 1041–1046.

——, McHugo, G. J. & Noordsy, D. L. (1993) A pilot study of outpatient treatment of alcoholism in schizophrenia: four-year outcomes. *American Journal of Psychiatry*, **150**, 328–329.

Duke, P. J., Pantelis, C. & Barnes, T. R. E. (1994) South Westminster schizophrenia survey: alcohol use and its relationship to symptoms, tardive dyskinesia and illness onset. *British Journal of Psychiatry*, **164**, 630–636.

Glass, I. B. (1989) Alcoholic hallucinosis: a psychiatric enigma – 1. The development of an idea. *British Journal of Addiction*, **84**, 29–41.

Jablensky, A., Sartorius, N., Ernberg, G., *et al* (1992) Schizophrenia: manifestations, incidence and course in different cultures. *Psychological Medicine*, **suppl. 20**, 79.

Kofoed, L., Kania, J., Walsh, T., *et al* (1986) Outpatient treatment of patients with substance abuse and coexisting psychiatric disorders. *American Journal of Psychiatry*, **143**, 867–872.

Lehman, A. F., Myers, C. P. & Corty, E. (1989) Assessment and classification of patients with psychiatric and substance abuse syndromes. *Hospital and Community Psychiatry*, **40**, 1019–1025.

Linszen, D. H., Dingemans, P. M. & Lenior, M. E. (1994) Cannabis abuse and the course of recent-onset schizophrenic disorders. *Archives of General Psychiatry*, **51**, 273–279.

McGuire, P. K., Jones, P., Harvey, I., *et al* (1995) Morbid risk of schizophrenia for relatives of patients with cannabis-associated psychosis. *Schizophrenia Research*, **15**, 277–281.

Martinez-Arevalo, M. J., Calcedo-Ordonez, A. & Varo-Prieto, J. R. (1994) Cannabis consumption as a prognostic factor in schizophrenia. *British Journal of Psychiatry*, **164**, 679–681.

Menezes, P. R., Johnson, S., Thornicroft., G., *et al* (1996) Drug and alcohol problems among individuals with severe mental illnesses in South London. *British Journal of Psychiatry*, **168**, 612–619.

Regier, D. A., Farmer, M. E., Rae, D. S., *et al* (1990) Comorbidity of mental disorders with alcohol and other drug abuse: results from the Epidemiological Catchment Area (ECA) study. *Journal of the American Medical Association*, **264**, 2511–2518.

Salloum, I. M., Moss, H. B. & Daley, D. C. (1991) Substance abuse and schizophrenia: impediments to optimal care. *American Journal of Drug and Alcohol Abuse*, **17**, 321–336.

Schneier, F. R. & Siris, S. G. (1987) A review of psychoactive substance use and abuse in schizophrenia: patterns of drug choice. *Journal of Nervous and Mental Diseases*, **175**, 641–652.

Selzer, J. A. & Lieberman, J. A. (1993) Schizophrenia and substance abuse. *Psychiatric Clinics of North America*, **16**, 401–412.

Siris, S. G. (1990) Pharmacological treatment of substance-abusing schizophrenic patients. *Schizophrenia Bulletin*, **16**, 111–122.

Smith, J. & Hucker, S. (1994) Schizophrenia and substance abuse. *British Journal of Psychiatry*, **165**, 13–21.

Strakowski, S. M., Tohen, M., Stoll, A. L., *et al* (1993) Comorbidity in psychosis at first hospitalization. *American Journal of Psychiatry*, **150**, 752–757.

Thomas, H. (1993) Psychiatric symptoms in cannabis users. *British Journal of Psychiatry*, **163**, 141–149.

Misuse of amphetamines and related drugs

Nicholas Seivewright & Charles McMahon

This chapter discusses the misuse of drugs which act as stimulants, an effect mainly produced by enhancement of the central transmission of catecholamines, particularly dopamine. Stimulant misuse is extremely widespread in the UK and elsewhere, but primary users of such drugs present relatively rarely for treatment at drug services. At present such services mainly see heroin users, not only because the greater addictiveness of heroin produces generally higher levels of problems, but because a substitute treatment can be used in that group in the form of methadone.

There are several reasons, however, why it is important to have a good working knowledge of stimulant misuse. Drug services consider amphetamine misuse a hidden epidemic, in which the heaviest users experience many of the same problems as heroin users without receiving similar treatment, and various policy initiatives are under way to attract this group into services.

Meanwhile in recent years cocaine usage has transferred to the much more potent form known as 'crack', which is causing severe problems in some of the UK's inner cities. Use of methylenedioxymethamphetamine (MDMA, 'ecstasy') by young people, associated with the 'rave' nightclub scene, is on a huge scale and the drug is proving to have some disturbing adverse effects in a minority of cases, including the well-publicised fatalities. Most importantly for psychiatrists, stimulant misuse is the form of drug misuse most associated with psychiatric complications, which often require management within general mental health services.

Table 1 describes the main stimulant drugs and indicates the ways in which they are used, approximate current street prices, and their classification under the 1971 Misuse of Drugs Act which dictates severity of penalties for the offences of possession or supplying.

Stimulant drugs of abuse

Amphetamine

The form of amphetamine predominantly used by drug misusers is a powder, substantially adulterated with other substances, which is known as 'speed' or 'whizz'. The amphetamine contained is a racemic mixture of the d- and l-isomers, the l-form being relatively inactive. Many recreational users simply swallow the drug, licking it from a finger or else putting it in a drink or swallowing an amount in cigarette paper, but it can also be snorted or injected. Sometimes pharmaceutical preparations are misused, the only preparation of amphetamine itself now routinely available being dexamphetamine sulphate tablets.

Cocaine

Cocaine hydrochloride is a white powder for which many claims have been made over the years proclaiming this form as a drug entirely compatible with an executive lifestyle. Such use is by snorting, while polydrug users also inject the powder, often along with heroin in the apparently inappropriately named 'speedball'. Starting in the USA however, and now also in the UK, cocaine use is increasingly in the form of 'crack', a chemically altered preparation which is purer, more potent in its effects and withdrawal effects, and more likely to lead to heavy compulsive use. The chemical process is a simple one, involving heating with sodium bicarbonate. The appeal of the volatile crack is that an intense euphoria is experienced rapidly by smoking, reflecting blood concentrations rising at a rate normally only seen after injecting drugs. Some

Table 1. The main stimulant drugs of misuse				
Drug	Description	Routes of administration	Street price	Misuse of Drugs Act classification
Amphetamine	Usually light coloured powder, very low purity (approx 5%). Some pharmaceutical preparations, e.g. dexamphetamine sulphate tablets	Swallowed, snorted, IV	£10–15 per gram	B, but A if prepared for injection
Cocaine HCl	White powder, moderate purity (up to 50%)	Snorted, IV	£45–65 per gram	A
Crack cocaine	Crystalline 'rocks'	Smoked, IV	£20 per 150 mg rock	A
MDMA	Various manufactured tablets, often with characteristic motifs	Swallowed	£5–20 per 100–120 mg tablet	A

individuals do inject crack, but this confers no major advantage. In some areas crack is becoming the only available form of cocaine, which polydrug users may inject if that is their preferred route of drug usage. Interestingly, the equivalent purified form of amphetamine, known as 'ice', is by contrast hardly encountered in the UK.

Methylenedioxymethamphetamine (MDMA, 'ecstasy')

This methylated amphetamine has a long history, but is currently popular as a recreational drug which has hallucinogenic properties as well as the stimulant effect. It appears in the form of tablets, which it is believed are mainly imported from other parts of Europe. Many have a characteristic motif or imprint, and users may try to seek out a type with which they are familiar, especially if they consider that it produces genuine MDMA effects, as there are many bogus preparations in circulation. Some such imitations contain amphetamine and lysergide (LSD), while a range of other drugs which produce hallucinations, such as the general anaesthetic agent ketamine, have been passed off as MDMA. Substances which on analysis prove to be chemically closely related analogues of MDMA also appear, produced in attempts to bypass specific drug legislation. Although MDMA users may also use other drugs, including amphetamine, MDMA is very rarely used by methods other than swallowing the tablets.

Others

Other stimulant drugs which have been or are misused to a minor degree include the appetite suppressants, such as diethylpropion (Apisate, Tenuate Dospan) and fenfluramine (Ponderax), decongestants containing ephedrine or pseudo-ephedrine, methylphenidate, and the monoamine oxidase inhibitor tranylcypromine. Although these may be associated with clinical problems in individuals, there is little systematic evidence and they will not be discussed further here.

Of the illicit drugs, amphetamine and cocaine are similar enough in many aspects to be considered together. MDMA is significantly different in terms of epidemiology, type of usage, and clinical features and so is discussed separately.

Amphetamine and cocaine

Epidemiology

The true prevalence of any form of drug misuse is unknown, as it is an illicit activity. Apart from enforcement statistics, two sources of data which are of interest are surveys and Drug Misuse Database (DMD) figures, the former because they probably come closest to true estimates of usage, and the latter because they are from treatment services.

Surveys necessarily collect limited information, commonly whether individuals have 'ever used' various drugs. In UK surveys, up to 10–12% of young people reported having tried amphetamines by the age of 19, whereas less than 1% had tried cocaine, a similar figure to heroin (Institute for the Study of Drug Dependence, 1994). It is of course important to know what proportion of such experimenters progress to regular use, but this is a relatively uncharted area, until users come into contact with treatment services.

The DMD system incorporated the notification of addicts to the Home Office Addicts Index before the latter was stopped, but has always been a much wider reporting system. Of the drugs discussed here, only cocaine was notifiable (along with opiates), whereas the DMD records the use of all drugs in the previous month by anyone considered to be a problem drug misuser presenting to a range of medical and non-medical services, including community drug teams, street agencies, psychiatric drug misuse services, and general practitioners. These are best referred to as 'treated prevalence' data.

In the six months to March 1997, the last period for which full figures are available, out of a total of 25 925 individuals presenting in England, 8% were using amphetamine as their main drug and 4% cocaine. An additional 9 and 11%, respectively, were using amphetamines and cocaine as secondary drugs, usually to opiates, confirming the common clinical impression of polydrug use. Of individuals using amphetamine, 41% were injecting it, with considerable regional variation. Undoubtedly, this figure from clinical treatment contacts is a much higher rate of injecting than would relate to amphetamine use in general, while the equivalent figure for cocaine was 16%, indicating the prominence of the smokable crack form (Department of Health, 1998). The rise in crack cocaine was demonstrated by Strang *et al* (1990) who examined drug use in 441 attenders at a south London community drug team between 1987 and 1989, and found that in that period subjects using cocaine increased from 13 to 29%, and within that group, use of smokable forms increased from 15 to 75%.

Many drug misusers who use stimulants terminate episodes of use of such drugs, and alleviate withdrawal effects, by using various sedatives, including benzodiazepines, cannabis or alcohol. This is reflected in DMD statistics and is commonly reported clinically, the most worrying combination being users of crack cocaine who turn to heroin for this purpose, with the result that they then become physically dependent on the opiate.

Clinical features

The main actions of amphetamine and cocaine resulting in a stimulant effect involve increased presynaptic release and inhibition of reuptake of catecholamines, with a direct action on dopaminergic terminals and effects in the 'reward pathway' common to most drugs of misuse (Holman, 1994). The main clinical effects and withdrawal effects of stimulant drugs are shown in Box 1. The effects

---

Box 1. Effects of stimulant drugs

Effects
Early – increased energy, elation, reduced appetite
Late – overactivity, confusion, paranoia
Withdrawal – depression, irritability, agitation, craving, hyperphagia, sleep disturbances (hypersomnia, nightmares)

---

are categorised into early effects, which are generally the desired effects, the late features, which most users recognise as indicating that they should terminate their episode of stimulant use, and withdrawal effects.

Amphetamine has a slower onset of action than cocaine and a longer elimination half-life, and of the two forms of cocaine, crack has the quicker onset and withdrawal. The patterns of usage reflect this, and an amphetamine user may use the drug over a period of 2–3 days, going without sleep or much food. The undesirable effects then accumulate and he or she will stop the amphetamine, perhaps with the aid of sedatives as referred to above. By contrast, the whole process including height of action and experience of withdrawal effects is measured in a crack user in minutes rather than hours, and both aspects are usually much more intense.

The experience of paranoid feelings is very characteristic with both drugs, and is related to the complication of psychosis. As indicated, many users will stop at this stage, and in the relatively slow process of amphetamine symptoms it is debatable whether the subsequent depression, hyperphagia and hypersomnia represent a true withdrawal syndrome or whether the last two features are simply catching up after a period without eating or sleeping. The similar more acute withdrawal effects from cocaine are often referred to as a 'crash', in which profound depression and craving are thought to be related to a rebound depletion in central dopamine transmission.

Gawin & Kleber (1986) have described a three-stage withdrawal syndrome in which these acute features are followed by more prolonged depressive symptoms, and then a normalisation of those features but the re-experience of withdrawal symptoms if exposed to cues associated with previous usage. The entity of a withdrawal syndrome, however, still remains controversial, leading to these drugs generally being described as not physically addictive. The aspect of cues does appear important in relation to cocaine, in that individuals who have experienced severe withdrawal distress in their own situations may demonstrate few symptoms if admitted to hospital (Weddington *et al*, 1990).

Complications

One of the reasons why the massive recent USA cocaine epidemic caused such concern was a high rate of medical complications, and stimulants also have the propensity to cause a range of psychiatric effects including psychosis. The main complications of amphetamine and cocaine misuse are listed in Box 2.

The infective and general complications can occur in misuse of any drug which involves injection or heavy usage. The cardiovascular complications are more specific to stimulant misuse, and clearly relate to the increase in catecholamine secretion. Stimulants cross the placenta and although defining the links between drug misuse and obstetric complications is difficult research to do, as drug misusers tend to also be high-risk in other ways such as diet, smoking and poor living conditions, it appears that stimulants are more likely to be associated with such problems than most other drugs of misuse.

Irritability, agitation and depression have already been noted as withdrawal effects of stimulant drugs, and it is to some extent a matter of 'caseness' as to when such problems become clinical anxiety or depressive disorders. Similar problems of separation apply to antisocial behaviours such as aggressiveness, when there is the additional aspect that antisocial personality disorder is a frequent accompanying diagnosis in drug misusers (Seivewright & Daly, 1997). It is difficult, but important, to distinguish in drug misusers between 'secondary' antisocial behaviours, which may be related to the process of drug misuse itself, and definitely pre-existent personality disorder, which requires a history pre-dating drug misuse. The crack cocaine 'scene' is considered by enforcement authorities to be associated with particularly high levels of violence, which partly relates to aspects of dealing in this drug, where especially large amounts of money tend to be at stake, but which may also reflect desperate behaviour in those users who experience most acutely the intense withdrawal craving that can occur.

The best-known complication of stimulant misuse is a paranoid psychosis. Once again this can be seen as a development of the paranoid feelings that many stimulant users experience in their ordinary use of the drugs, but a full-blown psychotic disorder seems to require heavy continuous usage. The paranoid delusions and associated features such as auditory hallucinations may exactly resemble schizophrenia, and indeed the fact that amphetamine can produce this was part of the evidence for the dopamine hypothesis of causation of schizophrenia. Tactile and visual hallucinations may occur and overactive, repetitive or compulsive behaviour may give a clue to stimulant use. Confusion and cognitive impairment are not usually present.

Urine screening for drugs of misuse should be done on young patients with psychosis, and if stimulants are present, another part of making the diagnosis of drug-induced psychosis is expectant management, as the psychosis may clear within a short number of days if the individual stops misusing drugs. Poole & Brabbins (1996) have criticised the diagnosis of drug-induced psychosis, observing that clear criteria are not usually applied, and that although relationships such as drugs worsening a functional psychosis, or individuals susceptible through family history developing psychosis after relatively small amounts, are likely, there is little proper evidence. It is important in differential diagnosis to remember that use of drugs which can cause psychosis, such as amphetamines or cannabis, is extremely widespread and evidence of such use in an individual may not account for all of their symptoms, and also that other major drugs of misuse such as heroin do not have the propensity to cause psychosis at all.

Box 2. Complications of amphetamine and cocaine misuse

Medical
Cardiovascular – hypertension, arrythmias, myocardial infarction, cerebrovascular accident
Infective – abscesses, hepatitis, septicaemia, HIV
Obstetric – reduced foetal growth, miscarriage, placental abruption, premature labour
Other – weight loss, dental problems, epilepsy

Psychiatric
Anxiety
Depression
Antisocial behaviours
Paranoid psychosis

Management

Assessment

The routine assessment of any form of drug misuse is indicated in Box 3. The points of history, examination and investigation mentioned relate to drug misuse itself rather than to its complications, for which additional assessment may be required. It is also important to establish a drug misuser's personal situation and the context in which they use drugs, as well as his or her motivation to change behaviour, including any external factors such as family pressure or legal trouble.

Harm reduction

Stimulant misuse is not a form of drug misuse for which an obviously effective treatment exists, like methadone for heroin users. Also, not all users are inclined to stop using drugs completely, especially individuals who consider that their drug use has brought them no significant problems. Therefore, it is necessary that measures are adopted aimed at reducing harm from drug misuse, including the general provision of information, education about health risks, advice to reduce damaging injecting practices, and the provision of clean injecting equipment. This work is usually done by community drug agencies, who will also provide counselling aimed at encouraging lifestyle and social changes. Members of drug misuse psychiatric teams, such as community psychiatric nurses or clinical psychologists, may counsel drug misusers in a more structured way, using behavioural methods to reduce usage, or the techniques of motivational interviewing.

Box 3. Assessment of drug misuse

History
How often?
How much?
Routes of administration?
Duration of usage?
Significant drug-free periods?
Previous treatment?
Other associated drug misuse?

Examination
Features of individual drugs
Injection marks

Investigation
Urine testing

Pharmacological treatments

There is a substantial literature from the USA on medications which may reduce cocaine withdrawal symptoms, which has been reviewed by Withers *et al* (1995). A large number of compounds have been tried, which both reflects the scale of the cocaine epidemic in the USA, but also the generally limited effectiveness of the medications involved. Because cocaine withdrawal effects are considered to be due to dopamine depletion, some trials have been of the dopaminergic agents, bromocriptine and amantadine, which have been found to reduce craving in some cases. Use of these drugs has not been significantly taken up in the UK, but there appears to be more use of desipramine, which is the most investigated drug in this indication in the USA, where a meta-analysis of studies indicated significant benefit over placebo in promoting abstinence from cocaine (Levin & Lehman, 1991). Carbamazepine is another medication which can reduce cocaine craving, and in general the same range of medications has been tried in the situation of reducing adjunctive cocaine use in patients on methadone. An alternative approach, again both in the acute withdrawal state and in attempting to achieve a general reduction in stimulant usage, is to use fluoxetine, as there is evidence, mainly from animal studies, that compounds which enhance serotonin transmission reduce consumption of substances of misuse, including stimulants. In the UK, fluoxetine has been found to help some amphetamine users reduce or stop their drug (Polson *et al*, 1993). Given the general difficulties in pharmacological management of drug misusers, these specialised treatments for which only limited evidence exists should probably only be used within drug misuse services.

In general, substitute prescribing for stimulant misusers is not considered suitable in the way that methadone is used for heroin users. This is because stimulants are inherently more destabilising drugs, and a true physical dependence is doubtful. While most would not support prescribing cocaine, some authorities in drug misuse feel that amphetamine prescribing should be considered for heavy daily users who appear unable to curtail their usage by any other method. Some services are experimenting with limited amphetamine prescribing, but the relatively short-acting dexamphetamine sulphate is not very satisfactory for the purpose.

Treatments for psychiatric complications

The management of psychiatric complications of stimulant misuse, including the use of antidepressants and antipsychotics, can be identical to treating the same disorders in other contexts. Medications are generally not effective in the face of ongoing drug misuse, and efforts must be directed to ensuring that this does not occur, including frequent urine monitoring. Some specialists would consider that if an antidepressant is required, there is a theoretical advantage in using a selective serotonin reuptake inhibitor, probably fluoxetine, while benzodiazepines should usually be avoided in managing anxiety symptoms.

Admission

Admission to a psychiatric ward, or sometimes alternatively to a drug rehabilitation centre, is indicated in three main situations. First, individuals in states of extreme withdrawal distress can require admission urgently, in a way that is hardly required in heroin users where methadone can effectively alleviate the situation. Secondly, there is a less urgent group of users who nevertheless feel unable to stop their drug use outside hospital in their own social situation, and request admission as the only way successfully to detoxify. It is important in assessment to establish what is going to be different about the individual's social situation when they return to it, in order to attempt to avoid relapse. Finally, admission can be required for severe psychiatric complications, notably psychosis, especially if an individual lacks insight or is acting on delusional ideas.

Other

Because of the lack of definitely effective conventional treatments for stimulant misuse, such individuals may present for complementary therapies. The only systematic evidence for effectiveness relates to some limited benefits for acupuncture (Lipton *et al*, 1994).

MDMA ('ecstasy')

Epidemiology

MDMA was originally synthesised as an appetite suppressant, and was later used both as a recreational drug in US student circles, and as an aid to psychotherapy. Current usage centres on 'rave' nightclubs and parties within youth culture, notably in the UK. Recent surveys have found that 9% of 16- to 19-year-olds and 8% of 16- to 29-year-olds had tried what they believed to be MDMA; analysis of drugs seized show the related chemicals MDA (methylenedioxyamphetamine) and MDEA (methylenedioxyethylamphetamine) to be gaining

ground (Institute for the Study of Drug Dependence, 1994). It is estimated that there are approximately 1 000 000 users of this group of drugs in the UK, and that most are weekend users, with a small minority progressing to more frequent use. The overlap with other drug usage occurs where amphetamine and LSD feature in the same youth culture, or where sedatives, rarely including heroin, are taken to terminate episodes of MDMA use.

Clinical features

The stimulant features of MDMA are as described above, but the drug also has so-called hallucinogenic, or psychedelic, effects which more resemble those of LSD. These include visual illusions, general enhancement of sensory perceptions, and states of altered consciousness, which are desired parts of the experience at raves. The most sought-after effect, which is achieved by many users of the drug, is a feeling of predominantly non-sexual affection towards others, hence the sobriquet 'the love drug'. Common physical effects include tachycardia, dry mouth, dilated pupils, facial muscle stiffness and parasthesiae.

Peroutka *et al* (1988) described effects of MDMA which occurred more than 24 hours after taking the drug, which become increasingly adverse and can broadly be seen as withdrawal effects. These can include tiredness, muscle aching, depression, headache and irritability.

Complications

Although large numbers of people use MDMA apparently unproblematically, there are specific complications which appear to relate to the complex pharmacology of the drug, which is well described by Steele *et al* (1994). Although complications in common with other stimulants may occur, particular interest has focused on deaths, and a range of psychiatric adverse effects.

Deaths

A number of deaths in recreational users have occurred (Henry *et al*, 1992; Milroy *et al*, 1996). It is notable that these do not seem particularly associated with heavy high-dose usage, and neither is there reliable evidence of exposure to single doses only, as might be expected in a hypersensitivity reaction. Individuals have died with a range of pathology, including disseminated intravascular coagulation, rhabdomyolysis, renal and liver failure, shock, brain haemorrhages and pulmonary infarcts. A characteristic syndrome of hyperthermia is considered to relate both to the drug's direct effect on thermoregulation and also the environment in which MDMA is taken, involving vigorous non-stop dancing. One of the ways in which MDMA differs from other stimulants is that the effect on serotonergic neurones appears to be of more significance, and serotonin is involved in internal heat regulation. It is not known why some individuals are susceptible to fatal effects, while even the common harm reduction advice to drink plenty of water when taking MDMA has proved controversial, given evidence in some cases of inappropriate antidiuretic hormone secretion.

Psychiatric disorders

Although the systematic data largely rely on a series of case studies, it appears common for MDMA to cause psychiatric disturbance. A typical history is the individual who used MDMA recreationally over a period, possibly along with amphetamine or LSD, decided to stop, and "hasn't felt right since". In this context, clinicians encounter anxiety states, depression, panic disorder, 'flashback' experiences and psychoses. The evidence for these is reviewed by Steele *et al* (1994) and by McGuire *et al* (1994), in which the link between MDMA and subsequent psychiatric problems in some of the cases is tenuous. Largerscale research needs to be done, but one feature that is emerging is that cases of psychiatric disorder which follow MDMA use are often resistant to treatment. MDMA is neurotoxic to serotonergic neurones, and so there is concern that resistance to treatment may reflect this form of brain damage.

Management

The general management of MDMA use resembles the approach to other forms of drug misuse. No specific treatments have been described, and for the psychiatric complications conventional medication should be used. Because one of the effects of MDMA is to cause a shut-down in

serotonin transmission, serotonergic antidepressants may be preferable, and may be useful when resistance to psychotropic treatments is encountered even if depressive features are not prominent.

References

Department of Health (1998) *Statistical Bulletin: Drug Misuse Statistics 1998/17*. London: HMSO.

Gawin, F. H. & Kleber, H. D. (1986) Abstinence symptomatology and psychiatric diagnoses in cocaine abusers: clinical observations. *Archives of General Psychiatry*, **43**, 107–113.

Henry, J. A., Jeffreys, K. J. & Dawling, S. (1992) Toxicity and deaths from 3,4-methylenedioxymethamphetamine ('ecstasy'). *Lancet*, **340**, 384–387.

Holman, R. B. (1994) Biological effects of central nervous system stimulants. *Addiction*, **89**, 1435–1441.

Institute for the Study of Drug Dependence (1994) *Drug Misuse in Britain*. London: ISDD.

Levin, F. R. & Lehman, A. F. (1991) Meta-analysis of desipramine as an adjunct in the treatment of cocaine addiction. *Journal of Clinical Psychopharmacology*, **11**, 374–378.

Lipton, D. S., Brewington, V. & Smith, M. (1994) Acupuncture for crack-cocaine detoxification: experimental evaluation of efficacy. *Journal of Substance Abuse Treatment*, **11**, 205–215.

McGuire, P. K., Cope, H. & Fahy, T. A. (1994) Diversity of psychopathology associated with use of 3,4-methylenedioxymethamphetamine ('Ecstasy'). *British Journal of Psychiatry*, **165**, 391–395.

Milroy, C. M., Clark, J. C. & Forrest, A. R. W. (1996) Pathology of deaths associated with "ecstasy" and "eve" misuse. *Journal of Clinical Pathology*, **49**, 149–153.

Peroutka, S. J., Newman, H. & Harris, H. (1988) Subjective effects of 3,4-methylenedixoymethamphetamine in recreational users. *Neuropsychopharmacology*, **1**, 273–277.

Polson, R. G., Fleming, P. M. & O'Shea, J. K. (1993) Fluoxetine in the treatment of amphetamine dependence. *Human Psychopharmacology*, **8**, 55–58.

Poole, R. & Brabbins, C. (1996) Drug induced psychosis. *British Journal of Psychiatry*, **168**, 135–138.

Steele, T. D., McCann, T. D. & Ricaurte, G. A. (1994) 3,4-Methylenedioxymethamphetamine (MDMA, "ecstasy"): pharmacology and toxicology in animals and humans. *Addiction*, **89**, 539–551.

Strang, J., Griffiths, P. & Gossop, M. (1990) Crack and cocaine use in South London drug addicts: 1987–1989. *British Journal of Addiction*, **85**, 193–196.

Weddington, W. W., Brown, B. S., Haertzen, C. A., *et al* (1990) Changes in mood, craving, and sleep during short-term abstinence reported by male cocaine addicts. *Archives of General Psychiatry*, **47**, 861–868.

Withers, N. W., Pulvirenti, L., Koob, G. F., *et al* (1995) Cocaine abuse and dependence. *Journal of Clinical Psychopharmacology*, **15**, 63–78.

Psychiatric illness and learning disability: a dual diagnosis

Jane Bernal & Sheila Hollins

The prevalence of moderate to profound learning disability is roughly 3 per 1000 and of mild learning disability about 3 per 100 (Abramowicz & Richardson, 1975). There are estimated to be more than 120 million people with learning disability worldwide.

Most adults and children with learning disability do not live in hospitals but at home or in some type of residential accommodation. Psychiatric problems are fairly common, and learning disability can be thought of as a risk factor for psychiatric disorder. The presence of learning disability can alter presentation, and psychiatric diagnosis is likely to be based more on behavioural signs than on self-reported mental state.

Definitions

The Department of Health in England now uses the phrase 'people with learning disability'. This is preferred also by those who have such disabilities. People with learning disabilities have made it clear that 'mental retardation', 'mental handicap' and 'mental subnormality' are as offensive as terms previously used, and contribute to social marginalisation. The names have often been changed but unless underlying social injustices are addressed each new term will become pejorative (Sinason, 1992).

The ICD and DSM classifications, and computer databases that follow international codings, still use the term 'mental retardation'. In North America the preference is for the term 'developmental disabilities' (Grossman, 1983).

The ICD–10 (World Health Organization (WHO), 1992) defines mental retardation as a condition of arrested or incomplete development of the mind, characterised especially by impairment of skills manifested during the developmental period which contribute to the overall level of intelligence, that is, cognitive, language, motor and social abilities. Retardation can occur with or without any other mental or physical disorder. However, the prevalence of other mental disorders is at least three to four times greater in this population than in the general population, and mentally retarded individuals are at greater risk of exploitation and physical, emotional and sexual abuse. Adaptive behaviour is always impaired, but in protected social environments where support is available this impairment may not be at all obvious in subjects with mild mental retardation.

A brief description of the level of function expected for each level of retardation is given. If standardised IQ tests are used, the levels fall within these ranges: 50–69 is indicative of mild mental retardation; 35–49 of moderate retardation; 20–34 of severe retardation and <20 of profound retardation.

The WHO has now issued an ICD *Guide for Mental Retardation* (World Health Organization, 1992) to enable those working with people with mental retardation to make best use of the classification. It recommends a multi-axial classification (Box 1). The guide brings together useful diagnoses that are widely scattered in ICD–10. It describes classification of the severity of mental retardation in considerable detail, pointing out that the diagnosis of mental retardation must be made using all available data rather than relying on IQ tests alone.

The codes for the severity and type of behaviour disturbance are placed, perhaps confusingly, after the dot on axis I. Thus, for example, the code F73.11 would describe a person with profound learning disabilities who showed significant repetitive self-injury. Associated physical diagnoses are coded. It is also possible to specify whether physical diagnoses are believed to have caused the mental retardation.

The terms impairment, 'disability' and 'handicap' are often used interchangeably in everyday speech. In the WHO schedule they are not interchangeable.

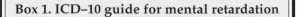

> **Box 1. ICD–10 guide for mental retardation**
>
> **Axis I** – severity of retardation and problem behaviours
> **Axis II** – associated medical conditions
> **Axis III** – associated psychiatric disorder
> **Axis IV** – global assessment of psychosocial ability
> **Axis V** – associated abnormal psychosocial situation

In this context an 'impairment' is any loss of abnormality of psychological, physiological or any anatomical structure or function. A 'disability' is any restriction or lack (resulting from impairment) of ability to perform an activity in the manner or within the range considered normal for a human being. A 'handicap' is a disadvantage for an individual, resulting from an impairment or a disability, that limits or prevents the fulfilment of a role that is normal according to age, gender and social and cultural factors for that individual. This medical model of impairment, disability and handicap is not acceptable to the disability movement (Oliver, 1990). The social model of disability defines disability as a failure of society or the environment to be accessible to disabled people.

'Challenging behaviour'

This term was originally coined to draw attention to the interactive nature of the problem. Whether or not a behaviour occurs or is perceived as challenging depends on features in the service as well as the individual (Mansell, 1993).

Severely challenging behaviour refers to behaviour of such an intensity, frequency or duration that the physical safety of the person or others is likely to be placed in serious jeopardy, or behaviour which is likely seriously to limit or deny access to the use of ordinary community facilities. (Emerson *et al*, 1991). The term 'challenging behaviour' neither necessitates nor excludes a formal psychiatric diagnosis.

Depending on the definitions used, up to 7% of people with learning disabilities show behaviour that seriously disrupts their lives or that of those around them (Qureshi & Alborz, 1992). Challenging behaviour is more common in people living in hospital or in their own homes than in local authority residential accommodation.

Prevalence of psychiatric disorders

Estimates vary according to the age and location of the populations studied, the definitions of both psychiatric disorder and learning disability, and the instruments used. People with learning disabilities tend to have a significantly higher life-time prevalence of psychiatric disorders (Table 1).

Studies based in mental handicap hospitals tend to show higher prevalence rates, probably because people with behavioural or psychiatric problems are more likely to be admitted to hospital, and they are harder to discharge. Hospitalisation may exacerbate problems, especially in understaffed, poor-quality institutions.

People with learning disability sent to hospital by the courts may not be typical of offenders with learning disability; for example, arson and sexual offences may be over-represented in hospital populations.

Aetiology of psychiatric disorder in people with learning disability

The aetiology of psychiatric disorder in people with learning disability can be understood in terms of dynamic interactions between biomedical and psychosocial processes.

Biological

Genetic

A number of disorders are linked to genetic causes. Down's syndrome is significantly associated with Alzheimer's disease, but by no means inevitably, both clinically and on neuropathology, and is also associated with depression (Holland & Oliver, 1995).

Tuberous sclerosis and various other conditions show higher than expected rates of autism and pervasive developmental disorders. It is not clear whether this is a specific association or whether it simply reflects overall brain damage.

Certain genetic syndromes have a very characteristic behavioural presentation (Holland, 1994; O'Brien & Yule, 1995; Turk & Hill, 1995). Prader-Willi syndrome (partial deletion of chromosome 15) is associated with overeating, a failure of satiety

Table 1. Prevalence of psychiatric disorder in people with learning disabilities (PLD): epidemiological studies (adapted from Bregman & Hodapp, 1991)

Study	Age (years)	Sample	Method	Psychiatric disorder(%) PLD	Controls
Rutter *et al* 1970	9–11	Entire age cohort IOW	Comprehensive assessment – multi-axial	30–42	6–7
Gillberg *et al* 1986	13–17	Representative cohort	Comprehensive DSM–III	57 (mild) 64 (severe)	5
Jacobson 1982	All ages	Receiving services for people with MR in New York State	Survey of behaviour frequency data	14 (children) 17 (adults)	0
Lund 1985	<20	Sample from Danish MR register	Comprehensive DSM–III	27	0
Gostason 1985	20–60	Sample from Swedish register	Comprehensive DSM–III	33 (mild) 71 (severe)	23
Patel *et al* 1993	>50	All people with learning disability in one district	Parallel interviews of subjects and informant and 3-year cognitive testing Mental illness only	21	
Cooper 1997*b*	>65 <65	All adults on Leicester LD register	Comprehensive semi-structured instrument with informant. ICD–10	69 (>65) 47.9 (<65)	

IOW, Isle of Wight; MR, mental retardation.

and massive obesity. Lesch–Nyhan syndrome (sex-linked recessive defect of uric acid metabolism) gives rise to self-injurious behaviour.

It should be noted that most obesity and self-injury that occurs in people with learning disability is not caused by these rare conditions.

Fragile X syndrome is the most common cause of an X-linked learning disability. Men are more commonly affected, but women can have the syndrome. Some family members have learning disability with characteristic cognitive, language and social abnormality. Some but not all children with fragile X meet criteria for the diagnosis of autism (Turk, 1997). The underlying genetic defect is a CGG repeat on the X chromosome that can be detected using a gene probe. The length of the repeat determines the pattern of disability. Some affected family members present with emotional problems or psychiatric illness but no learning disability. Genetic screening is indicated when there is a family history of both learning disability and psychiatric illness.

It may be appropriate to offer genetic screening to adults who have not received an aetiological diagnosis in childhood.

Epilepsy

Epilepsy is common in people with learning disabilities (Corbett, 1988). It is associated with increased rates of psychiatric disturbance, probably due to a combination of underlying neurological damage and social factors.

Physical illness

People who cannot communicate well may express themselves behaviourally if they are in pain or have chronic ill health. Symptoms such as anorexia and restlessness may have been caused by infections or gastro-intestinal disorders. Physical and psychiatric pathology may be difficult to distinguish between.

Sensory impairment

Sensory impairment may cause disturbed behaviour or be a risk factor for psychiatric illness. About one in four adults with a learning disability has a significant hearing impairment, and visual impairments are common (Wilson & Haire, 1990).

Motor abnormalities

Tic-like phenomena and stereotypies are more common in people with known central nervous system damage. The phenomenologies of Gilles de la Tourette syndrome and the autistic spectrum disorders have been described, singly and together, in people with learning disabilities.

Prescribed medication

Drugs prescribed, for example, for epilepsy or disturbed behaviours, often have psychiatric and motor side-effects. Regular review of such prescriptions is often neglected (Wilson & Haire, 1990). Sedative anti-epileptic drugs (phenobarbitone, phenytoin) can produce drowsiness, paradoxical over-arousal or pseudo-dementia (Trimble, 1987). Vigabatrin may cause psychosis which can present as disturbed behaviour. People with learning disabilities may be particularly sensitive to the motor side-effects of neuroleptics, although apparently similar motor abnormalities also occur without neuroleptics (Rogers *et al*, 1991).

Psychological

Poor communication skills

Difficulties in understanding or in being understood may predispose to frustration, loss of motivation, challenging behaviour and psychiatric illness. Behaviour serving a communicative function may be wrongly attributed to psychiatric illness.

Limited range of coping behaviours

Impaired learning and restricted environments mean that people with learning disabilities acquire few coping skills, leaving them vulnerable to psychosocial stresses.

Low self-esteem

Some degree of parental loss and disappointment is described following the birth of a child with learning disabilities (Bicknell, 1983). Inability to keep up with other children and the experience of repeated failure at academic tasks, together with social marginalisation and stigmatisation, tend to interfere with the development of self-esteem. This is an established risk factor for depression.

Autism

Autistic spectrum disorders are much more common in people with learning disability than in the general population (Gillberg, 1990). This adds to the considerable body of evidence that autism has a neurodevelopmental rather than psychogenic basis. There is an increased prevalence of both 'Kanner' autism and the severe social and language impairments described by Wing & Gould (1979), which are common at lower IQ levels. The lack of a theory of mind postulated by Frith (1989) and others may explain the increased incidence of disturbed behaviour seen in people with autism. The inability to understand and predict the behaviour of others, and to understand everyday social rules, often leads to disturbed behaviour and may predispose to psychiatric illness. Some of the psychiatric disturbance in this group may also be secondary to the underlying brain pathology (Gillberg, 1988; Rutter *et al*, 1994) the precise nature and cause of which has yet to be determined.

Social

Biological impairment

People who function at a very low level because of biological impairment are often unable to live independently or to find work. Their living expenses are often increased, but they tend to have lower incomes than average.

Labelling

Being labelled may itself lower self-esteem and predispose to psychiatric illness. It may also lead to exclusion from opportunities for employment and an adequate income, leisure activities, marriage and a valued social role.

Arrangements for care

Most families continue to function well when they have a member who has a learning disability (Carr, 1985). Where family adjustment fails, or inadequate services are provided, people with learning disabilities may live in very unusual or restrictive family circumstances. Residential care provision may fail to provide exposure to many normal learning experiences and be inappropriately tolerant of behaviour that would be unacceptable in people without disabilities.

Abuse

There is an increased likelihood of physical and sexual abuse among children and adults with learning disabilities (Sobsey *et al*, 1991), both at home and in service settings.

Loss

People who are dependent on others may be more vulnerable to the effects of loss, especially of a care-taker. Disturbed behaviour may follow major life events but carers and others often deny that the person with learning disabilities is aware of any loss. The person with learning disability may thus be denied the opportunity to grieve. Such exclusion compounds the problem, delaying the person's understanding of the loss event and reducing the likelihood of them coming to terms with it (Hollins & Esterhyzen, 1997).

Sexuality

The development of sexuality may be denied by care-givers (Craft *et al*, 1987). This may lead to someone being diagnosed as sexually deviant when in fact they have never been given any appropriate sexual knowledge.

Psychiatric assessment and diagnosis

The psychiatric assessment of a person with learning disabilities involves an assessment of their social circumstances, as well as history-taking and examination, modified as necessary (see Box 2).

People with learning disabilities rarely present themselves to the doctor. Instead, it is the concern of the family, or workers in care settings, that brings them to psychiatric attention. Assessment of the wider family and caring system is essential.

The history should be obtained both from the person with learning disabilities, if communication skills permit, and from an informant or informants.

Physical examination and investigations are particularly necessary in people who cannot complain or describe their symptoms. Pain or discomfort often present behaviourally. Hypothyroidism is associated with Down's syndrome and may mimic depression or dementia. Sensory assessment is also important.

An informant can be asked to record target behaviours, such as sleep or aggressive outbursts, to facilitate diagnosis. Recordings also permit monitoring of treatment, whether the intervention is behavioural, psychodynamic or pharmacological. Functional behavioural analysis is extremely useful.

Specific conditions

Affective disorders

Major depressive disorder occurs and can be diagnosed at all IQ levels, although the diagnosis is easily missed or simply seen as challenging behaviour.

Box 2. History taking – points of interest

Mother's reproductive and obstetric history
Family history
Childhood – including milestones
Aetiology of the learning disability, if known
How the family were told and how they responded
Highest level of functioning – do not assume that a current low level of functioning is caused by the learning disability
Life events, especially changes of placement or staff, loss and abuse
Circumstances immediately before current problem
History of presenting complaint – particular attention to behavioural correlates of psychiatric illness, e.g. sleep, appetite, level of activity, interest in previous pursuits (however limited)

Depressive cognition and suicidal ideation are rare but anhedonia, changes in activity level or appetite and other biological symptoms can be used to make the diagnosis (Collacott *et al*, 1992). Both physical and psychological interventions can be used.

Mania also occurs, but should be differentiated from other causes of overactivity. Individualised recording schedules are particularly useful in managing cyclical disorders.

Schizophrenia

The relationship between schizophrenia, learning disability and autism has been a recurring debate in psychiatry (Turner, 1989). People with learning disabilities show a higher prevalence of schizophrenia (3–4%) which tends to be inversely related to IQ. Schizophrenia cannot be diagnosed reliably below IQ approximately 45 (Reid, 1994). Below this level, if there is evidence of delusions or hallucinations, a diagnosis of 'psychosis not otherwise specified' may be used.

Dementia

The pathological features of Alzheimer's disease are common in middle-aged people with Down's syndrome, as are deafness, hypothyroidism, cataracts and depression. It is particularly important to exclude treatable conditions in older people with learning disabilities who may develop physical health problems as they age (Moss *et al*,

1993; Cooper, 1997*a*). These, like dementia, can present as loss of skills or disturbed behaviour. Psychometric diagnosis is difficult unless the results of adult, premorbid testing are available.

Obsessive–compulsive disorder

Repetitive ritualised behaviour is common. It is often life-long and associated with social impairment and language abnormalities: indeed, the presence of such behaviour is used in the diagnosis of autism. People with autism, unlike those with typical obsessive–compulsive disorder, gain obvious pleasure from, and seldom resist carrying out, their rituals although they do characteristically become very anxious if they are prevented from doing so.

Adjustment reactions

People with learning disabilities are more vulnerable to the adverse effects of loss life events. Bereavement may entail more life changes than for other people (e.g. loss of house, change of carer). The changes are often greater than for other people and denial often compounds the problem. The presentation may be behavioural. Counselling techniques, using pictures and objects as well as words, are effective (Hollins & Sireling, 1994*a,b*). Prevention involves the education of families and services. People with autism need particularly careful management of change. Moves should be well planned and new staff introduced by careful steps (Howlin & Rutter, 1987)

Post-traumatic stress disorder

Traumatic events, particularly abuse and accidental injury, may be followed by anxiety in or avoidance of similar situations, with flashbacks, nightmares and rumination over the event. In people who cannot talk this may present as sudden, otherwise inexplicable, change in arousal, or avoidance of certain activities and obvious fear in the presence of a history of trauma (Ryan, 1994). Treatment involves acknowledgement of the trauma, appropriate drug treatment and psychotherapy. Again, pictures may help (Hollins & Sinason, 1993*a,b*).

Autism

A diagnosis of autism does not preclude the diagnosis of other psychiatric disorders (except, according to some diagnostic schedules, obsessive–compulsive disorder). However, the motor phenomena, language pathology and social impairments of autism may lead to an over-diagnosis of schizophrenia. Prolonged episodes of severely disturbed behaviour may follow apparently trivial change or excessively demanding situations.

Hyperkinetic/attention deficit disorder

Children with learning disability are more likely to develop attention deficit disorder and the disorder is more likely to persist into adult life. Stimulant drugs are thought to be less effective in children with learning disability. They are relatively contraindicated in Tourette's and autism, where they may precipitate tics.

Diagnostic guidelines

Where there is no spoken or signed language it is not possible to diagnose delusions, hallucinations or obsessive–compulsive phenomena reliably. Even when there is language it may be impossible to distinguish between a wish, an over-valued idea, and a delusion, or between a day-dream, a pseudo-hallucination and a hallucination. An interpreter who knows the client well is helpful.

Some instruments standardised on general psychiatric populations can be used in people with mild learning disability. Specialist research instruments are being developed. For example, Moss *et al* (1993) have developed a valuable family of diagnostic instruments, the Psychiatric Assessment Schedule for Adults with Developmental Disabilities (PAS-ADD), based on the Present State Examination to screen for and diagnose psychiatric disorder in people with learning disabilities. They include both direct and informant interviews. The direct interview is less useful in people with severe and profound learning disabilities. Not all psychiatric disorders are included in PAS-ADD, in particular personality disorder is excluded. Additional instruments must be used to make a firm diagnosis of autism and classify behavioural problems (Moss *et al*, 1993). The use of standardised instruments is still less developed than it is for other psychiatric populations.

A concise diagnosis on axis III of the ICD–10 classification may not always be possible. It is often more reliable to stick to wider categories such as 'somatoform disorder' or 'schizophrenia' rather than trying to decide on subtypes. In any case a multi-dimensional formulation should be used, describing the developmental and environmental context in which the diagnosis occurs

Intervention, treatment and management

Assessment for treatment, treatment itself, and checking the effectiveness of treatment should be multi-disciplinary and requires good inter-professional communication. Parents and providers of social care should be involved in decision-making unless this would breach confidentiality. A communicable plan of management should always be attainable.

Many people with learning disabilities will be able to consent or withhold consent to medical procedures, especially if the information is carefully presented. Some will not be able to consent either because they cannot understand the implications or because they are not able to make a free choice (Curran & Hollins, 1994). If an adult is not able to consent, no other person (in English law) can consent on their behalf, and treatment decisions are based on the duty of care that doctors owe their patients and their obligation to act in the patient's best interests. It is good practice to consult all those concerned with the care of the patient.

This use of the doctrine of necessity was called into question by the appeal court ruling on L. *v.* Bournewood, which was subsequently overturned in the House of Lords. The appeal court ruled that where statute law could be applied (e.g. the Mental Health Act 1983) the use of the common law doctrine of necessity was unlawful. The Department of Health therefore recommended that if a patient was not competent to consent and needed admission, she or he should be formally detained even if she or he made no attempt to leave (Brown, 1998). This obviously had enormous implications for clinical practice. The Law Lords, taking into account the deliberations of the Percy Commission (Percy, 1957), which underpins both the 1959 and 1983 Mental Health Acts, ruled that the Bournewood Trust had not acted unlawfully. Legally incompetent patients can now be treated informally.

The debate has drawn further attention to the unsatisfactory nature of the law in this area. The Law Commission has already undertaken extensive consultation on decision-making on behalf of mentally incapacitated adults (Lord Chancellor's Department, 1997). It is likely that there will be new legislation.

Behavioural treatments, based on functional behavioural analysis, have been shown to be effective in managing, reducing or eliminating challenging behaviour such as aggression or self-injury in individuals (Emerson, 1993). Most studies have been done in staffed settings. Less information is available about other psychological methods. Rational emotive therapy, cognitive therapy and individual and group psychotherapies have all been described. Evaluation of psychotherapy outcomes is similar to that seen in other groups (DesNoyers Hurley, 1989; Hollins & Evered, 1990).

Medication

Because of the underlying neuropathology drug treatment is always to some extent a therapeutic trial and particularly careful monitoring of side-effects is essential. Ineffective medication should be discontinued and long-term treatment regularly reviewed (Einfeld, 1990; Sovner & DesNoyers Hurley, 1992). Consensus guidelines on psychotropic medication were produced by an internationally convened panel in 1995 and, except for the section on consent which does not conform to UK law, should be used to inform practice (Kalachnik *et al*, 1995).

There is evidence that long-term neuroleptics are over-prescribed for behavioural indications, and that other effective drug regimes, such as selective serotonin reuptake inhibitors, are under-used often because no diagnostic formulation has been attempted.

Tricyclic antidepressants and selective serotonin reuptake inhibitors may be used to treat depression. Clomipramine and fluoxetine may also lessen distressing repetitive behaviour in people with autism.

Phenothiazines, butyrophenones and the newer antipsychotic drugs are all used in schizophrenia. People with learning disabilities may be partic-

---

Box 3. Current controversies in service provision

What is the role of the general psychiatrist in the treatment of people with mild or moderate learning disabilities?

Are linked posts in psychiatry of learning disability and general psychiatry the answer? What is the place of dual certificates of completion of specialist training?

Specialist psychiatric learning disability teams or multi-disciplinary health care teams – which is the way forward?

Life span *v.* adult-only learning disability services – which makes more sense?

Do all psychiatric trainees need competencies in examining the mental state of adults with learning disabilities?

'Borderline' learning disability could include 16% of the population. Should forensic learning disability services accept referrals of people with IQ >70?

Specialist in-patient units are needed. What extent of NHS residential or nursing home provision is required?

ularly vulnerable to motor side-effects. Neuro-leptics should be avoided as a treatment for behavioural disorders wherever possible.

Carbamazepine and valproate are usually the drugs of first choice for epilepsy. Phenobarbitone and phenytoin contribute to learning problems and may precipitate over-arousal or pseudo-dementia. There are few controlled trials of the newer anti-epileptic drugs in this population. Both vigabatrine (despite adverse behavioural side-effects) and lamotrigine have been shown to improve seizure control in people with learning disabilities.

Service organisation

The Royal College of Psychiatrists have published a report, jointly authored by the Psychiatry of Learning Disability and General Psychiatry Faculties, which describes "how to meet the mental health needs of adults (including elderly people) with learning disabilities" (Royal College of Psychiatrists, 1997). Its recommendations covered training issues and suggested the use of locally agreed protocols to achieve seamless services.

Many consultants in this speciality are single-handed and welcome being more fully included within the psychiatric fraternity, so that their expertise can be better understood (Bouras & Szymanski, 1997).

In some larger trusts with more than one consultant there are opportunities to develop special interests, for example, in psychotherapy or neuropsychiatry.

On the other hand, the separation of some specialist health care services, including specialist mental health services, for people with learning disabilities into different National Health Service trusts from the rest of psychiatric practice has made close working relationships harder. A number of controversies remain about the way services should be delivered (Box 3).

References

Abramowicz, H. K. & Richardson, S. A. (1975) Epidemiology of severe mental retardation in children: community studies. *American Journal on Mental Retardation*, **80**, 18–39.

Bicknell, D. J. (1983) The psychopathology of handicap. *British Journal of Medical Psychology*, **56**, 167–178.

Bouras, N. & Szymanski, L. S. (1997) Services for people with mental retardation and psychiatric disorders: US–UK comparative overview. *International Journal of Social Psychiatry*, **43**, 64–71.

Bregman, J. D. & Hodapp, R. J. (1991) Current developments in the understanding of mental retardation. Part 1: Biological and phenomenological perspectives; Part II: Psycho-pathology. *Journal of American Academy of Child and Adolescent Psychiatry*, **30**, 707–719; 861–872.

Brown, M. (1998) *Court of Appeal Judgement: L. v. Bournewood Community and Mental Health Trust. Letter to Chief Executives of NHS Trusts.* London: Department of Health.

Carr, J. (1985) The effect on the family of a severely mentally handicapped child. In *Mental Deficiency: The Changing Outlook* (eds A. M. Clarke, A. D. B. Clarke & J. M. Berg), pp. 512–548. London: Methuen.

Collacott, R. A., Cooper, S.-A. & McGrother, C. (1992) Differential rates of psychiatric disorders in adults with Down's syndrome compared with other mentally handicapped adults. *British Journal of Psychiatry*, **161**, 671–674.

Cooper, S.-A. (1997a) High prevalence of dementia amongst people with learning disabilities not attributed to Down's syndrome. *Psychological Medicine*, **27**, 609–616.

— (1997b) Epidemiology of psychiatric disorders in elderly compared with younger adults with learning disabilities. *British Journal of Psychiatry*, **170**, 375–380.

Corbett, J. (1988) Some special problems of epilepsy. In *A Textbook of Epilepsy* (eds J. Laidlaw, A. Richens & J. Oxley), pp. 533–538. Edinburgh: Churchill Livingstone.

Craft, A., Heshuis, L., Johnson, P. J., et al (1987) *Mental Handicap and Sexuality: Issues and Perspectives.* Tunbridge Wells: Costello.

Curran, J. & Hollins, S. (1994) Consent to medical treatment and people with learning disability. *Psychiatric Bulletin*, **18**, 691–693.

DesNoyers Hurley, A. (1989) Individual psychotherapy with mentally retarded individuals: a review and call for research. *Research in Developmental Disabilities*, **10**, 261–275.

Einfeld, S. L. (1990) Guidelines for the use of psychotropic medication in individuals with developmental disabilities. *Australian and New Zealand Journal of Developmental Disabilities*, **16**, 71–73.

Emerson, E., Cambridge, P. & Harris, P. (eds) (1991) *Evaluating the Challenge. A Guide to Evaluating Services for People with Learning Difficulties and Challenging Behaviour.* London: King's Fund.

Emerson, E. (1993) Challenging behaviours and severe learning disabilities: recent developments in behavioural analysis and intervention. *Behavioural and Cognitive Psychotherapy*, **21**, 171–198.

Frith, U. (1989) *Autism. Explaining the Enigma.* Oxford: Basil Blackwell.

Gillberg, C. (1988) The neurobiology of infantile autism. *Journal of Child Psychology and Psychiatry*, **29**, 257–266.

— (1990) Autism and pervasive developmental disorders. *Journal of Child Psychology and Psychiatry*, **31**, 99–120.

—, Persson, E., Grufman, M., et al (1986) Psychiatric disorders in mildly and severely mentally retarded urban children and adolescents: epidemiological aspects. *British Journal of Psychiatry*, **149**, 68–74.

Gostason, R. (1985) Psychiatric illness among mentally retarded: a Swedish population study. *Acta Psychiatrica Scandinavica*, **71** (suppl. 318), 1–117.

Grossman, H. J. (ed.) (1983) *Classification in Mental Retardation.* Washington, DC: American Association on Mental Deficiency.

Holland, A. J. (1994) Learning disability and psychiatric/behavioural disorders: a genetic perspective. In *The New Genetics of Mental Illness* (eds P. McGuffin & R. Murray), pp 245–258.

— & Oliver, C. (1995) Down's syndrome and the links with Alzheimer's disease. *Journal of Neurology, Neurosurgery and Psychiatry*, **59**, 111–115.

Hollins, S. & Evered, C. (1990) Group process and content: the challenge of mental handicap. *Group Analysis*, **23**, 56–67.

— & Sinason, V. (1993a) *Jenny Speaks Out.* London: St George's Mental Health Library.

— & — (1993b) *Bob Tells All.* London: St George's Mental Health Library.

— & Sireling, L. (1994a) *When Mum Died.* London: St George's Mental Health Library.

— & — (1994b) *When Dad Died.* London: St George's Mental Health Library.

—— & Esterhuyzen A. (1997) Bereavement and grief in adults with learning disabilities. *British Journal of Psychiatry*, **170**, 497–501.

Howlin, P. & Rutter, M. (1987) *Treatment of Autistic Children*. Chichester: John Wiley and Sons.

Jacobson, J. (1982) Problem behaviour and psychiatric impairment within a developmentally disabled population. I: Behaviour frequency. *Applied Research in Mental Retardation*, **3**, 121–140.

Kalachnik, J. E., Leventhal, B. L., James, D. H., *et al* (1995) *Guidelines for the Use of Psychotropic Medication*. International Consensus Panel on Psychopharmacology.

Lord Chancellor's Department (1997) *Who Decides? Making Decisions on Behalf of Mentally Incapacitated Adults. A Consultation Paper*. London: HMSO.

Lund, J. (1985) The prevalence of psychiatric morbidity in mentally retarded adults. *Acta Psychiatrica Scandinavica*, **72**, 563–570.

Mansell, J. L. (1993) *Services for People with Learning Disabilities and Challenging Behaviour or Mental Health Needs*. London: HMSO.

Moss, S., Patel, P., Prosser, H., *et al* (1993) Psychiatric morbidity in older people with moderate and severe learning disability. I: Developmental and reliability of the Patient Interview (PAS-ADD). *British Journal of Psychiatry*, **163**, 471–480.

O'Brien, G. & Yule, W. (1995) *Behavioural Phenotypes*. Cambridge: MacKeith Press.

Oliver, M. (1990) *The Politics of Disablement*. London: Macmillan.

Patel, P., Goldberg, D. & Moss, S. (1993) Psychiatric morbidity in older people with moderate and severe learning disability. II: The prevalence study. *British Journal of Psychiatry*, **163**, 481–491.

Percy, Lord (1957) *Report of the Royal Commission on the Law Relating to Mental Illness and Mental Deficiency 1954–1957*. Cmnd 169. London: HMSO.

Qureshi, H. & Alborz, A. (1992) Epidemiology of challenging behaviour. *Mental Handicap Research*, **5**, 130–145.

Reid, A. H. (1994) Psychiatry and learning disability. *British Journal of Psychiatry*, **164**, 613–618.

Rogers, D., Karki, C., Bartlett, C., *et al* (1991) The motor disorders of mental handicap. An overlap with the motor disorders of severe psychiatric illness. *British Journal of Psychiatry*, **158**, 97–102.

Royal College of Psychiatrists (1997) *Meeting with Mental Health Needs of People with Learning Disability*. Council Report CR56. London: Royal College of Psychiatrists.

Rutter, M., Graham, P. & Yule, W. (1970) A neuropsychiatric study in childhood. *Clinics in Developmental Medicine*, vols 35 & 36 (eds M. Rutter & L. Hersov). London: Heinemann Medical.

——, Bailey, A., Bolton, P., *et al* (1994) Autism and known medical conditions: myth and substance. *Journal of Child Psychology and Psychiatry*, **35**, 311–322.

Ryan, R. (1994) Post-traumatic stress disorder in persons with developmental disabilities. *Community Mental Health Journal*, **30**, 45–54.

Sinason, V. (1992) *Mental Handicap and the Human Condition*. London: Free Association Books.

Sobsey, D., Gray, S., Wells, D., *et al* (1991) *Disability, Sexuality and Abuse : An Annotated Bibliography*. Baltimore, MD: Paul H. Brookes.

Sovner, R. & DesNoyers Hurley, A. (1992) The diagnostic treatment formulation for psychotropic drug therapy. *Habilitative Mental Healthcare Newsletter*, **11**, 81–89.

Sturmey, P., Reed, J. & Corbett, J. (1991) Psychometric assessment of psychiatric disorders in people with learning difficulties (mental handicap): a review of measures. *Psychological Medicine*, **21**, 143–155.

Trimble, M. (1987) Anticonvulsant drugs and cognitive function: a review of the literature. *Epilepsia*, **28** (suppl. 3), S37–S45.

Turk J. (1997) Fragile X syndromes, autism and autistic features. *Autism*, **1**, 175–197.

—— & Hill, P. (1995) Behavioural phenotypes in dysmorphic syndromes. *Clinical Dysmorphology*, **4**, 105–115.

Turner, T. H. (1989) Schizophrenia and mental handicap: an historical review, with implications for further research. *Psychological Medicine*, **19**, 301–314.

Wilson, D. N. & Haire, A. (1990) Health care screening for people with mental handicap living in the community. *British Medical Journal*, **301**, 1379–1381.

Wing, L. & Gould, J. (1979) Severe impairments of social interaction and associated abnormalities in children: epidemiology and classification. *Journal of Autism and Developmental Disorders*, **9**, 11–30.

World Health Organization (1992) *The ICD–10 Classification of Mental and Behavioural Disorders. Research Criteria*. Geneva: WHO.

Suggested reading

Anonymous (1998) *Psychotropic Medications and Developmental Disabilities: The International Consensus Handbook*. Ohio: Ohio State University Nisonger Center.

ARC & NAPSAC (1993) *It Could Never Happen Here! The Prevention and Treatment of Sexual Abuse of Adults with Learning Disabilities in Residential Settings*. Nottingham: ARC & NAPSAC.

Hogg, J. & Raynes, N. V. (eds) (1987) *Assessment in Mental Handicap – A Guide to Assessment Practices, Tests and Checklist*. London: Croom Helm.

Livingston, G., Hollins, S., Katona, C., *et al* (1998) Treatment of patients who lack capacity. *Psychiatric Bulletin*, **22**, 402–404.

Russell, O. (1985) Mental handicap. *Current Reviews in Psychiatry*. No 1 (eds E. S. Paykel & H. G. Morgan). London: Churchill Livingstone.

—— (ed.) (1997) *Seminars in the Psychiatry of Learning Disabilities*. London: Gaskell.

Thompson, D. (1993) *Learning Disabilities: The Fundamental Facts*. London: Mental Health Foundation.

Treatment of psychoses in the elderly

A. Phanjoo

Psychotic disorders in the elderly can be divided into three types: disorders that have started in earlier life and persist into old age; disorders that start *de novo* after the age of 60; and psychoses associated with brain disease, including the dementias. The classification of psychoses in late life has provoked controversy for nearly a century. The debate concerns whether schizophrenia can present at any stage of life or whether functional psychoses, arising for the first time in late life, represent different illnesses. The nomenclature of such disorders consists of numerous terms including late-onset schizophrenia, late paraphrenia, paranoid psychosis of late life and schizophreniform psychosis. This plethora of terms has made research difficult to interpret.

Historical overview

Although the term paraphrenia was used by Kahlbaum as early as 1861, the concept of paraphrenia was first described by Kraepelin (1909). He used the term to differentiate a certain type of psychotic illness from schizophrenia (dementia praecox) because he believed that, unlike schizophrenia, paraphrenia was not associated with a deterioration of personality, volition was not affected and such patients could engage in a rational argument outside of their delusions. There was also an absence of catatonic symptoms.

In 1921, Mayer published an important literature review and a follow-up study of patients diagnosed as suffering from paraphrenia; he showed that, over a period of time, 70% of such patients develop symptoms which are almost indistinguishable from those of schizophrenia. The impact made by this paper gave the term paraphrenia a 'death blow' according to Manfred Bleuler and the general view was to consider paraphrenia as a variant of schizophrenia and therefore not a separate entity.

The controversy was revived in 1955 with a series of studies by Roth and co-workers, who investigated more fully the range of these disorders. They described a condition, late paraphrenia, which accounted for 10% of mental hospital admissions after the age of 65. The main characteristics of this disorder were florid paranoid delusions and hallucinations occurring in clear consciousness. Unlike the patients followed-up by Mayer, Roth's cohort did not undergo personality deterioration. He also found that the condition was more common in women, was associated with sensory deficits, social isolation and a reduced marriage rate, as well as reduced fertility. Roth's subjects seemed to have an excess of abnormal personality traits of the paranoid or schizoid type.

Over the next 20 years, a number of researchers confirmed the findings of Roth and colleagues, most of whom concurred with their view that late paraphrenia probably represented a variant of schizophrenia (Kay & Roth, 1961).

The situation changed dramatically in 1987 when DSM–III was revised and the age of 45 as the upper limit for a diagnosis of schizophrenia was removed (American Psychiatric Association, 1987). Consequently, people in the USA who develop schizophrenic symptoms after the age of 45 are described as having late-onset schizophrenia. ICD–10 (World Health Organization, 1992) does not have a diagnosis of late paraphrenia. There has been some concern about the loss of the diagnosis of late paraphrenia because some authors still believe that the major differences in phenomenology, genetic risk and brain imaging do not readily fit within the pattern of changes reported in younger individuals with schizophrenia. Almeida *et al* (1995) have demonstrated the high prevalence of persecutory delusions and auditory hallucinations in this group of people and commented on the high female to male ratio (8 : 1) and the importance of deafness as a risk factor.

The issue has recently been discussed in an editorial in the *British Journal of Psychiatry* (Howard & Rabino, 1997).

Treatment strategies

Use of drugs

A variety of treatment strategies have been proposed for the management of psychosis in the elderly, including family therapy, psychotherapy and cognitive–behavioural therapy, but the mainstay of treatment remains the use of antipsychotic drugs. There are a number of factors, however, which make the use of drugs problematical. They include:

(a) altered pharmacokinetics in old age;
(b) poor drug compliance (especially relevant in the elderly, many of whom live alone);
(c) drug interactions; and
(d) high incidence of serious side-effects including extrapyramidal side-effects, tardive dyskinesia and the neuroleptic malignant syndrome.

Identifying the cause

Treatment with psychotropic drugs must be preceded by a careful attempt to identify the cause of the psychosis. In some elderly patients, the symptoms may well represent a recurrence of a previous illness. In individuals who present with psychotic symptoms *de novo*, potentially remediable aetiological factors should be sought, for example, infection, altered metabolism, drugs or alcohol. Paranoid symptoms may be secondary to delirium or may be seen in the context of organic syndromes as both reversible or irreversible. A psychosis of sudden onset will suggest an organic cause which should be sought for, whereas an illness which has developed over a period of months, if not years, may allow the clinician to make a diagnosis of late paraphrenia with some confidence.

Choice of drugs

A considerable range of antipsychotic drugs are now available for clinical use (see Box 1). A few compounds are available for depot intramuscular injections. There is relatively little information in the literature to guide the clinician in the choice of an antipsychotic – clinicians vary widely in their choice of drug, its dosage or its method of administration (oral or intramuscular). Considering that many antipsychotic drugs have been in use for 25 years or more, personal experience of one compound or a class of compounds can be considerable and it is not surprising that anecdotal evidence has accumulated to convince some psychiatrists that one drug is particularly good for one group of symptoms whereas another may be used preferentially for different symptoms. Yet there is little scientific evidence for such preferences. Indeed, before the advent of clozapine, it was recognised that in equivalent doses no antipsychotic had been shown to be consistently superior to chlorpromazine.

Whereas there is a considerable literature on the treatment of psychoses of patients up to the age of 70, there is a dearth of good research on the treatment of psychoses in older people. Early reports (Kay & Roth, 1961) describe remissions after treatment with electroconvulsive therapy or medication with tranquillisers. Of the 43 patients reported in that series, approximately 25% experienced a temporary remission. Of the 12 patients who received electroconvulsive therapy, seven showed a good to moderate response but the improvement was not maintained at follow-up. Post (1966) described a series of 71 patients who had received antipsychotic treatment in the form of trifluoperazine or thioridazine. Forty-three of the 71 patients had complete response to treatment and 22 were described as showing moderate improvement. In the same study, Post

---

Box 1. Commonly used antipsychotics

Oral medication
Phenothiazines
  Chlorpromazine, thioridazine, fluphenazine
Diphenylbutylpiridines
  Pimozide
Thioxanthenes
  Flupenthixol, zuclopenthixol
Butyrophenones
  Haloperidol
Benzamide derivatives
  Sulpiride
Dibenzodiazepines
  Clozapine
Benzisoxazoles
  Risperidone

Intramuscular depot medication
Butyrophenones
  Haloperidol decanoate
Phenothiazines
  Fluphenazine decanoate
Thioxanthenes
  Flupenthixol decanoate

also showed that maintenance on antipsychotics was associated with reduced admission. More recent reports have been less sanguine and improvement has been reported in 26–48% of patients (Pearlson *et al*, 1989; Howard & Levy, 1992).

Since 60% of psychoses in the elderly are characterised by paranoid ideation, drug compliance remains a major problem, particularly as a large proportion of elderly people with psychosis live on their own and show extreme suspiciousness. It is logical to assume that parenteral depot preparations would be associated with more consistent improvement. This has indeed been shown in studies comparing depot with oral preparations. Depot preparations, however, are not guaranteed to produce a complete remission of symptoms and many patients still harbour bizarre ideas, although they may not readily express them. Many patients are reluctant to comply with medication because of unpleasant side-effects. Howard & Levy (1992) have shown that the monitoring of patients by community psychiatric nurses and the use of depot rather than oral medication improved compliance, with a concomitant improvement in psychotic symptoms, although there was little effect on social adjustment and insight.

It is important for patients to have a trusting relationship with their therapist, and many patients can be maintained in the community once this has been achieved. The development of this therapeutic relationship may be difficult and time-consuming but once established it will enable the therapist to persuade the patient of the necessity to take some form of medication, if only to alleviate the distress provoked by the symptoms. The therapist should focus on how the patient's symptoms interfere with his or her day-to-day living, going on to suggest ways in which the patient's level of functioning could improve. Therapists should be able to deal with patients' anger and criticism and take their complaints seriously.

Treatment is all too often hindered when a junior doctor moves on after six months without sufficient time to develop trusting relationships with her or his patients. Experienced community psychiatric nurses who are attached to a psychogeriatric unit over a longer period of time may achieve a great deal in the management of elderly people with psychosis.

Once compliance with a drug regime is assured, due consideration must be given to the choice of medication, the dosage and the method of administration. A simple drug schedule involving one tablet taken once a day is preferable to a combination of antipsychotics which have to be taken at different times of the day. Patients on depot preparations should be managed as far as possible without any oral preparations, although some patients on a depot preparation may take another antipsychotic as a hypnotic. It is important that the patient and her or his relatives are given a full description of the side-effects of any drug, as well as the importance of complying with the drug regime.

Range of antipsychotics

Individual studies suggest that high-potency antipsychotics are more effective than low-potency ones, but have more side-effects. There is no evidence to suggest that the clinical efficacy of an antipsychotic drug is related to its sedative effect. The use of the novel antipsychotics in the elderly has been poorly researched. These novel or atypical antipsychotics can be divided according to Gerlach's classification (Gerlach, 1991):

(a) selective dopamine receptor blockers (e.g. sulpiride);
(b) partial dopamine agonists;
(c) non-dopamine drugs (e.g. ondansetron); and
(d) combination receptor blockers (e.g. clozapine and risperidone).

Selective dopamine receptor blockers

The usefulness of these compounds in treating psychosis in the elderly is much less obvious than with younger patients. A good example of the benzamide group is sulpiride which has been shown to have an antipsychotic efficacy equal to that of haloperidol and chlorpromazine, although its effect on negative symptoms is questionable. Another compound of a similar nature, remoxipride, which was introduced in 1989 but subsequently withdrawn because of its propensity to cause blood dyscrasias in some patients, had been tested against haloperidol in a number of studies and was shown to have the same efficacy as haloperidol but a reduced incidence of side-effects. Sulpiride is a useful drug in the elderly because it has fewer extrapyramidal side-effects than the conventional neuroleptics.

Combination receptor blockers

Clozapine belongs to the the dibenzoxazepine group of compounds. This drug has proved to have beneficial effects in cases of treatment-resistant schizophrenia and, despite early reports of fatalities due to agranulocytosis, the Food and Drug Administration decided to continue its use on a named-patient basis (McKenna & Bailey,

1993). Clozapine has been found to be superior to chlorpromazine in six out of 13 studies. Studies in treatment-resistant schizophrenia culminated in a multi-centre trial (Kane *et al*, 1988) which showed the superiority of clozapine over chlorpromazine in negative symptoms as well as a reduced incidence of side-effects. Although this study was criticised by some researchers on the basis that the high doses of chlorpromazine may have been detrimental to some patients, most authorities have become convinced that clozapine is an important addition to the range of antipsychotic drugs.

A note of caution has been introduced regarding the use of clozapine in the elderly since it has been shown to be associated with a decline in memory function, perhaps because of its potent anticholinergic effects (Goldberg *et al*, 1993). However, Lee *et al* (1994) have produced evidence that clozapine is superior to conventional drugs in improving cognitive function in schizophrenia with particular reference to impaired social function and poor work performance. The UK Clozapine Study Group (1993) have reported that out of 54 in-patients with a diagnosis of severe treatment-resistant schizophrenia treated with clozapine, 26 completed the study and 20 of these patients showed improvement in both positive and negative symptoms. The use of clozapine is no longer restricted to treatment-resistant patients or patients with predominantly negative symptoms. It certainly produces a much lower incidence of extrapyramidal side-effects and is claimed to have a beneficial effect on tardive dyskinesia. On the other hand, it has a tendency to produce hypersalivation and in a few cases will lower the seizure threshold.

The question of agranulocytosis was addressed by Alvir *et al* (1993). The American data of 11 555 patients treated with clozapine showed that 73 patients had developed this problem, which in two cases led to death. It is important to note that 61 out of the 73 patients developed agranulocytosis within three months of starting medication and only three patients developed it after six months. The risk increases with age and women are at greater risk of developing agranulocytosis.

Negative symptoms are far more common in younger than in older people with psychosis. Indeed, there is some evidence that these symptoms tend to decline with advancing age. Consequently there has been little justification for the use of clozapine in the elderly. Two of the limiting factors have been the high cost of the drug and the necessity for regular blood monitoring. However, there are a number of elderly patients with psychosis whose illness fails to improve either because of their unresponsiveness to conventional antipsychotics or because of their propensity to develop unpleasant side-effects. Clozapine is an obvious drug to be tried on such patients.

Risperidone, a benzisoxazole, was launched in 1993 and is claimed to be beneficial in both positive and negative symptoms in schizophrenia. The most effective dose of risperidone in younger people has been shown to be 6 mg; this is slightly more effective than 20 mg haloperidol in controlling acute psychotic symptoms and has the added benefit of a reduced incidence of extrapyramidal side-effects. This drug, however, should be used in smaller doses in the elderly and it is advisable to start with a dose of 0.5 mg per day and gradually increase this to about 2 mg daily. Higher doses in the elderly may result in marked sedation and the development of extrapyramidal side-effects. There is still controversy as to whether this drug is as effective as clozapine in treating the negative symptoms of schizophrenia. A number of newer antipsychotics such as sertindole, quetiapine, olanzapine, amisulpiride and ziprasidone have become available, and further studies are needed regarding their safety and efficacy in the elderly. Olanzapine in a starting dose of 2.5 mg daily is an alternative to risperidone.

Other uses of antipsychotics

Apart from schizophrenia and paraphrenia, psychotic symptoms are also found in affective disorders and in organic psychosis. Patients suffering from various types of dementia are liable to have psychotic symptoms such as delusions and hallucinations, which may well lead to disruptive behaviour. The use of antipsychotics is popular in the geriatric population. It has been shown recently (Nygaard *et al*, 1994) that on admission to nursing homes 63% of elderly patients were receiving psychotropic medication and that this figure increased to 68% after three months. Another study of long-stay elderly patients in hospital in Perth, Scotland, showed that 37.5% of the 104 patients were receiving antipsychotic drugs for a variety of reasons (Connelly, 1990).

Antipsychotics are useful in the treatment of Charles Bonnet syndrome but patients suffering from Lewy body dementia with psychotic symptoms show neuroleptic sensitivity to conventional antipsychotics and may well benefit from drugs like risperidone instead. A meta-analysis of double-blind trials comparing neuroleptics with placebo in agitated patients with a diagnosis of dementia (Schneider *et al*, 1990) found that antipsychotics were marginally more effective than placebo, no single antipsychotic drug was superior to another and that low doses of medication are often sufficient in controlling target symptoms. Indeed, there have been a number of reports in the literature in the past 10 years suggesting that ultra-low doses are equally effective (Gottlieb *et al*, 1988). Treatment sometimes consists of a delicate balancing act between a low dose, which may be ineffective, and a high dose, which may be effective but is associated with unpleasant side-effects.

Side-effects

The elderly are particularly prone to a variety of side-effects including acute dystonic reactions, extrapyramidal symptoms, tardive dyskinesia and neuroleptic malignant syndrome.

Extrapyramidal symptoms

High-potency drugs such as haloperidol and trifluoperazine are more likely to cause severe extrapyramidal side-effects than low-potency drugs such as chlorpromazine. The only reaction which appears to be more common in younger than in elderly patients is acute dystonia. One should not forget, however, that the elderly are sometimes prone to dystonic reactions such as torticollis and oculogyric crises. Such dystonic reactions can be treated on a short-term basis by anticholinergic drugs but their administration should not be prolonged because of the risk of anticholinergic toxicity. Parkinsonian reactions or neuroleptic-induced Parkinsonism appear to be more common in the elderly. Symptoms include rigidity, tremor and bradykinesia though tremor and festinating gait appear less common than in Parkinson's disease. If symptoms are particularly troublesome, the antipsychotic dose should initially be reduced. If there is no improvement in the symptoms, anticholinergic medication can be prescribed over a short period (e.g. 8–10 weeks).

Akathisia

This is commonly found in the elderly. It is characterised by a desire or a need to move all the time, motor restlessness, frequent changes in posture, various rocking movements, and abnormal movements of the legs and feet. Treatment involves a reduction in the offending medication and, if symptoms persist, short-term anticholinergic treatment.

Neuroleptic malignant syndrome

This is a serious disorder which is potentially fatal. It develops over a period of 24–72 hours and is characterised by hyperpyrexia and muscular incontinence. Leucocytosis and an elevated serum creatine phosphokinase are usually seen. Patients may require intensive care and treatment should consist of immediate discontinuation of the antipsychotics and administration of dantrolene, which reduces muscular rigidity, and bromocriptine, which restores brain dopaminergic function. Although neuroleptic malignant syndrome is more rarely seen with the new antipsychotics, there are reports that it has been caused by risperidone in elderly patients with brain damage. Various other effects have been described on the endocrine, cardiovascular, gastro-intestinal and autonomic nervous systems. Blood dyscrasias and agranulocytosis may rarely occur with any antipsychotic but it has been reported in 1% of patients taking clozapine. Remoxipride, prior to its withdrawal, had been implicated in bone marrow suppression.

Tardive dyskinesia

Tardive dyskinesia is a serious complication of antipsychotic medication which is particularly common in the elderly. It arises after at least three months' treatment with antipsychotics and is associated with choreoathetoid movements of the face, mouth and hands. As the disorder progresses, the upper limbs and trunk may be involved and more rarely the diaphragm, pharynx and inter-costal muscles may show incoordination. Risk factors have been shown to be advancing age, female gender and affective disorder. In addition, the length of neuroleptic exposure, brain damage, elevated serum neuroleptic concentration and late-onset psychosis may be regarded as possible risk factors. It was shown (Jeste & Wyatt, 1987) that the increased incidence of tardive dyskinesia in the elderly is a true finding which may be related to the higher serum neuroleptic concentration found in older patients and also to central mechanisms such as neuronal loss and changes in neuro-chemical receptors. These authors also noticed that oral facial dyskinesia seems to be more common in the elderly, and that elderly patients are less likely to show a reversal of their symptoms following antipsychotic withdrawal (for reviews see Lohr & Bracha, 1988; Szabadi, 1995).

There is good evidence in the literature on younger people with psychosis that the management of first episodes should consist of anti-psychotic medication being given for at least one year. Approximately 40–50% of patients are likely to remain well after cessation of medication but the remainder will require continuing medication, preferably of the depot type. Of those patients who require long-term medication, 60–70% are likely to relapse within a year and about 85% in two years. There is little information to guide the clinician about continuation of medication in the elderly but the aforementioned suggestions should prove useful in practice. Some guidelines for the use of antipsychotics in the elderly are listed in Box 2.

Non-pharmacological approaches

Many criticisms have been levelled at hospitals which have failed to provide adequate follow-up care for their patients with psychosis. Many elderly individuals with psychosis live on their own and returning to the community may equate with social isolation and increasing distortion of reality. The role of the community psychiatric nurse is paramount in maintaining contact with the patient and also in promoting liaison between hospital-based services and community agencies. It has been shown with reference to younger people with schizophrenia that families who react with hostility and criticism (high expressed emotion) increase the risk of the patient relapsing. It is not uncommon to find an elderly couple where the 'well' partner becomes involved in the psychopathology of the patient and may in fact encourage the patient not to cooperate with treatment. Such situations require delicate and diplomatic handling by experienced nurses. Particular attention should be paid to the standard of accommodation, social contacts and daytime activities. The availability of day facilities in many areas has proved valuable – in such settings the progress of people with psychosis can be monitored and adequate attention paid to their diet and self-care.

Psychosocial therapies

In the past few years there has been interest in developing various forms of treatment including social skills training, psychosocial rehabilitation and cognitive–behavioural interventions for patients with psychosis (Liberman & Corrigan, 1993). The value of such treatments has yet to be proven but the rationale behind cognitive–behavioural interventions appears sound. Problem-solving focuses on breaking down problems

---

> **Box 2. Guidelines for antipsychotic use in the elderly**
>
> **Assess hepatic, renal and cardiac function prior to antipsychotic treatment**
> **Patients and their carers should be fully informed of the benefits and risks of the treatment**
> **Treatment should be titrated, starting with very small doses and gradually increasing to the lowest effective dose**
> **Treatment should be time-limited, if at all possible**
> **Patients should be closely monitored for extrapyramidal side-effects as well as for postural hypertension**
> **Anticholinergic agents should be used with caution**
> **Antipsychotic medication is more effective in florid symptoms such as delusions, hallucinations and severe agitation**

---

resulting from the illness into small elements spanning a course of action and setting objectives. If the patient employs strategies successfully to cope with psychotic symptoms, then these are enhanced by various techniques (Bellack & Mueser, 1993).

Conclusions

Relatively little is known about the value of medication, the choice of drugs, the duration of treatment and outcome of illness in patients who refuse treatment or whose compliance is poor. Many old age psychiatrists will be familiar with elderly patients living on their own in the community who harbour bizarre delusions for years. Whether such patients should be coerced into accepting treatment is debatable. Recent publicity about the 'dangerousness' of patients with psychosis in the community may well influence psychiatrists into imposing treatment on such individuals. The identification of psychosis in elderly people living in the community is problematic because many such patients live in isolation and do not share their bizarre ideas with their doctor or other professional helpers. Although Roth and his co-workers (Kay & Roth, 1961) found that 10% of all their admissions could be given a diagnosis of late paraphrenia, the prevalence of such disorders is probably much less in the community.

For further information see Jeste & Zisook (1988), Katona & Levy (1992) and Phanjoo (1995).

References

Almeida, O. P., Howard, R. J., Levy, R., *et al* (1995) Psychotic states arising in late life (late paraphrenia). *British Journal of Psychiatry*, **166**, 205–228.

Alvir, J. J., Lieberman, J. A., Safferman, A. Z., *et al* (1993) Clozapine induced agranulocytosis; incidence and risk factors in the USA. *New England Journal of Medicine*, **329**, 162–167.

American Psychiatric Association (1987) *Diagnostic and Statistical Manual of Mental Disorders* (3rd edn, revised) (DSM–III–R). Washington, DC: APA.

Bellack, A. S. & Mueser, K. T. (1993) Psychosocial treatment for schizophrenia. *Schizophrenia Bulletin*, **19**, 317–338.

Clozapine Study Group (1993) The safety and efficacy of clozapine in severe treatment-resisant schizophrenic patients in the UK. *British Journal of Psychiatry*, **163**, 150–154.

Connelly, P. J. (1990) An audit of the use of antipsychotics in a geriatric psychiatry continuing care unit in Scotland. *International Journal of Geriatric Psychiatry*, **7**, 447–454.

Gerlach, J. (1991) New antipsychotics: classification, efficacy and adverse effects. *Schizophrenia Bulletin*, **17**, 289–309.

Goldberg, T. E., Greenburg, R. D. Griffin, S. J., *et al* (1993) The effect of clozapine on cognition and psychiatric symptoms in patients with schizophrenia. *British Journal of Psychiatry*, **162**, 43–48.

Gottlieb, G. L., McAllister, T. N. & Gur, R. (1988) Depot neuroleptics in the treatment of behavioural disorders in AD. *Journal of the American Geriatric Society*, **36**, 619–621.

Howard, R. & Levy, R. (1992) Which factors affect treatment response in late paraphrenia? *International Journal of Geriatric Psychiatry*, **9**, 415–417.

—— & Rabins, P. (1997) Late paraphrenia revisited. *British Journal of Psychiatry*, **171**, 406–408.

Jeste, D. V. & Wyatt, R. J. (1987) Aging and tardive dyskinesia. In *Schizophrenia and Aging* (eds N. E. Miller & G. D. Cohen), p. 275. New York: Guildford Press.

—— & Zisook, S. (eds)(1988) Psychosis and depression in the elderly. *Psychiatric Clinics of North America*, **11**, 1–33.

Kane, J., Honigfeld, G., Singer, J., *et al* (1988) Clozapine for the treatment resistant schizophrenic: a double-blind comparison versus chlorpromazine/benztropine. *Archives of General Psychiatry*, **45**, 789–796.

Katona, C. & Levy, R. (eds) (1992) *Delusions and Hallucinations in Old Age*. London: Gaskell.

Kay, D. W. K. & Roth, M. (1961) Environmental and hereditary factors in the schizophrenia of old age (late paraphrenia) and their bearings on the general problems of causation in schizophrenia. *Journal of Mental Sciences*, **107**, 649–686.

Kraepelin, E. (1909) *Psychiatrie, Ein Lehrbuch fur Studierende und Artzte* (8th edn). Leipzig: Barth.

Lee, M. A., Thompson, P. A. & Meltzer, H. Y. (1994) Effects of clozapine on cognitive function in schizophrenia. *Journal of Clinical Psychiatry*, **55** (suppl.), 82–87.

Liberman, R. P. & Corrigan, P. W. (1993) Designing new psychosocial treatments for schizophrenia. *Psychiatry*, **56**, 238–249.

Lohr, J. B. & Bracha, H. S. (1988) Association of psychosis and movement disorders in the elderly. *Psychiatric Clinics of North America*, **11**, 61–82.

Mayer, W. (1921) On paraphrenic psychoses. *Zentralblatt Gesamte Neurologie und Psychiatrie*, **71**, 187–206.

McKenna, P. J. & Bailey, P. E. (1993) The strange story of clozapine. *British Journal of Psychiatry*, **162**, 32–38.

Nygaard, H. A., Brudvik, O. B., Juvik, W. E., *et al* (1994) Consumption of psychotropic drugs in nursing home residents. *International Journal of Psychiatry*, **6**, 171–175.

Pearlson, G., Kreger, L., Rabins, P., *et al* (1989) A chart review study of late onset and early onset schizophrenia. *American Journal of Psychiatry*, **146**, 1568–1574.

Phanjoo, A. L. (1995) Novel antipsychotics in the elderly. In *Developments in Dementia and Functional Disorders in the Elderly* (eds R. Levy & R. Howard), pp. 151–166. Petersfield: Wrightson.

Post, F. (1966) *Persistent Persecutory States in the Elderly*. Oxford: Pergamon Press.

Roth, M. (1955) The natural history of mental disorder in old age. *Journal of Mental Science*, **101**, 281–292.

Schneider, L. S., Pollock, V. E. & Lyness, S. A. (1990) A meta analysis of controlled trials of neuroleptic treatment in dementia. *Journal of American Geriatric Society*, **38**, 553–563.

Szabadi, E. (1995) Adverse reaction profile of antipsychotic drugs. *Prescribers Journal*, **35**, 37–44.

World Health Organization (1992) *The Tenth Revision of the International Classification of Diseases and Related Health Problems* (ICD–10). Geneva: WHO.

Risk and childbirth in psychiatry

Margaret Oates

The relationship between childbirth and serious mental illness has been known since the time of ancient Greece. It was first described in the psychiatric literature by Esquirol and later by his pupil Marcé in 1857. A substantial number of women become mentally ill, often for the first time, following childbirth. There are few events associated with such a measurable and predictable risk to mental health as childbirth, with its nine months' warning. Despite this, there is little awareness among general psychiatrists of the predictable and manageable risk that faces many of their female patients should they become pregnant, or of the risks that mothers with mental illness may pose for their children.

This chapter discusses the likely contribution of childbirth and parity to the excess of affective morbidity in women. It considers the risks in women who were previously well and in those with pre-existing psychiatric disorder. It identifies predictive factors, and offers advice concerning risk management with mentally ill mothers and their children.

Classifying postpartum disorders

One of the reasons why childbirth-related psychiatric disorders attract little attention in general adult psychiatry may be that officially they do not exist. From ICD–7 and DSM–I onwards the special category of postpartum disorder disappeared.

The prevailing view is expressed in ICD–10 (World Health Organization, 1992), which states that "the clinical picture of puerperal psychosis is so rarely if ever reliably distinguishable from affective disorder or schizophrenia that a special category is not justified". This view largely results from earlier studies which showed that both the family history of affective disorder and the subsequent rates of affective illness in women who suffered from puerperal psychosis were similar to those who suffered from such an illness outside of childbirth. Childbirth was therefore seen as a life event, provoking illness in a vulnerable group, and

any distinctive clinical characteristics were seen as pathoplastic effects of childbirth. However, Kendell *et al* (1987) argue that the life event theory does not explain the dramatic increase in risk, particularly in the first 90 days following childbirth. Others (Kadrmas *et al*, 1979; Dean *et al*, 1989; Cooper & Murray, 1995) have suggested that women who have a first episode of severe affective illness following childbirth may have a greater risk of developing a further episode of illness following subsequent childbirths, and a lower order of risk following non-puerperal events.

Future research may reveal two groups of women who become mentally ill following childbirth: those whose mental illnesses are provoked by childbirth only, and those for whom childbirth is one of many events which may provoke such an illness. In the meantime, it would seem reasonable to define postnatal psychiatric disorder as a new episode of mental illness arising in temporal relationship to childbirth. It should be classified according to ICD–10 or DSM–IV (American Psychiatric Association, 1994) in a non-postpartum category but should receive an additional classification of a psychiatric disorder associated with childbirth.

Most of the studies referred to in this text, using standardised and operational clinical criteria, place postpartum psychiatric disorder within the spectrum of affective disorders. However, these diagnoses do not do justice to the condition's heterogeneity, lability and complexity, particularly with regard to postpartum psychoses. First-rank symptoms of schizophrenia are often present (Kadrmas *et al*, 1979) and may be sufficient to result in categorisation of the illness as 'schizoaffective'.

Risks for previously well mothers

Risks of depressive illness

A substantial proportion of the excess depressive morbidity in young married women is accounted

Table 1. Incidence of postnatal affective disorders	
Diagnosis	Rates (% of women delivered)
All types of depression	15–30
Major depressive illness	10
Major illness with melancholia	3–5
Referred to a psychiatrist	1.7
Admitted	0.4
Admitted, psychosis	0.2

for by childbirth. Ten per cent of women suffer from a postnatal depressive illness (DSM–III–R major depression; American Psychiatric Association, 1987). Between 3 and 5% of all women would satisfy the criteria for moderate to severe depressive illness following childbirth, which represents an increase in risk estimated at between five- and ten-fold (Cox et al, 1993). Two per 1000 women delivered are admitted to hospital suffering from non-psychotic conditions (Meltzer & Kumar, 1985; Kendell et al, 1987).

Risks of puerperal psychosis

It is now well established that a further two out of every 1000 women delivered are admitted to a psychiatric hospital suffering from puerperal psychosis. It is remarkable that the incidence has remained broadly constant for over a century and in different countries (Kendell et al, 1987). It is likely, therefore, that this incidence will be the same in the future. This figure represents a dramatic increase in risk compared with non-childbearing women (Kendell et al, 1987), although admission for puerperal psychosis remains relatively rare.

The majority of admissions for psychosis take place within 16 days of delivery and presentations of severe illness within 90 days. Risk is, therefore, highest in the first three months following delivery.

As well as the rate of admission, the rate of referral to psychiatric services is increased following childbirth (Kendell et al, 1987; Oates, 1988). The risk of a woman developing a bipolar illness in the first 90 days following delivery is said to be a 16-fold increase over lifetime risk, and the risk of admission for a psychotic episode to be a 32-fold increase in relative risk. The risk of a woman being referred to a psychiatrist in the year following childbirth is five times greater than at other times in her life (Oates, 1994).

Childbearing can thus be seen to pose a major risk to the mental health of women who were previously well. This risk is particularly high in Western societies for first childbirth.

Risks for those with pre-existing disorders

This section considers the risk to the mental health of a woman who is already suffering from a psychiatric disorder, or receiving treatment for it, at the time of conception, that is women with chronic or recurrent mental illnesses. This group of illnesses, therefore, encompasses the entire range of psychiatric conditions that afflict women during their reproductive life span.

Apart from depression and anxiety, the prevalence of a given condition in pregnancy is the same as it is in the general age-matched female population. Obvious exceptions include anorexia nervosa, which reduces fertility. Some epidemiological studies (Kendell et al, 1976) suggest that there may be a slight reduction in the prevalence of mental illness, as judged by contact rates with psychiatric services during pregnancy, including contacts for deliberate self-harm. Schizophrenia has also in the past been associated with reduced fertility (a contribution being made by neuroleptic medication). However, the move towards community care may result in an increase in reproductive activity in women with chronic psychiatric illness (Lane et al, 1992).

Women with chronic or episodic mental illness who become pregnant are the poor relations of those who develop postnatal disorders in terms of the amount of research effort and service provision they receive. It is common for a woman with severe mental illness to remain as an in-patient on a general adult psychiatric ward until she starts labour, following which her infant is usually cared for by others.

Manic–depressive psychosis

Woman with multiple episodes of bipolar disorder are probably not at increased risk of a deterioration in their state during pregnancy. However, they are at particularly high risk of having a puerperal relapse, perhaps as high as one in two (Wieck et al, 1991; Marks et al, 1992). This risk may be even higher if the disorder has been predominantly manic.

Schizophrenia

Women who suffer from paranoid schizophrenia with episodes of acute relapse may be at an equivalent risk of relapse following childbirth as those suffering from manic–depressive illness (Davies *et al*, 1995). However, in general, the risk for schizophrenic relapse during pregnancy or in the early months following delivery is not elevated (Kendell *et al*, 1987), provided that maintenance neuroleptic medication is continued.

Although the risk of relapse of a serious chronic or recurrent mental illness is not increased during pregnancy, such a relapse will have major implications for both the developing foetus and the newborn infant. Disturbed behaviour may severely compromise antenatal care and pose a direct and indirect risk to the baby through self-neglect, substance misuse, poor nutrition and hygiene, concealed pregnancies and unassisted delivery. In a small minority of cases, conception may occur while a patient is acutely psychotic, because of altered judgement or the inability to consent. In such cases the resultant distress may cause a deterioration in mental health.

Predicting postnatal psychiatric illness

Non-psychotic depressive illness

Research suggests that psychosocial factors are at least as important as, if not more important than, biological factors in the causation of major depressive illnesses in the puerperium.

The risk factors for mild depressive illness, dysthymia and adjustment problems in the puerperium include youth, being single, recent marriage, social adversity, recent life events, psychiatric history, lack of a female confidante, ambivalence about the baby, previous miscarriage or termination of pregnancy. It has been suggested by Elliott (1989) that women who have several of these risk factors suffer from twice as much postnatal depressive illness as those who do not. However, the majority of women who suffer from postnatal depressive illness following their first childbirth will not have been predicted, and the majority of women with identified risk factors will not go on to suffer from postnatal depression. Because these risk factors are relatively non-specific and widely found in the population they are useful for targeting groups of people for special resources rather than for predicting individuals at risk.

There may be a subgroup of severely ill patients for whom biological factors are in the ascendancy. They present within the first four weeks after birth with very severe postnatal depressive illnesses,

comprising one-third of all referred severe depressive illnesses (Kendell *et al*, 1987; Oates, 1988) (see Box 1).

Puerperal psychosis

The most consistent predictors from research are a family history of severe affective disorder and a prior history of psychiatric disorder. These patients are not otherwise distinguishable from the normal obstetric population. Studies from Western countries report first-time (probably emergency) Caesarean section as a risk factor for puerperal psychosis. It may be that high levels of obstetric concern during pregnancy and foetal loss are also risk factors. Some studies have reported a trend towards severe affective disorder being more common in women who are rather older and longer married at the time of their first pregnancy and therefore more likely to have had higher education. Large-scale studies have yet to be completed on the effects of new techniques, such as *in vitro* fertilisation, but the clinical impression from specialist services is that these women are more vulnerable to mental illness than women who conceive spontaneously.

Although factors such as previous severe unipolar or bipolar disorder or family history of severe affective disorder pose a high degree of risk, approximately 80% of women with severe affective disorder following their first childbirth have none of these risk factors. Puerperal psychosis will take most women, their families and their care-takers by surprise.

The prevailing opinion is that in the causation of puerperal psychoses, biological factors (including genetic factors) are likely to be as important if not more important than psychosocial and obstetric factors. The most plausible explanation for these conditions is that the majority of them are a variant of bipolar disorder and that the women carry this genetically determined susceptibility into childbirth, following which the illness is triggered by some factor. One explanation for this 'triggering' mechanism is development of a hypersensitivity of the central D_2 receptors, which may be related to the effects of oestrogen

---

Box 1. Risk factors for severe illness

Previous psychiatric history
Previous postnatal illness
Family history of affective disorders
Caesarean section (psychosis only)

withdrawal on the function of the dopamine systems. Other steroid hormones have also been implicated (Wieck, 1989).

Risk management

One of the main purposes of identifying risk factors for the development of common and serious illnesses is to be able to reduce risk to future maternal mental health and to the developing child (see Box 2). If possible, this primary prevention would be an unusual if not unique event in psychiatry.

Postnatal depression

In milder cases of postnatal depression it is generally assumed that psychosocial factors play the major role. A study of the effects of psychological intervention (modified antenatal classes) during pregnancy in an identified 'at-risk' population (Elliott, 1989) revealed a reduced rate of postnatal depression at three months, compared with those at-risk women who received standard care. Although these findings have yet to be replicated, they suggest that relatively simple intervention might reduce risk.

For those women with a previous history of early presentation of severe postnatal depressive illness it might appear rational to engage in primary prevention, using hormonal or psychotropic medication. However, there is little evidence from randomised controlled trials to support this strategy. None the less, women who have suffered

---

Box 2. Risk management in obstetrics

Pre-conception
Counselling 'at-risk' women

Booking clinic
Screen – for family history or past history of psychiatric disorder
Vigilance – depression, anxiety in pregnancy, infertility, complications in Caesarean section

After delivery
Monitor closely

Six-week postnatal examination
Screen all mothers for postnatal depression

---

from a previous episode of postnatal depression will approach their general practitioners for advice on the possibility of avoiding it after their next baby. In such cases it would be reasonable to start these women on a small dose of a suitable antidepressant (tricyclic if breast-feeding), gradually increasing the dose to the therapeutic range. Progesterone prophylaxis (Dalton, 1985) is popular but not of proven efficacy.

Secondary prevention of postnatal depression is a practical possibility. The postnatal examination carried out on all women in the UK at six weeks after birth should include either a brief routine clinical examination to detect depressive illness or the use of the Edinburgh Postnatal Depression Scale (Cox *et al*, 1987). Such a strategy would go a long way towards detecting the 10% of women likely to be suffering from postnatal depressive illness and would ensure early treatment of this condition, thus reducing avoidable and prolonged psychiatric morbidity and limiting the consequences for the child. Such early treatment for the more severe cases would include antidepressants, and for the less severe cases, non-directive counselling or a cognitive psychotherapeutic approach (Elliott, 1989; Appleby *et al*, 1997). A better understanding of the numerous psychosocial risk factors for the development of postnatal depressive illness would enable obstetricians, midwives, health visitors and general practitioners to be more aware of the vulnerable patients that they treat and more alert to the early signs of the illness, as well as to the possibility of reducing certain risk factors.

Puerperal psychosis and postpartum relapses of bipolar disorder

Some women at high risk of severe affective disorder, and in particular puerperal psychosis, can be identified at the booking clinic by virtue of a prior history of bipolar disorder (postnatal or non-postnatal) or a family history. Such women are at high risk (1 : 3 or 1 : 2) of becoming seriously ill in the first 90 days following childbirth, the maximum risk being in the first 16 days for puerperal psychosis.

A woman with a personal history of affective psychosis should be referred during her pregnancy to a psychiatrist with a special interest. This, at the very least, offers the psychiatrist a unique opportunity to know the patient when well and to engage in forward planning. It will also enable those caring for the patient, both professionals and family, to be alert and after delivery to watch for the early signs of the illness and to ensure prompt and appropriate treatment (secondary prevention).

At best, it offers the opportunity to engage in prophylactic treatment (primary prevention). Lithium carbonate, started on the first postpartum day, and aiming at a therapeutic level between day 3 and day 5, may prevent the onset of postpartum affective psychoses (Kadrmas *et al*, 1979; Stewart *et al*, 1991). However, this remains to be confirmed by randomised controlled trials. Alternatives, particularly for breast-feeding mothers, include using small doses of neuroleptic medication such as haloperidol or chlorpromazine. This regime should also begin on the first postpartum day. The findings of Wieck *et al* (1991) suggest a rationale of avoiding the postpartum drop in oestrogen levels. However, a trial of transdermal oestrogens in the prevention of recurrent postpartum psychosis has so far not shown this to be possible (Henderson *et al*, 1991). The use of progesterone, given intramuscularly before birth and rectally for a period of time afterwards, has much popular support (Dalton, 1985). However, neither its scientific basis nor its clinical effectiveness has been confirmed.

Implications for the general adult psychiatrist

One of the most important aspects of risk reduction is an awareness on the part of general adult psychiatrists that women with severe affective disorder or enduring mental health problems might become pregnant. Discussing contraception, the likely effects of pregnancy upon their mental health and their capacity to care adequately for their child physically and emotionally should be part of ordinary psychiatric practice.

Women with manic–depressive psychosis

The lithium that many women will be receiving to stabilise their mental state is potentially teratogenic. They should be advised to take contraceptives as long as they are taking lithium, and to plan their conceptions carefully so that lithium can be withdrawn before they conceive and be reinstated immediately following delivery.

Women with chronic schizophrenia

There is no evidence that neuroleptic medication is teratogenic. However, there is no information about the long-term effects on the developing child of having received such medication *in utero* or through breast milk. The theoretical risk of dopamine blockade in the developing foetus has to be balanced against the practical risk of a maternal relapse in pregnancy and the puerperium. As there is some evidence (Ruben, 1987) that babies born to mothers on large doses of neuroleptic medication may suffer from both anticholinergic and extrapyramidal side-effects, it would seem reasonable to reduce the neuroleptic medication to the lowest possible maintenance dose before delivery, increasing it again after delivery.

The most tangible risk to a mother with chronic schizophrenia is the stress and high expressed emotion involved in raising a small child. Clinical outcomes from mother and baby units which offer an assessment programme for mothers with enduring mental health problems suggest that the outcome for mothers suffering from chronic schizophrenia is poor, particularly if they are single and suffer from social adversity (Davies *et al*, 1995). Most of them are unable to care for their children upon leaving the unit, necessitating their removal into care. In order to minimise the risks to both mother and infant it would seem sensible for all general adult psychiatrists managing fertile women with chronic schizophrenia to include advice on contraception and pregnancy in their care programme approach, which will include a realistic appraisal of the woman's ability to meet the needs of her child. Her pregnancy should be collaboratively managed by the obstetrician and psychiatrist, with an early involvement of social services so that appropriate plans can be made for her and the infant's care following delivery. One such appropriate plan could be the admission of the mother/infant pair immediately following delivery to a mother and baby unit. Skilled staff can then undertake an assessment of her ability to care for her infant and of her needs to continue this care in the community. Such an admission would also serve to provide the new mother with an understanding environment in which she can develop the best possible attachment to her child and the skills she needs to care for it (Appleby & Dickens, 1993).

Risks to children

Effects on emotional development

The evidence for adverse effects on the well-being and development of the infant and child broadly comes from two different types of studies with different methodologies. The first follows-up the children of large numbers of parents with psychiatric illness, using indirect outcome measures such as health statistics and parents' and teachers' assessments. Similar methods have been used for prospective studies of women identified in antenatal clinics, comparing the outcome of children of mothers with postnatal depression with those of well mothers. In general, these studies reveal that there is an association between maternal psychiatric disorder and many parameters of childhood morbidity. Their findings support a view that the effects of maternal psychiatric disorder are strongly associated with social adversity and marital disharmony and that chronic disability and personality dysfunction are more important than single episodes in hospital suffering from a major psychiatric disorder (Harder, 1980).

The second kind of study, usually involving smaller numbers, involves the direct assessment of mother–infant interactions and infant and child development using naturalistic, observational techniques. Such studies consistently report the adverse effects of maternal depression on mother–infant attachment, the infant's social and language development and later cognitive development at school. This effect is particularly marked in boys and again appears to be strongest when associated with social adversity and marital conflict (Murray, 1992; Sharp *et al*, 1995).

Physical injury

Few studies have examined the psychiatric status of abusive parents using standardised criteria, but there is little evidence to implicate serious mental illness as a major contributor to non-accidental injury in children. The most consistent findings implicate parental youth, prematurity, previous abuse of the parents themselves and in men a previous criminal record for violence. On the other hand, mild depression and anxiety are commonplace in mothers who have abused their children (Oates, 1987).

Suicide and infanticide are rare but occasional consequences of puerperal psychosis and profound postnatal depression. Very occasionally a child is killed as the direct result of a delusional state in its parents. Numerically these cases are insignificant when compared with the numerous cases of non-accidental injury in small children in the population as a whole.

In contrast, most studies of those who kill their children reveal a significant minority of women with serious mental illness. The preliminary report of the Confidential Inquiry into Homicides & Suicides by Mentally Ill People (Steering Committee, 1994) found that a third of all such murders were committed by women and that 85% of their victims were their own children. A study of parental psychiatric disorder and fatal child

abuse (Falcov, 1996) found that 25% of the perpetrators had a mental illness (the majority of women). Of those who were ill 40% had schizophrenia, with high rates of service contact – only one individual was suffering from puerperal psychosis.

Reducing risks to children

Emotional damage

The most important factors in the reduction of risk to both child and mother from mental illness are prompt detection, early intervention and vigorous treatment of the maternal psychiatric disorder. Attention needs to be paid by those caring for the mother to her relationship with her child. Any specific problems with feeding, sleeping, the need for social support and marital work should be addressed.

Women who require hospitalisation following delivery should be admitted, if possible, to a specialist mother and baby unit, where the skills to manage the mother–infant relationship and meet the needs of the child will be found.

The less severe illnesses will usually be treated in the community. For serious depressive illness antidepressant medication will be a critical agent in recovery, whereas for less severe conditions psychological treatments may be at least as effective as antidepressants (Holden *et al*, 1989; Appleby *et al*, 1997). Counselling using a cognitive–behavioural approach may be helpful for mother–infant relationships. For all types of psychiatric disorder where physical contact is encouraged between mother and child, verbal and social interaction and breast-feeding (see Box 3) can help minimise the possibility of adverse sequelae.

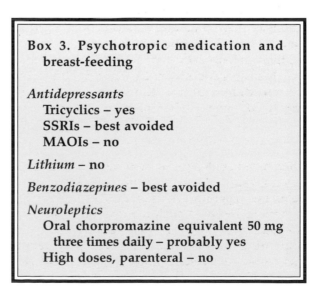

Box 3. Psychotropic medication and breast-feeding

Antidepressants
 Tricyclics – yes
 SSRIs – best avoided
 MAOIs – no

Lithium – no

Benzodiazepines – best avoided

Neuroleptics
 Oral chorpromazine equivalent 50 mg three times daily – probably yes
 High doses, parenteral – no

Physical injury

Although there is probably not an increased risk of child abuse in women with severe postnatal psychiatric disorder, complaints of irritability towards children and the expression by the mother of fears that she might harm her child should always be taken seriously, and discussions with the mother about her ability to care for her children and her feelings towards them should be part of every assessment.

References

American Psychiatric Association (1987) *Diagnostic and Statistical Manual of Mental Disorders* (3rd edn, revised) (DSM–III–R). Washington, DC: APA.

—— (1994) *Diagnostic and Statistical Manual of Mental Disorders* (4th edn) (DSM–IV). Washington, DC: APA.

Appleby, L. & Dickens, C. (1993) Mothering skills of women with mental illness. *British Medical Journal*, **306**, 348–349.

——, Warner, R., Whitton, A., *et al* (1997) A controlled study of fluoxetine and cognitive behavioural counselling in the treatment of postnatal depression. *British Medical Journal*, **314**, 932–936.

Cooper, P. J. & Murray, L. (1995) Course and recurrence of postnatal depression. Evidence for the specificity of the diagnostic concept. *British Journal of Psychiatry*, **166**, 191–195.

Cox, J. L., Holden, J. M. & Sagovsky, R. (1987) Detection of postnatal depression. Development of the 10-item Edinburgh Postnatal Depression Scale. *British Journal of Psychiatry*, **150**, 782–786.

——, Murray, D. & Chapman, G. (1993) A controlled study of the onset, duration and prevalence of postnatal depression. *British Journal of Psychiatry*, **163**, 27–31.

Dalton, K. (1985) Progesterone prophylaxis used successfully in postnatal depression. *Practitioner*, **229**, 507–508.

Davies, A., McIvor, R. I. & Kumar, R. (1995) Impact of childbirth on a series of schizophrenic mothers. *Schizophrenia Research*, **16**, 25–31.

Dean, C., Williams, R. J. & Brockington, I. F. (1989) Is puerperal psychosis the same as bipolar manic-depressive disorder? A family study. *Psychological Medicine*, **19**, 637–647.

Elliott, S. A. (1989) Psychological strategies in the prevention and treatment of postnatal depression. *Baillière's Clinical Obstetrics & Gynaecology*, **3**, 879–904.

Falcov, A. (1996) *Fatal Child Abuse & Parental Psychiatric Disorder*. Working Together Part 8 Reports. Department of Health ACPC Series, no. 1. London: HMSO.

Harder, D. W. (1980) Child competence and psychiatric risk, IV: Relationships of parent, diagnostic classification and parent psychopathology severity to child functioning. *Journal of Nervous and Mental Disease*, **186**, 343–347.

Henderson, A., Gregoire, A. & Kumar, R. C. (1991) Treatment of severe postnatal depression with oestradiol skin patches. *Lancet*, **338**, 816–817.

Holden, J. M., Sagovsky, R. & Cox, J. L. (1989) Counselling in a general practice setting: a controlled study of health visitors; intervention in treatment of postnatal depression. *British Medical Journal*, **298**, 223–226.

Kadrmas, A., Winokur, G. & Crowe, R. (1979) Postpartum mania. *British Journal of Psychiatry*, **135**, 551–554.

Kendell, R. E., Wainwright, S., Hailey, A., *et al* (1976) The influence of childbirth on psychiatric morbidity. *Psychological Medicine*, **6**, 297–307.

——, Chalmers, J. C., Platz, C. (1987) Epidemiology of puerperal psychoses. *British Journal of Psychiatry*, **150**, 662–673.

—— (1985) Pregnancy, childbirth and mental illness. In *Progress in Obstetrics and Gynaecology*, vol. 5 (ed. J. Studd), pp. 146–159. Edinburgh: Churchill Livingstone.

Lane, A., Mulvaney, M., Kinsella, A., *et al* (1992) Evidence of increased fertility in male schizophrenics. *Schizophrenia Research*, **6**, 94–99.

Marks, M. N., Wieck, A., Checkley, S. A., *et al* (1992) Contribution of psychological and social factors to psychotic and non-psychotic relapse after childbirth in women with previous histories of affective disorder. *Journal of Affective Disorder*, **29**, 253–263.

Meltzer, E. S. & Kumar, R. (1985) Puerperal mental illness, clinical features and classification: a study of 142 mother-and-baby admissions. *British Journal of Psychiatry*, **147**, 647–654.

Murray, L. (1992) The impact of postnatal depression on infant development. *Journal of Child Psychology and Psychiatry*, **33**, 543–562.

Oates, M. R. (1987) Different types of abusing parents. In *Understanding Child Abuse*, 2nd edn (ed. D. Jones), pp. 82–98. London: Hodder & Stoughton.

—— (1988) The development of an integrated community-orientated service for severe postnatal mental illness. In *Motherhood and Mental Illness*, vol. 2 (eds R. Kumar & I. F. Brockington), pp. 133–158. London: Wright.

—— (1994) Postnatal mental illness: organisation and function of a services. In *Perinatal Psychiatry: Use and Misuse of the Edinburgh Postnatal Depression Scale* (eds J. Cox. & J. Holden), pp. 8–33. London: Gaskell.

Ruben, P. C. (1987) *Prescribing in Pregnancy*. London: British Medical Association.

Sharp, D., Hay, D., Pawlby, S., *et al* (1995) The impact of postnatal depression on boys' intellectual development. *Journal of Child Psychology & Psychiatry*, **36**, 1315–1336.

Steering Committee of the Confidential Inquiry into Homicides & Suicides by Mentally Ill People (1994) *A Preliminary Report on Homicide*. London: Confidential Inquiry into Homicides & Suicides by Mentally Ill People.

Stewart, D. E., Klompenhouwer, J. L., Kendell, R. E., *et al* (1991) Prophylactic lithium in puerperal psychosis. The experience of three centres. *British Journal of Psychiatry*, **158**, 393–397.

Wieck, A. (1989) Endocrine aspects of postnatal mental disorders. *Baillières Clinical Obstetrics & Gynaecology*, **3**, 857–877.

——, Kumar, R., Hirst, A. D., *et al* (1991) Increased sensitivity of dopamine receptors and recurrence of affective psychosis after childbirth. *British Medical Journal*, **303**, 613–616.

World Health Organization (1992) *The ICD–10 Classification of Mental and Behavioural Disorders*. Geneva: WHO.

Fit to be interviewed by the police?

Keith J. B. Rix

Although police surgeons (or forensic medical examiners; FMEs) usually assess fitness to be interviewed by the police (Norfolk, 1996), psychiatrists may also be asked for an opinion (Protheroe & Roney, 1996).

Importance of fitness to be interviewed

Recent miscarriages of justice have occurred as a consequence of unreliable confessions to the police. A well-known illustration is the case of Engin Raghip, who was convicted of the murder in the Broadwater Farm riots of PC Blakelock. Prior to his trial it was known that he had a history of what were described as "serious learning difficulties" and had been recommended to attend a special school (Gudjonsson, 1992). His successful appeal (R v Raghip, 1991) turned on the evidence of Gudjonsson, a forensic psychologist responsible for research relating to factors such as suggestibility and compliance as they affect the reliability of confessions (Gudjonsson & MacKeith, 1988; Gudjonsson et al, 1993). His evidence included reference to Raghip having a verbal IQ of 73 and a performance IQ of 77.

The law on fitness to be interviewed

Although 'fitness to be interviewed' is not in the Police and Criminal Evidence Act 1984 (PACE) or its Codes of Practice (Home Office, 1995; hereafter, the Codes), except in relation to intoxication, it may arise as an issue in relation to PACE.

Section 76(2) allows the judge to exclude confession evidence if the prosecution cannot prove beyond reasonable doubt that it was not obtained by oppression or in consequence of anything said or done which was likely to have made it unreliable. Section 78(1) gives the judge discretion to exclude a confession when the defence can prove, on a balance of probabilities, that its admission would adversely affect the fairness of the proceedings. Relevant circumstances include psychiatric aspects of the accused. If attempts to have confession evidence excluded fail under sections 76 and 78, section 82(3) gives the judge further discretionary power to exclude evidence. There is also similar power under common law.

The Police and Criminal Evidence Act 1984 also includes specific provision for the mentally handicapped. The judge must warn the jury that there is special need for caution before convicting a mentally handicapped person if the confession was not made in the presence of an independent person and the case depends wholly or substantially on it. R. v. McKenzie (1992) established that when the prosecution's case depends wholly on a confession and the defendant suffers from "a degree of mental handicap" and the confession is "unconvincing to a point where a jury properly directed could not properly convict", the judge should withdraw the case from the jury. The law does not define "a degree of mental handicap".

Against this background, the police may seek an opinion on 'fitness to be interviewed'. This should be distinguished from the broader notion of the 'reliability' of interview material. Someone may be 'fit to be interviewed' but there might still be a question as to the degree of reliability that should be attributed to the interviews. The interviews might be removed from the trial entirely following a voir dire (see below), or there might be expert evidence that downgrades the evidential weight given to the interview within the trial and before the jury.

The police interview

When a possible crime has been committed the police gather evidence. They interview witnesses and suspects. If the suspect is charged, the interview is likely to become evidence. The prosecution may use it to try to prove guilt. The defence may either rebut it or attempt to use it to infer not the defendant's guilt but his or her innocence. Or they may use it to attempt to infer the defendant's guilt of a lesser offence, or that she or he has a psychiatric defence such as insanity or diminished responsibility.

Conduct of interviews is a subject of the Codes. Compliance should ensure that the courts have reliable, accurate and complete evidence. This reduces the likelihood of a miscarriage of justice. Interviews usually take place in designated rooms in police stations. Two police officers are present and both may ask questions. The suspect's legal representative may be present and, in some cases, an 'appropriate adult'. A solicitor may object to inappropriate questions or reference to matters not material to the enquiry. The appropriate adult may intervene if he thinks that a question is misleading or has not been understood. Subsequently, selective, typed transcripts are prepared. If necessary, complete transcripts can be prepared and part or all of the tapes may be played to assist a jury in reaching a verdict.

Provisions for mental disorder

Code C states that:

> "If an officer has any suspicion, or is told in good faith, that a person of any age may be mentally disordered or mentally handicapped, or mentally incapable of understanding the significance of questions put to him or his replies, then that person shall be treated as a mentally disordered or mentally handicapped person."

and

> "A... person who is mentally disordered or mentally handicapped, whether suspected or not, must not be interviewed... in the absence of the appropriate adult... "

Definitions of mental disorder and mental handicap

'Mental disorder' is as defined in section 1(2) of the Mental Health Act 1983:

> "mental illness, arrested or incomplete development of mind, psychopathic disorder and any other disorder or disability of mind."

The Code does not exclude substance-related disorders. 'Mental handicap' is different but calls for the same provision. Even if IQ test results are known before the interview, the courts do not adhere to IQ 69/70 as an absolute dividing line for identifying mental handicap. In R. *v.* Raghip (1991), the Court of Appeal judges stated that they were:

> "not attracted to the concept that the judicial approach to submissions under section 76(2)(b) should be governed by which side of an arbitrary line, whether at 69/70 or elsewhere, the IQ fell."

Role of the appropriate adult

The Code acknowledges that although

> "people who are mentally disordered or mentally handicapped are often capable of providing reliable evidence, they may without knowing or wishing to do so, be particularly prone in certain circumstances to provide information which is unreliable, misleading or self-incriminating."

Therefore:

> "special care should ... always be exercised in questioning such a person, and the appropriate adult should be involved, if there is any doubt about a person's ... mental state or capacity."

The Code states who can be an appropriate adult (Box 1) and advises that:

> "it may ... be more satisfactory ... if [he or she] is someone who has experience or training in their care rather than a relative."

It cannot be a solicitor or 'lay visitor' who is present at the police station in that capacity.

The Code states the role of the appropriate adult:

> "He is not expected to simply act as an observer ... the purposes ... are, first, to advise the person being questioned and to observe whether or not the interview is being conducted properly and fairly, and secondly, to facilitate communication."

Box 1. Paragraph 1.7(b) of Code C of the Police and Criminal Evidence Act 1984 states that 'the appropriate adult' means

A relative, guardian or other person responsible for his care or custody;

Someone who has experience of dealing with mentally disordered or mentally handicapped people but is not a police officer or employed by the police (such as an approved social worker as defined by the Mental Health Act 1983 or a specialist social worker); or

Failing either of the above, some other responsible adult aged 18 or over who is not a police officer or employed by the police

It is therefore necessary to see the suspect beforehand.

In R. *v.* Dutton (unreported case no. 4627.G1/87, details available from author), a 42-year-old man, who was born in a psychiatric ward where his mother was an in-patient, attended a residential school for retarded pupils and was considered mildly mentally handicapped with a mental age of 13 years and an IQ of 60, was convicted of sexual offences. The trial judge acknowledged that the police should have requested an appropriate adult for the interview with a prisoner whom they knew had attended a school for retarded pupils and been subject to a hospital order under the Mental Health Act. However, he allowed the confession evidence to be put to the jury. The appellant successfully appealed against conviction and the Court of Appeal judges explained:

"... paragraph C13 is intended to deal with ... an interview by the police of a person who is mentally handicapped or at least probably so. It is notorious that such people may be prone to fantasize and may on occasions admit to crimes they have not committed ... we believe that ... (a) the appropriate adult would, before the police interview, have ascertained ... quietly and without any pressure, what he wished to say; and/or (b) ... ensured that Mr Dutton had the advice of a solicitor before he was interviewed. It follows that if Mr Dutton had been accorded the assistance of a responsible adult, he might well have made no admission at all. Certainly, we cannot be sure that he would nevertheless have made the admissions he did make."

Assessing fitness

Preparation

The psychiatrist should obtain as much information as possible before seeing the suspect (Box 2). If the suspect is in police custody, there may be time constraints imposed by compliance with PACE ('the PACE clock').

The custody record details what happens to the person in custody and is used to prompt and record compliance with PACE. The records of assessments and reviews may give clues concerning the mental state of the suspect. Many decisions about fitness to be interviewed are made by FMEs. Discussion with the FME may not only assist the psychiatrist in addressing the issue but the FME will usually be more familiar with police procedures and PACE. With modern electronic communications it is occasionally possible to have access to a suspect's medical records with his or her consent.

Consent

The suspect is under no obligation to undergo psychiatric examination, whether at the request of the police or his own solicitors. However, few refuse. As in any medical consultation, consent, which does not need to be written, must be based on a proper understanding of the nature and purpose of the consultation and must be freely given.

The psychiatrist introduces himself and where he works, and explains who has requested that he attend, referring to his provision of a second opinion on the suspect's health so as to advise the police officers who question and look after the suspect. Impartiality and independence are explained, reference is made to the records, their location, their evidential status, their availability to both the prosecution and the defence and how anything said about the alleged offence may be used at trial. The suspect is advised that he does not have to say anything about the alleged offence. Finally, the psychiatrist explains that he will write a brief summary in the custody record where it can be read by the custody and interviewing officers and by the suspect's own solicitor, and later, if requested, prepare a report or statement for the police, the Crown Prosecution Service or the suspect's solicitors.

The suspect is asked whether he understands, questions are answered and with agreement the examination proceeds.

Setting

The examination will usually be in the FME's room. If not, the psychiatrist should insist on a room with chairs and a desk or table. Exceptionally, a police officer may be present. Solicitors have no right to be present but the doctor has no right to exclude them, particularly if the suspect wants the solicitor to be present. The solicitor can usually accept exclusion if either the psychiatrist indicates that his records will be available or if the psychiatrist agrees not to ask about the alleged offence.

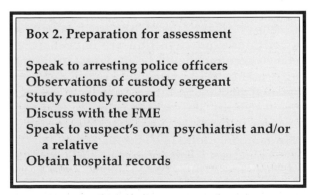

Box 2. Preparation for assessment

Speak to arresting police officers
Observations of custody sergeant
Study custody record
Discuss with the FME
Speak to suspect's own psychiatrist and/or
   a relative
Obtain hospital records

Format of the examination

Flexibility is important. Slavish adherence to a scheme can be counter-productive. Psychiatrists who are frequently called to police stations develop their own styles. Nevertheless, there is much to be said for history, mental state and physical examination.

In view of the importance of the suspect's ability to understand the police caution in assessing fitness to be interviewed (Gudjonsson, 1995), an important aspect of the psychiatric examination is the suspect's ability to understand the psychiatrist's explanation. In the case of a woman with an IQ of 73 who was aged 19 years and was six months pregnant when charged with murder (R. *v.* McGovern, 1990), it was part of her successful appeal against conviction for manslaughter that the incriminating confession occurred without a solicitor when she was

"physically ill, emotionally distressed and unable to understand the caution until it was explained in simple language."

The first element of the history is the arrest. Sensitive and empathic questioning about this helps establish rapport through focus on the suspect's current distress. Also, there may be clues at this stage concerning disorientation, memory impairment or clouding of consciousness.

An account is taken of the family and personal history, including recent life events and circumstances. Enquiry about special schooling, reading or writing difficulties and extra tuition or special classes may identify those with learning difficulties. Personality is assessed. Submissiveness, compliance with authority figures and dependence on others may point to suggestibility and compliance, which can affect reliability. While taking a history, the psychiatrist notes the intellect of the person and notes how easily he or she understands questions.

An account of the suspect's medical and psychiatric history is obtained with enquiry as to current physical symptoms. Evidence for physical illness in the appeal of McGovern was that she had been vomiting in her cell before the interview.

Mental state examination begins as soon as the suspect enters the room. Relevant observations can be made under the usual headings. Form of thought or speech, mood, abnormal beliefs or perceptions, and cognition are important. A detailed account should be recorded, including performance on any tests of intelligence or cognition. Standardised tests have the advantage of repeatability and help to compare findings. However, tests of more immediate relevance may assist more (Norfolk, 1997; Box 3).

In some cases reliability may be challenged on the basis of the suspect's suggestibility, compliance

---

> **Box 3. Norfolk's suggestions for assessing cognition and intellect**
>
> *Is he aware of why he is at the police station?*
>
> *Does he understand his rights?*
> **Do you need money in order to have a solicitor help you at the police station?**
> **If you don't want a solicitor to help you now, can you change your mind later?**
>
> *Does he understand the police caution?*
> **('You do not have to say anything. But it may harm your defence if you do not mention when questioned something which you later rely on in court. Anything you do say may be given in evidence.')**

---

or intelligence. Tests are available to measure these. However, psychiatrists would be wise to avoid the use of psychological tests with which they are not familiar. In order to examine the reliability of the interview, further and more expert assessment may be essential. Proper assessment of compliance, suggestibility or acquiescence depends on sophisticated assessment of 'traits' by a psychologist. Part of the assessment of reliability involves relating such traits to the actual interviews in order to show whether or not they are unreliable as a consequence of their influence.

The FME may have conducted a physical examination but the psychiatrist should be equipped to do so. This is particularly important when an organic disorder is suspected, or if the suspect may be under the influence of, or withdrawing from, intoxicants.

Psychiatric disorders affecting fitness to be interviewed

Only exceptionally may a 'person who is unfit through drink or drugs to the extent that he is unable to appreciate the significance of questions put to him and his answers' (Code C, 12.3; Home Office, 1995) be interviewed. In such a circumstance it is likely that an FME will have advised, but occasionally the psychiatrist may suspect intoxication which has been missed.

Box 4 lists psychiatric disorders that, in most cases, will render a suspect unfit to be interviewed because there would be a substantial risk of an unreliable confession. It is not an exhaustive list.

The criterion should probably be that the person's mental state is such that there is a substantial risk that reliance on their answers to questions put by the police could result in a miscarriage of justice.

Box 5 lists psychiatric disorders that may make a suspect vulnerable but do not necessarily lead to 'strictly inadmissible' evidence if an appropriate adult is present. Even in the presence of mental disorder the courts may rely on interviews with mentally disordered persons in the absence of an appropriate adult if a doctor assessed the suspect first and was satisfied that he or she was fit to be interviewed and this opinion can be sustained. In R. *v.* Crampton (1990), an unsuccessful appeal was made by a drug addict whose incriminating admission had been made when he was withdrawing from opioid drugs. It was ruled:

> "Whether or not someone who is a drug addict is fit to be interviewed, in the sense that his answers can be relied upon as being truthful, is a matter for judgment of those present at the time."

Other relevant factors affecting fitness to be interviewed

Gudjonsson (1992) has identified three types of false confession: voluntary, coerced–compliant and coerced–internalised. His voluntary type is illustrated by the person with schizophrenia who is deluded concerning his involvement in a crime, or the person with a depressive illness who makes a false confession as a means of expiating guilt. Routine psychiatric assessment ought to identify these. The other types may not be so readily recognisable and considerations concerning their reliability may require psychological assessment.

Although a psychiatrist may be able to make a preliminary assessment of IQ or personality characteristics such as compliance and suggestibility, these areas should be explored by a psychologist who can also administer the Gudjonsson Suggestibility Scales (Gudjonsson, 1984; 1987) and Compliance Questionnaire (Gudjonsson, 1989). These instruments are useful in assessing

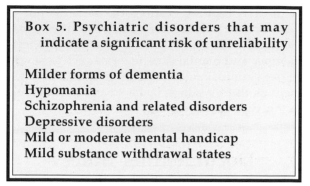

Box 5. Psychiatric disorders that may indicate a significant risk of unreliability

Milder forms of dementia
Hypomania
Schizophrenia and related disorders
Depressive disorders
Mild or moderate mental handicap
Mild substance withdrawal states

those who make a coerced–compliant false confession, where the main feature is the need to escape from a stressful or intolerable situation. Gudjonsson (1992) has identified factors that make people vulnerable to this type of confession. They include fear of being locked in a cell, and mental states that may interfere with coping mechanisms, such as extreme anxiety, depression and bereavement.

The Codes are intended to prevent admissions being made by suspects subject to physical discomfort, pain or exhaustion, which may also lead to coerced–compliant false confessions. Code C lays down requirements concerning heating, cleaning, ventilation and lighting of cells. It calls for particular care when deciding about using handcuffs with mentally handicapped persons. It specifies standards with regard to bedding, requirements as to toilet and washing facilities, clothing for the interview, refreshment, medical attention in the case of suspected illness or injury, even if the detainee does not request it, and rest. The suspect should be asked about the conditions, how he feels about being in custody, how he is drinking, eating and sleeping, and noting any concern about which immediate representation could be made and later reference made if there is an issue of an unreliable confession.

In the case of R. *v.* Delaney (1988) a 17-year-old educationally subnormal man had his conviction for indecent assault quashed. The court heard that he had an IQ of 80 and his emotional arousal was such that he might wish to rid himself of an interview as rapidly as possible. The Court of Appeal judges ruled that:

> "the [trial] judge ... should have ruled against the admission of these confessions, particularly so against the background of the appellant's age, his subnormal mentality and the behaviour of the police and what they admittedly said to him."

Coerced–internalised false confessions are related to the 'memory distrust syndrome', in which people distrust their own memories and

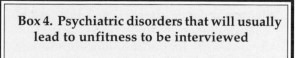

Box 4. Psychiatric disorders that will usually lead to unfitness to be interviewed

Acute organic reactions (including severe alcohol or drug withdrawal states)
Mania
Severe dementia
Severe mental handicap

begin to accept suggestions or scenarios put to them by their interrogators. Gudjonsson (1992) has identified a history of mental trauma which affects memory and mental state features such as severe anxiety, confusion, feelings of guilt and bereavement as factors which make suspects vulnerable to this type of confession.

Documenting fitness

Clinical records should bear the date and time. The psychiatrist must indicate in the custody record the location of the notes. The Codes require this. The psychiatrist should indicate whether or not the person is fit to be interviewed and, if fit, whether or not the interview should be in the presence of an appropriate adult. It may be appropriate to mention any special precautions for the police (such as keeping language simple) or the appropriate adult (such as being ready to intervene if particular delusional material begins to be introduced).

The records should be kept at least until the trial and in case there is an appeal it may be necessary to keep them for some years. The clinical records, if requested, must be disclosed by the prosecution to the defence.

If the Crown Prosecution Service considers that more information is needed about the basis or significance of the psychiatrist's opinion, he may be asked to prepare a report or a Criminal Justice Act statement (Hiscox & Davies, 1995). This should be in the form of evidence as it might be given orally at the trial. Box 6 suggests a format.

Limits of expertise

There are limits to how far fitness to be interviewed can be explored in the police station. Specialist registrars should not hesitate to consult the consultant or the consultant indicate that there is some aspect which ought to be addressed later by a consultant in, for example, old age psychiatry or learning disability.

In R. *v.* Heaton (1993), in which the defendant was convicted of the manslaughter of his child, the Court of Appeal upheld the trial judge's decision to exclude the evidence of a psychiatrist who stated, from a single interview, that the defendant was "not exceptionally bright," of "dull normal intelligence and is highly suggestible". Collins (1995) has advised barristers:

"unless the expert evidence is based on some scientific data or expert analysis outside the experience of the

judge and jury, a mere impression even of a highly qualified doctor will not be admissible [and] one interview by the expert might not be sufficient."

It may be appropriate to recommend examination by a forensic psychiatrist or a forensic psychologist. However, it is important to remember 'the PACE clock'. An opinion on fitness to be interviewed needs to be communicated in time for the police to comply with time limits.

With the benefit of hindsight and in light of subsequent reports by experts, the psychiatrist may have doubts about his opinion. If the psychiatrist is honest and can justify the decision reached at the time, he is unlikely to be criticised. He should

---

Box 6. Format for a statement or report on fitness to be interviewed.

Introduction
Full name, date of birth and address of suspect
Full name, qualifications (including Section 12 status) and professional address of psychiatrist
Where, when and at what time the suspect was examined
Name of anyone else present
At whose request the examination was carried out

Statement of suspect's consent to examination

Basis of opinion
History and examination
Any other relevant history (e.g. police officers, family)
Medical records or other psychiatrists consulted

Diagnosis **(including its justification) explained in lay terms**

Whether or not suspect is fit to be interviewed

Reasons for opinion **(usually only if considered unfit to be interviewed)**

If fit to be interviewed
Whether or not an appropriate adult should be present
Any assistance for police and/or appropriate adult to enhance reliability

Any recommendations as to re-examination (if unfitness is likely to be temporary)

Any recommendations as to examination by other psychiatrists or psychologists pre-trial

admit these doubts and allow the judge to decide whether or not to admit the interview as evidence.

Going to court

In cases in which there is an issue concerning fitness to be interviewed or reliability, the judge usually hears arguments at a 'trial within a trial' or *voir dire* and in the absence of the jury. The judge may listen to the interviews and may hear evidence from those who examined the defendant, police officers, the appropriate adult and experts subsequently instructed. The judge then hears arguments by prosecuting counsel and defence counsel as to whether or not the interviews can be admitted and put before the jury. A psychiatrist called to give evidence at such a trial should not hesitate to admit the limits of his expertise. If he has retained legible, detailed, contemporaneous records of the history and mental state, those with greater expertise will be assisted in giving their opinion as to the admissibility or reliability of the interview.

If there are breaches of PACE and they are "significant and substantial" (R. *v.* Absolam, 1988) then, *prima facie*, the evidence obtained in consequence ought to be excluded. It does not matter whether the police acted in good or bad faith. If the judge rules the interview evidence inadmissible, the prosecution may take the opportunity to offer no further evidence and the defendant is acquitted. If the judge rules that the jury would be assisted by experts in understanding the mental state of the defendant at the time of the interview, and thus assisted in determining the evidential weight to be placed on the admissions, they may be called again to give evidence before the jury.

Conclusions

Although the Court of Appeal has considered a number of cases in which fitness to be interviewed by the police is an issue, it is unwise to draw any definite conclusions of law or principle from these decisions. These cases have tended to turn on their own facts and not lay down any specific principle.

The expression "such an adverse effect on the fairness of the proceedings" (s. 78, PACE) requires the judge to look at the circumstances (including any breaches) in the round. He has a very wide discretion as to what evidence he does or does not admit. Where breaches of PACE are established, it makes it difficult but by no means impossible for him to exercise his discretion against a defendant. Whether or not breaches are established, it is in practice very difficult to challenge such an exercise of discretion on appeal.

For the psychiatrist the determination of fitness to be interviewed calls for the highest standards of history-taking and examination, supplemented by the careful consideration of relevant information from appropriate written and oral sources. Upon this assessment may hinge the decision of the court to convict the guilty or acquit the innocent.

References

*Collins, J. (1995) *Confessions by Mentally Handicapped Persons*. Archbold Practical Research Papers. London: Sweet and Maxwell.

Gudjonsson, G. (1984) A new scale of interrogative suggestibility. *Personality and Individual Differences*, **5**, 303–314.

—— (1987) A parallel form of the Gudjonsson Suggestibility Scale. *British Journal of Clinical Psychology*, **26**, 215–221.

—— (1989) Compliance in an interrogation situation: A new scale. *Personality and Individual Differences*, **10**, 535–540.

—— (1992) *The Psychology of Interrogations, Confessions and Testimony*. Chichester: Wiley.

—— (1995) 'Fitness for interview' during police detention: A conceptual framework for forensic assessment. *Journal of Forensic Psychiatry*, **6**, 185–197.

*—— & MacKeith, J. A. C. (1988) Retracted confessions: Legal, psychological and psychiatric aspects. *Medicine, Science and the Law*, **28**, 187–194.

——, Clare, I., Rutter, S., *et al* (1993) *Persons at Risk During Interview in Police Custody: The Identification of Vulnerabilities*. Research Study No. 12, Royal Commission on Criminal Justice. London: HMSO.

Hiscox, J. & Davies, H. de le Haye (1995) Section 9 police statement: A guide for junior doctors. *British Journal of Hospital Medicine*, **53**, 283–287.

Home Office (1995) *Police and Criminal Evidence Act 1994 (s.60(1)(a) and s.66) Codes of Practice*. London: Her Majesty's Stationery Office.

Norfolk, G. (1996) Fitness to be interviewed and the appropriate adult scheme: A survey of police surgeons' attitudes. *Journal of Clinical Forensic Medicine*, **3**, 9–13.

—— (1997) 'Fitness to be interviewed' – a proposed definition and scheme of examination. *Medicine, Science and the Law*, **37**, 228–234.

Protheroe, D. & Roney, G. (1996) Assessing detainees' fitness to be interviewed. Implications for senior registrars' training. *Psychiatric Bulletin*, **20**, 104–105.

* indicates articles of particular interest

Law reports

R. *v.* Absolam (1988) *Criminal Appeal Reports*, **88**, 332.

R. *v.* Crampton (1990) *Criminal Appeal Reports*, **92**, 369.

R. *v.* Delaney (1988) *Criminal Appeal Reports*, **88**, 338.

R. *v.* Heaton (1993) *Criminal Law Review*, 593.

R. *v.* McGovern (1990) *Criminal Appeal Reports*, **92**, 228.

R. *v.* McKenzie (1992) *The Independent*, 28 July.

R. *v.* Raghip (1991) *The Times Law Reports*, 6 December.

Preparing a medico-legal report

Robert Bluglass

Preparation of medico-legal reports is an increasingly important responsibility for the psychiatrist as legislation and administrative regulations become more complex and litigation increases.

The report may be prepared by a patient's consultant (or responsible medical officer) who has a specialised knowledge of the patient's history, illness, care and treatment, or by a psychiatrist acting as an independent expert who is providing an evaluation to assist a court or other tribunal.

Examples of the first category include reports required routinely under the provisions of the Mental Health Act 1983 (Box 1), reports to the coroner following sudden death, and reports to a tribunal of inquiry following a serious incident involving a patient or a hospital.

The second category includes cases such as the assessment of a person of whom the psychiatrist has no previous knowledge, and who is charged with an alleged offence and suspected of suffering from a form of mental disorder. Other examples include the request for an independent assessment by an applicant to a mental health review tribunal, the provision of an opinion for a hospital trust or patient with reference to an allegation of medical or nursing negligence, the assessment of a plaintiff claiming compensatory damages resulting from an accident or injury (on behalf of either the plaintiff or the defendant), or the provision of evidence of good psychiatric practice in less common actions such as libel suits involving medical practitioners.

Psychiatrists are often required to assist in criminal or civil proceedings and take the role of either a professional or an expert witness, depending upon the function they have been requested to perform.

If the psychiatrist is providing a report relating to facts of which he has prior knowledge, he is usually acting as a professional witness. The expert provides evidence which is outside the experience of a court, judge or jury. When acting as a professional witness, the psychiatrist may also be invited to give an opinion upon the inference to be drawn from the facts which he reports, and so take on the role of expert. Experts acting in an independent capacity will usually not know the subject or circumstances previously.

The general rule relating to evidence is that witnesses give evidence on facts, while the inference to be drawn from these facts is a matter for the judge or jury. If the witness offers an opinion, the function of the jury is usurped. There are, however, exceptions to this rule. The opinion of experts is admissible where competency to form an opinion upon a subject can only be acquired by a course of special study, and where the judge or jury could not otherwise form an opinion. The scope and limitations of expert opinion are established by the law of evidence of each jurisdiction (there are differences between the jurisdictions of the UK; see for example May (1998)). It is helpful to have some basic understanding of these rules, which indicate what evidence is admissible and what should be avoided and may lead to objection in court. Although 'hearsay' is usually inadmissible by witnesses as to fact (e.g. what a witness reports someone else told him), more flexibility is accepted in a psychiatric report if it can be justified to support the assessment. Clearly the account given to the doctor by a patient is crucial in determining a diagnosis.

Psychiatrists assisting criminal courts most commonly provide a medico-legal report about disposal following conviction and may, for example, ask for a hospital order or probation order with a requirement of treatment as an alternative to any other disposal the court may have in mind. There

> **Box 1. Examples of reports required under the Mental Health Act 1983**
>
> Managers' application
> Mental health review tribunals
> Reports to Home Secretary on restricted patients
> Recommendation to transfer convicted or remanded prisoners to hospital
> Court protection
> Supervised discharge review (subject to legislation)

> **Box 2. Matters requiring expert opinion in the criminal court**
>
> Fitness to appear in court
> Fitness to plead and stand trial
> Criminal responsibility of defendant
> Insanity
> Diminished responsibility
> Infanticide
> Automatism
> Effects of drugs or medication
> Disposal of convicted defendant
> Fitness of a witness to give reliable evidence

are, however, a range of other issues which also often require an opinion (see Box 2). The list provided is not exhaustive. For civil proceedings some of the issues which often require expert opinion are summarised in Box 3. The rules of evidence differ between criminal and other courts or tribunals.

General principles

The opinion provided in a medico-legal report is dependent upon the accuracy and validity of the facts upon which it is based. The facts will usually result from the examination of a patient, reading of papers and interviews with relatives or others.

Interviewing the patient

It is important to allow sufficient time for the interview of the patient and to extend it to more than one session if necessary. When the examination is for an expert opinion, this should be made clear to the patient. He should understand that the interview is for a medico-legal report, not a diagnostic opinion or for the prospect of treatment. The normal expectation of confidentiality between doctor and patient does not exist, or is limited, and the report may be seen by others including a solicitor, judge, counsel or others. The patient should understand the purpose of the interview, who has requested it, and to whom the doctor will report.

The examiner is not an advocate representing a client's interests but an independent medical expert who will be as dispassionate as he can. It is the lawyers whose principal duty is to represent their client's best interests as they see it. The psychiatrist reporting to one side or the other may find it difficult to maintain his objectivity once he is drawn into the complexities of adversarial legal conflict, but he should always endeavour to do so. Ways of rationalising the use of experts in the judicial system and ensuring their independence are currently under discussion.

Where appropriate, the psychiatric interview should be followed by a physical examination and any necessary tests. These procedures may require further time to be spent on preparation of the report.

Interviewing third-party members

It is also valuable as a routine to request an interview with a spouse or close relative who may be able to give an independent view of the patient's background and usual behaviour or performance.

Depending upon the nature of the report, the examiner will be provided with papers to study and digest. These may be voluminous, including reports from other specialists or hospital records, school reports, statements or depositions (witness statements). It is important to request whatever might be relevant if not provided. In criminal cases there are sometimes audio-tapes, and in compensation claims video surveillance cassettes may be available. Although sometimes difficult, the examiner should negotiate sufficient time to examine all this material carefully. It is unwise to depend upon the analyses of documentation undertaken by other experts involved in the case. Medical records often reveal important historical material, descriptions of behaviour or of treatment which may substantially differ from the account given by the subject and shed a different light on the case.

Structure of the report

The format of the report will vary depending on whether it is for a tribunal, statutory body or a

> **Box 3. Issues requiring expert opinion in the civil court**
>
> Compensation claims following injury or neglect
> Medical negligence and failure of duty of care
> Professional competence (doctor or other professional)
> Reports for children and youth courts
> Other litigation

court. If it is for legal proceedings, the content will vary between criminal and civil actions, but general principles apply.

Jargon-free language

It is important to bear in mind that a medico-legal report is usually an opinion addressed to laymen who are not themselves experts. Although lawyers and judges who frequently deal with medical matters gain a knowledge of psychiatric termin-ology, it can often be inaccurate and no assum-ptions should be made. The report should be written in clear and understandable English, with as little use of technical terms and professional jargon as possible. When a technical term is used it must always be explained (in parentheses if necessary) in a manner that can be easily under-stood. The writer should edit the report to ensure that any terms that have slipped in inadvertently, such as 'psychotic' or 'delusion', are qualified.

Facts v. opinion

Whatever the purpose of the report, the author should remember that opinion should be clearly differentiated from the facts upon which the report is based. The facts include the undisputed back-ground information, the history and the examin-ation findings. The opinion is the expert evaluation of the significance of these facts, together with a conclusion which should include specific recom-mendations relevant to the issue in hand and, if appropriate, an assessment of risk or danger-ousness and prognosis for the future. It is import-ant to remember that negative findings are of as much value to the judicial process as positive ones.

Keep to your subject

The psychiatrist should not stray beyond his expertise to provide an opinion upon matters about which he is unable to demonstrate special qualific-ation or experience, such as orthopaedics or cardiology.

Independence

The author should try to be as independent and unbiased as possible. A report requested on behalf of a plaintiff or a defendant does not imply that the psychiatrist has a responsibility to help to obtain damages or gain an acquittal. These are matters that concern the lawyers. If the conclusion does not assist the client, then the report may or may not be used. It may well, however, have assisted those who requested it in understanding the reality of the case.

Length of the report

The report should be comprehensive without being unnecessarily wordy and over-inclusive. Its length should be dictated by the complexity of the matter under consideration. This is a delicate balance to get right; reports of exceptional brevity are usually of little value. It is important to be clear at the outset what the issues in a particular case are and, if the report has been requested from an outside agent, to read the requesting letter from time to time to ensure that the issues are well in mind when writing the report and to check that they have been clearly addressed.

Layout of the report

No particular format is essential, but the following guidance may be helpful and is often adopted by those regularly preparing medico-legal reports (see also Box 4).

1. The report should be typed on A4 paper, using double or 1½-line spacing, with one-inch margins.

2. The first page should show:
(a) The name of the subject (and sometimes date of birth).
(b) A short summary indicating the purpose of the report, e.g. 'This report is prepared at your request to provide a psychiatric opinion upon Mr A.B. who was involved in a road traffic accident on 1 October 1994'.
(c) A paragraph indicating the source materials which provided the background to the report, listing all those interviewed, with dates and place of interview, and listing all the documents, materials, tapes and reports in the order in which they were examined. In civil cases solicitors may ask for this list to be omitted so long as the decision has not been made to disclose to the other party all the documents supplied to the expert.

3. A brief description of the subject of the report should be made, e.g. 'Mr A.B. is an unmarried man of 45 years of age, of Indian background, who is employed as a fitter'.

4. Indication should be given that the subject has understood the purpose of the interview and to whom the report will be sent.

5. The personal history of the subject should be provided with appropriate headings, in order that each section may easily be accessed and referenced by those using the report, e.g. 'family history', 'previous medical history', etc. Reference may be made to the source of information such as general practitioner records or specific hospital case notes in the text if the information does not derive from the interview with the person himself.

6. A previous history which is particularly relevant to the issue might be discussed under a separate heading, e.g. 'psychiatric history', relating to episodes of illness, treatment and outcome, serial admissions to psychiatric hospitals or referral to psychiatrists for assessment. A history of drinking behaviour, substance misuse, or of sexual problems may also merit a separate section. In criminal cases the history of delinquency is likely to be relevant and may not necessarily be consistent with a criminal record provided.

7. The background established above may conflict with information obtained from witnesses in statements provided or by interviews with relatives or others. These differences may be of minor significance and in appropriate cases, such as civil actions, may be reconciled before a final revised report is produced. The expert may draw attention at this stage to chronological or other anomalies remembering that this part of the report is concerned with the description of facts and not opinion.

8. The next section should report the account provided by the patient of his recollection of the matter with which the report is concerned (e.g. alleged criminal behaviour; accident; a medical treatment received; response to treatment and any previous assessment).

9. The report should continue with the findings arising from the psychiatric assessment of the patient, including positive and negative findings, describing the results of a comprehensive mental state assessment, and relevant observations of the presentation of the patient during the interview and the manner in which he gave his history and responded to questioning.

10. It can sometimes be helpful to the reader to include at this stage a discussion bringing together the salient points, explaining the relationship between them, and explaining in lucid terms complicated material. This section is often unnecessary but should be considered to assist lay readers in complex cases where the author wishes to draw attention to conflicting findings and their significance, to emphasise discrepancies or to discuss possible psychopathology before moving to the final opinion.

11. Having presented the facts and discussed the important principles in the report, the author should now give his opinion under a separate heading. The structure of this section, which can conveniently be laid out in numbered paragraphs, will of course depend upon the issues being addressed in the report. It is important not to confine the opinion to a few lines, but to range widely providing reasonable justification for conclusions and dealing with each important matter separately. For example, in a claim for compensation following injury, the history, previous personality and behaviour of the subject might be discussed first. A description of the psychological injuries resulting from the accident might follow, with an opinion on the nature of the patient's suffering, the longer-term disabilities and the degree of loss of function. An evaluation of the suffering and reduction in lifestyle compared with the pre-accident condition of the patient should be made.

The report should discuss the prognosis, likely response to treatment and, if it is possible to do so, the extent to which the accident is responsible for the present state. Any previous evidence of

---

Box 4. Layout of a medico-legal report

Topic of report
Introduction
When and where interviewed
Others interviewed
Papers, reports, documents examined
Brief description of subject
Patient's understanding of the interview
Personal history – childhood, education, employment, marital and sexual history, drinking behaviour, substance misuse, etc.
Family history
Previous medical history
Previous psychiatric history
Specific topics of relevance
Patient's account of matter under consideration
Examination
Discussion
Opinion
Name, qualifications and main appointment
Date

psychiatric illness may weigh against the case of the accident being totally, or even partially, responsible for the change in the patient's condition.

In criminal cases, a discussion of criminal responsibility with any indication of factors which might reduce or mitigate it should precede recommendations regarding disposal. Disposals should clearly indicate whether or not arrangements can be made for admission to hospital or for a form of treatment.

12. The report should conclude with the author's name, qualifications and principal appointment. In civil rather than in criminal cases, a brief curriculum vitae of the author may be requested; this can be sent on a separate sheet or included at the beginning or end of the report.

Specific issues requiring a medico-legal report

Requests for 'a psychiatric report' should not be accepted until the referring agent has made clear which issues should be addressed. The psychiatrist might otherwise reasonably conclude that the lawyer has embarked upon a 'fishing expedition'. The issues are usually relevant to a specific class of case and experts are, by definition, aware of this. Some cases are almost exclusively psychiatric questions, whereas others are primarily legal issues. When dealing with legal issues, the writer should be aware which among them are of specific concern so that he may address them using the appropriate legal wording.

The following are examples of legal issues which require an expert psychiatric opinion in the form of a report with a negative or positive conclusion.

Fitness to plead

Can the accused understand the nature of the charge against him and plead with understanding to it? Is he able to instruct his legal advisers? Could he follow and understand the evidence given in court? Would he be able to challenge a juror?

Insanity

At the time (of the act) was the accused labouring under such a defect of reason, from disease of the mind, as not to know the nature and quality of the act he was doing or, if he did know it, did he know that what he was doing was wrong? (McNaughton Rules 1843).

Diminished responsibility

At the time of the killing did he (the accused) suffer from such abnormality of mind (whether arising from a condition of arrested or retarded development of mind, or any inherent causes, or induced by disease or injury) as substantially impaired his mental responsibility for his acts or omissions in doing or being a party to the killing? (Section 2(1) Homicide Act 1957)

Infanticide

At the time of the death of her child was the balance of the woman's mind disturbed by reason of her not having fully recovered from the effect of giving birth to the child or by reason of the effect of lactation consequent upon the birth of the child? (Section 1(1) Infanticide Act 1938).

Opinions for mental health review tribunals

Just as it is important to be precise in completing the forms used in detaining a patient so that the specific requirements of the detaining section are met, it is equally necessary, when making a recommendation to a mental health review tribunal, to consider the conclusions that the tribunal will have in mind. For example, an application for discharge from detention under Section 3 of the Mental Health Act 1983 will be accepted if the tribunal is satisfied:

(a) that the patient is not suffering from mental illness, psychopathic disorder, severe mental impairment, or from any of those forms of disorder of a nature or degree which make it appropriate for him to be detained in hospital for medical treatment; *or*

(b) that it is not necessary for the health or safety of the patient or for the protection of other persons that he should receive such treatment; *or*

(c) that (in relevant cases) he would be likely to act in a manner dangerous to other persons or to himself (Section 72(1)(b) Mental Health Act 1983).

Reference to other appropriate sections of the Act should be made for the precise wording under consideration when discharging other categories of patients.

Where reference to a statute requiring psychiatric evidence is necessary (as above) it helps the court or tribunal for the author to consider the precise wording used in his report. It should be remembered that these are legal classifications and definitions which have a meaning that has usually been defined in law. They are not necessarily directly equivalent to clinical diagnoses and classifications. Reference should be made to forensic and medico-legal texts for discussions of the meaning of terms such as 'abnormality of mind' (Homicide Act) or the McNaughton Rules.

Additional information

Those preparing medico-legal reports for specific purposes such as a defence of diminished responsibility or fitness to plead should possess an appropriate knowledge of the law. This should be evident in the way the opinion is provided. Lawyers rarely request references to published work in civil and criminal cases to substantiate an opinion, and are not usually impressed by excessively legalistic presentations. They are seeking a psychiatric, not a legal, opinion. The psychiatrist should always try to anticipate the requirements of lawyers and the court.

Subsequent events

When the report is required in connection with court proceedings the psychiatrist should always expect that he may be called to give evidence. When preparing the report he should therefore always remember that he may be faced with it in public and it may be subject to detailed scrutiny. In both criminal and civil cases the report will, however, frequently be accepted without the need for oral evidence.

The report may require revision after a conference with counsel or, in civil cases, other experts. Lawyers may suggest changes but cannot insist on them or give any impression that they are influencing the final opinion.

Reports between experts may be exchanged under the guidance of lawyers; in civil and criminal cases, it is increasingly common for doctors briefed by opposing sides to consult each other.

Finally, it is worth remembering that the report required by a defending solicitor may not be used at the time. It is the prerogative of the solicitor to decide whether or not it is of assistance to his client.

The report may, for instance, be helpful in indicating to the lawyer that he is going in the wrong direction. It may also have a long life in the records and be consulted again, even after a considerable time, in connection with a new appeal, future offending, parole or other circumstances.

Further guidance

More detailed advice on writing a report, but with particular reference to psychiatric reports, mental health review tribunals, hospital managers, the Home Office for restricted patients and the transfer of patients to special hospitals and prisons, and for Mental Health Act Commission second opinions, is available from Faulk (1994) and Bluglass (1995), where further advice on compensation reports is also available with specimen reports for both criminal and civil proceedings. Bowden (1990) and Gunn & Taylor (1993) also provide valuable advice on reporting to the criminal court. Briscoe (1990) discusses court reports in civil cases involving children, and Storey (1990) and Cornes & Aitken (1990) discuss reports for compensation following injury. Black *et al* (1991) provide a helpful chapter on writing reports for cases involving children. Powers & Harris (1994) give comprehensive guidance on reports on medical negligence in a detailed textbook.

References

Black, D., Wolkind, S. & Harris Hendricks, J. (1991) *Child Psychiatry and the Law* (2nd edn). London: Gaskell.

Bluglass, R. (1995) Writing reports and giving evidence. In *Seminars in Practical Forensic Psychiatry* (eds D. Chiswick & R. Cope), pp. 134–163. London: Gaskell.

Bowden, P. (1990) The written report and sentences. In *Principles and Practice of Forensic Psychiatry* (eds R. Bluglass & P. Bowden). Edinburgh & London: Churchill Livingstone.

Briscoe, O. (1990) Court reports: civil cases involving children. In *Principles and Practice of Forensic Psychiatry* (eds R. Bluglass & P. Bowden). Edinburgh & London: Churchill Livingstone.

Cornes, P. & Aitken, R. C. (1990) Medical reports on persons claiming compensation for personal injury. *Journal of the Royal Society of Medicine*, **85**, 329–333.

Faulk, M. (1994) *Forensic Psychiatry* (2nd edn). Oxford: Blackwell Scientific.

Gunn, J. & Taylor, P. (1993) *Forensic Psychiatry: Clinical, Ethical and Legal Issues*. Oxford: Butterworth-Heinemann.

May, R. (1998) *Criminal Evidence* (4th edn). London: Sweet & Maxwell.

Powers, M. & Harris, N. (1994) *Medical Negligence* (2nd edn). London: Butterworths.

Storey, P. (1990) Reports for compensation after injury. In *Principles and Practice of Forensic Psychiatry* (eds R. Bluglass & P. Bowden). Edinburgh & London: Churchill Livingstone.

Index

Compiled by Caroline Sheard

abuse
  and learning disability 103
  and postnatal psychiatric illness 121
ACT *see* assertive community treatment
acute disturbance
  case history 2–5
  drug therapy 3–4, 5–6, 7–8, 10–11
  elderly/debilitated patients 11
  environment 9
  investigations 3
  management following aggressive incidents 11–12
  management guidelines 2–6, 7–13
  nursing supervision 9
  patient assessment 9
  physical examination 2
  physical support 11
  psychological and environmental factors in outcome 8–9
  psychological approaches 9–10
  staff support 11
  and sudden unexplained death 6, 7
adjustment reactions and learning disability 105
affective disorders, postnatal 117
after-care 76
agitation as risk factor for NMS 23
akathisia 8, 16, 30, 36, 113
alcohol use
  see also substance misuse
  effect on antipsychotic metabolism 91
alcoholic hallucinosis 86
altered consciousness, in NMS 23
Alzheimer's disease and learning disability 101, 104–5
amantadine 97
amoxapine 22
amphetamine 93, 94
  misuse
    assessment 97
    clinical features 95–6
    complications 96
    epidemiology 94–5
    management 97–8
  psychosis induced by 86
amylobarbitone sodium in acute disturbance 11
anticonvulsants
  in learning disability 107
  side-effects 103

antidepressants
  association with NMS 22
  and breast-feeding 121
  in dual diagnosis 91
  in psychiatric disorder with learning disability 106
  in stimulant misuse 98
antipsychotics
  action at non-dopamine D_2 receptors 18
  in acute disturbance 3, 4, 10–11
  association with NMS 22–3
  association with sudden death 6, 7, 16
  atypical 29, 37
  and breast-feeding 121
  classification 29, 111
  clinical use 15
  combination receptor blockers 111–12
  daily oral maximum doses 10, 14
  depot
    in dual diagnosis 91
    elderly patients 110, 111
    in schizophrenia 31–2, 36
  dopamine hypothesis 14–15
  in dual diagnosis 91
  during pregnancy 120
  effects on cognition 40
  elderly patients 110–13, 114
  first-generation 29
  high-dose 5–6, 7, 14, 19–20
    dangers 15–16
    definition 14
    efficacy 15
    rationale for 16–19
  mechanism of action 14–15
  polypharmacy 11, 30
  potency 15
  prescribing for homeless people 82
  prophylactic postpartum 120
  in psychiatric disorder with learning disability 106–7
  in rapid tranquillisation 5, 7–8, 10
  re-challenge in NMS 25–6
  in schizophrenia 28, 29–33, 43
    maintenance therapy 31–3, 36
  second-generation 29
  selective dopamine receptor blockers 111
  selectivity 15

side-effects 30, 36, 103
  in elderly patients 113–14
  and substance misuse 88
  third-generation 29
  toxicity 26
  see also neuroleptic malignant syndrome
Apisate 94
assertive community treatment (ACT) 51, 58–9, 63–4, 64–5
  clinical teams 59–60
  cross cover 62
  establishing local need 60–1
  extent of service 62
  key elements 59
  operational policy 62, 63
  resistance to 62–3
  supervision and leadership 62
  team meetings 62
  team model 62
  team structure 61
atropinism 24
attention deficit disorder and learning disability 105
autism 103, 105
autonomic disturbance in NMS 23

barbiturates in acute disturbance 11
bed management, community mental health teams 52–3
behavioural management in schizophrenia 39–40
benzodiazepines
  see also specific drugs
  in acute disturbance 3–4, 11
  and breast-feeding 121
  in dual diagnosis 91
  in rapid tranquillisation 5, 7–8
  side-effects 8
bereavement and learning disability 103–4, 105
breast-feeding and psychotropic medication 121
bromocriptine
  in cocaine use 97
  in NMS 25
butyrophenones in psychiatric disorder with learning disability 106

Camberwell Assessment of Need 51
cannabis
  and psychosis 86–7
  and schizophrenia 86

carbamazepine
  in acute disturbance 4
  in cocaine use 97
  initiating 6
  in learning disability 107
  in schizophrenia 37
cardiac arrhythmias associated
  with antipsychotics 6, 16
care management 76
Care Programme Approach (CPA)
  50, 59, 73, 77
    case studies 76
    ensuring continuity 75
    flexibility 74
    with homeless people 84
    individual care plans 75–6
    interprofessional collaboration
      in 73–5
    keeping contact with patients
      74–5
    keyworkers 74
    local implementation 73
    needs assessment 74
    prioritisation 75
    role of counsellors 75
    in schizophrenia 41
carers, education and support
  55
case management 51, 66–7
  homeless people 84
  training in 68
catatonia 21, 24
CBT *see* cognitive–behavioural
  therapy
challenging behaviour 101
Charles Bonnet syndrome 112
children, risks of maternal
  postnatal psychiatric illness
  120–2
chlorpromazine
  in acute disturbance 11
  and breast-feeding 121
  daily oral maximum dose 10,
  14
  dose–occupancy profile 18, 19
  prophylactic postpartum 120
  in rapid tranquillisation 5, 8,
  10
  in schizophrenia 30
  side-effects 8
clinical psychologists in ACT
  teams 61
clomipramine in psychiatric
disorder with learning disability
  106
clozapine 29
  daily oral maximum dose 10, 14
  dose–occupancy profile 18, 19
  effects on cognition 40, 112
  elderly patients 111–12
  and NMS 22
  in schizophrenia 30–1, 32, 37, 39,
    41
  side-effects 112
Clozaril Patient Monitoring Service
  30
CMHTs *see* community mental
  health teams

cocaine 93–4
  psychosis induced by 86
  use
    assessment 97
    clinical features 95–6
    complications 96
    epidemiology 94–5
    management 97–8
cognitive–behavioural therapy
(CBT)
    elderly patients 114
    in schizophrenia 29, 31, 37–8,
      43–8
cognitive impairment in
  schizophrenia 40–1
community mental health services
  assessment and consultation
    53–4
  bed management 52–3
  case management 51
  components 50–4
  crisis response 53
  day care 53
  levels of accommodation 52
  needs assessment 50–1
  and needs of people with
    schizophrenia 49–50
  strategic development 49, 50
community mental health teams
(CMHTs) 49
    assessment and consultation
      services 53–4
    bed management 52–3
    crisis response services 53
    day care services 53
    interventions in schizophrenia
      54–5
    management 56
    organisation 55–6
    primary care liaison 54
community psychiatric nurses
(CPNs)
    see also mental health nursing
      in ACT teams 61
    case loads 53–4
    family interventions in
      schizophrenia 44
    training in CBT techniques
      46–7
comorbidity *see* dual diagnosis
Compliance Questionnaire 127
compliance therapy in
  schizophrenia 36, 45
confidentiality
  in CPA 73–4
  and homeless people 83
consciousness, altered, in NMS 23
consent to assessment of fitness to
  be interviewed 125
continuous treatment team 59
coping behaviour in learning
  disability 103
counsellors, role in Care
  Programme Approach 75
CPA *see* Care Programme
  Approach
CPNs *see* community psychiatric
  nurses

crack 93–4
  use
    assessment 97
    clinical features 95–6
    complications 96
    epidemiology 95
    management 97–8
creatine kinase in NMS 3, 23–4
crisis response services 53

Daily Living Programme 59
dantrolene 25
day care services 53
de-escalation 8, 9
dehydration as risk factor for NMS
  23
delusions
  and learning disability 105
  in schizophrenia 37–8
dementia
  and learning disability 101, 104–5
  Lewy body 112
depression
  and learning disability 101, 104
  postnatal 116–17, 118, 119
  in schizophrenia 38
desipramine in cocaine use 97
developmental disabilities *see*
  learning disability
diazepam
  in acute disturbance 3, 3–4, 11
  in rapid tranquillisation 5
diethylpropion 94
diminished responsibility,
  medico-legal report 134
disability, definition 101
disulfiram 91
DLP 59
DMD 94, 95
dopamine, in aetiology of NMS 21
dopamine receptors
  actions of antipsychotics at
    14–15
  D_2 14–15
  D_3 18
  D_4 18
  incomplete blockade by
    antipsychotics 17
  subtypes 15
Down's syndrome, association
  with psychiatric disorder 101
droperidol
  in acute disturbance 11
  daily oral maximum dose 10, 14
  in rapid tranquillisation 5, 8, 10
  side-effects 8
Drug Misuse Database 94, 95
drug therapy
  acute disturbance 3–4, 5–6, 7–8,
    10–11
  and breast-feeding 121
  psychiatric disorder with
    learning disability 106–7
  schizophrenia 14–20, 27–34
dual diagnosis 86
  learning disability and
    psychiatric illness 100–8
  and mental health nursing 67

substance misuse and psychosis 86–92
dystonia associated with antipsychotics 16, 113

ecstasy *see* MDMA
ECT, elderly patients 110
Edinburgh Postnatal Depression Scale 119
EE 38, 43–4, 114
elderly
  with acute disturbance 11
  non-compliance 111
  psychoses 114–15
    classification 109
    drug side-effects 113–14
    history 109
    non-pharmacological therapies 114
    treatment strategies 110–13
electroconvulsive therapy, elderly patients 110
ephedrine 94
Epidemiological Catchment Area study 87
epidemiology in development of community mental health services 50
epilepsy and learning disability 102
expert witness 130
expressed emotion 38, 43–4, 114

false confessions 127–8
families
  adjustment to member with learning disability 103
  education and support 55
family therapy, schizophrenia 43–4
fenfluramine 94
fever
  differential diagnosis 24
  in NMS 23
fitness to be interviewed 123
  assessment 125–6
  documentation 128–9
  giving evidence on 129
  law relating to 123
  and mental disorder 124–5
  and mental handicap 123, 124–5
  psychiatric disorders affecting 126–8
  and role of appropriate adult 124–5
fitness to plead, medico-legal report 134
fluoxetine
  in amphetamine misuse 97
  association with NMS 22
  in psychiatric disorder with learning disability 106
flupenthixol 10
fluphenazine
  association with NMS 22
  daily oral maximum dose 10
fragile X syndrome 102

Gilles de la Tourette syndrome 103
Gudjonsson Suggestibility Scales 127

hallucinations
  alcohol-induced 86
  and learning disability 105
  in schizophrenia 37
haloperidol
  in acute disturbance 3, 4, 11
  association with NMS 22
  daily oral maximum dose 10, 14
  high-dose 5–6
  intramuscular 10
  prophylactic postpartum 120
  in rapid tranquillisation 5, 8, 10
  in schizophrenia 30
  side-effects 8
halothane–caffeine test in NMS 23
handicap, definition 101
Health of the Nation Outcome Scales 51
hearing impairment and learning disability 102
heat exhaustion 24
homeless people 78–9
  access to housing and benefits 82
  access to services 81
  accommodation 78
  barriers to care 79–81
  Care Programme Approach 84
  case management 84
  and confidentiality 83
  distrust of officialdom 81
  inter-agency working 80
  joint service provision with voluntary sector 83
  keyworker/advocate 82, 84
  lifestyles 81
  mobility 81
  no fixed abode rotas 80
  organisation of services 80
  prescribing for 82
  primary outreach services 83
  priorities 81
  problems for service providers 83
  professional attitudes to 80, 82–3
  residential stabilisation 83
  secondary outreach services 83
  service provision models 83–4
  service provision strategies 81–4
  support networks and agencies 79
homelessness, definition 78–9
Homicide Act 1957 134
homovanillic acid in NMS 21
hospital bed use by people with schizophrenia 51–2
Huntington's disease and NMS 22
hyperkinetic/attention deficit disorder and learning disability 105
hypotension associated with antipsychotics 16

ice 94
impairment, definition 101

infanticide
  medico-legal report 134
  and postnatal psychiatric illness 121
insanity, medico-legal report 134
interviews
  see also fitness to be interviewed police 123–5
IQ and learning disability 100
iron, serum, and NMS 23

keyworkers
  in Care Programme Approach 74, 84
  with homeless people 82, 84

labelling and learning disability 103
lamotrigine in learning disability 107
late paraphrenia 109
learning disability
  aetiology of psychiatric illness 101–4
  and challenging behaviour 101
  classification 100, 101
  and communication skills 103
  and coping behaviour 103
  and fitness to be interviewed 123, 124–5
  management of psychiatric illness 105–7
  mental health service organisation 106, 107
  prevalence 100
  prevalence of psychiatric illness 101, 102
  psychiatric assessment and diagnosis 104–5
  and psychiatric illness 100–8
  and self-esteem 103
  terminology and definitions 100–1
Lesch–Nyhan syndrome 102
leucocytosis, in NMS 24
Lewy body dementia 112
lithium
  association with NMS 22
  and breast-feeding 121
  in dual diagnosis 91
  prophylactic postpartum 120
  in schizophrenia 37
  teratogenicity 120
lorazepam 3–4, 11
loss and learning disability 103–4, 105
loxapine 10, 14

McNaughton Rules 134
major tranquillisers *see* antipsychotics
mania and learning disability 104
manic–depressive psychosis and pregnancy 117, 120
MAOIs *see* monoamine oxidase inhibitors
MDA 98
MDEA 98

MDMA 93, 94
   clinical features of use 98
   complications of use 98–9
   death associated 98–9
   epidemiology of use 98
   management of use 99
medico-legal reports 130–1
   additional information 135
   further guidance 135
   issues covered 134–5
   jargon 132
   layout 132–4
   patient interviews 131
   structure 131–2
   subsequent events 135
   third-party interviews 131
memory distrust syndrome 127–8
mental disorder and fitness to be
   interviewed 124–5
mental handicap
   see also learning disability
      and fitness to be interviewed
      123, 124–5
Mental Health Act 1983
   reports required under 130
   Section 2 10
   Section 3 10
   Section 5 (II) 10
mental health nursing 71–2
   and behaviour therapy 68
   contemporary services and roles
      66–7
   in dual diagnosis populations
      67
   education and training 68–9
   focus on serious mental illness
      66
   management 69–70
   and medication management 68
   neglected roles 67–8
   and physical health of patients
      67
   research 70
   review 66, 69
   undergraduate education 69
mental health review tribunals
   134–5
mental health services
   see also community mental health
      services
   organisation for people with
      learning disability 106, 107
mental retardation
   see also learning disability
   terminology 100
methadone 91
methotrimeprazine 10
methylenedioxyamphetamine
   98
methylenedioxyethylamphetamine
   98
methylenedioxymethamphetamine
   see MDMA
methylphenidate 94
metoclopramide, association with
   NMS 22
Minnesota model of treatment 90
Misuse of Drugs Act 1971 93

monoamine oxidase inhibitors
   (MAOIs)
      and breast-feeding 121
      in dual diagnosis 91

needs assessment
   in Care Programme Approach 74
   in planning of community
      mental health services 50–1
neuroleptic malignant syndrome
   (NMS) 2, 3, 11, 21
      aetiology 21
      associated with high-dose
         antipsychotics 16
      clinical course 25
      demographic factors 23
      diagnosis 23–5
      differential diagnosis 24–5
      dopamine shut-down
         hypothesis 21
      in the elderly 113
      epidemiology 22–3
      heredity 23
      incidence 22
      laboratory investigations 23–4
      management 25–6
      mortality 22
      neuroleptic re-challenge 25–6
      partial/forme fruste 24–5
      post mortem findings 24
      recurrence 23
      risk factors 22–3
      symptoms 23
neuroleptics *see* antipsychotics
NFA rotas 80
NMS *see* neuroleptic malignant
   syndrome
no fixed abode rotas 80
noradrenergic system in aetiology
   of NMS 21
nurse behaviour therapists 68
Nurse Therapy Training
   Programme 68

observation levels 9
obsessive–compulsive disorder and
   learning disability 105
occupational therapy in
   schizophrenia 29
oestrogens, prophylactic
   postpartum 120
olanzapine 29
   daily oral maximum dose 14
   dose–occupancy profile 18
   elderly patients 112
   in schizophrenia 30, 32, 37
overactivity as risk factor for NMS
   23

PACT 58, 59
paradoxical behaviour associated
   with high-dose antipsychotics
   16, 17
paraphrenia 109
parkinsonism associated with
   antipsychotics 16, 17, 18, 36, 113
Parkinson's disease and NMS 22
PAS-ADD 105

patient education in schizophrenia
   35–6, 55
pericyazine 10
perphenazine, association with
   NMS 22
phenobarbitone
   in learning disability 107
   side-effects 103
phenothiazines 106
phenytoin
   in learning disability 107
   side-effects 103
pimozide 10, 14
ping-pong effect 89
Police and Criminal Evidence Act
   1984 123, 125
      Codes of Practice 123, 124, 127
police interviews 123–5
   see also fitness to be interviewed
Ponderax 94
postnatal psychiatric illness 116
   classification 116
   prediction 118–19
   risk management 119–20
   risks for previously well mothers
      116–17
   risks for those with pre-existing
      disorders 117–18
   risks to children 120–2
post-traumatic stress disorder and
   learning disability 105
Prader–Willi syndrome 101–2
primary care liaison 54
primary outreach services for
   homeless people 83
prioritisation in Care Programme
   Approach 75
problem-solving 114
prochlorperazine 10
procyclidine 3
professional witness 130
progesterone, prophylactic
   postpartum 120
Programs in Assertive Community
   Treatment 58, 59
Project 2000 69
propranolol in schizophrenia 37
pseudoephedrine 94
Psychiatric Assessment Schedule
   for Adults with Developmental
   Disabilities 105
psychiatric diagnosis as risk factor
   for NMS 22
psychiatric intensive care unit 3, 5
psychoeducation 35–6, 55
psychological therapies in
   schizophrenia 29
psychosis
   and cannabis use 86–7
   drug-induced 86, 96
   in the elderly 109–15
   and substance misuse 86–7, 92
      extent of dual diagnosis 87
      implications of dual diagnosis
         88–9
      management 89–91
      reasons for substance use
         87–8

puerperal psychosis
  classification 116
  prediction of 118–19
  risk management 119–20
  risk of 117

quetiapine 29, 30, 32, 37

Raghip, Engin 123
rapid tranquillisation 5, 7–8, 10
rehabilitation in schizophrenia 31,
  40, 53
remoxipride 29, 111
reports
  on fitness to be interviewed 128–9
  medico-legal 130–5
restraint 9
rigidity in NMS 23
risperidone 29
  association with NMS 22
  daily oral maximum dose 10, 14
  dose–occupancy profile 18
  elderly patients 112
  in schizophrenia 30, 32, 37
Royal College of Psychiatrists'
  Research Unit, *Management of
  Imminent Violence* 5, 12

schizophrenia
  behaviour problems 39–40
  and cannabis 86
  Care Programme Approach 41
  cognitive–behavioural therapy
    29, 31, 37–8, 43–8
  cognitive impairment in 40–1,
    45–6
  deployment of community
    mental health team 49–57
  drug therapy 14–20, 27–34
  in the elderly 109
  family interventions 43–4
  first presentation 27
  follow-up after discharge 36
  and hospital bed use 51–2
  identification of people with 50,
    51
  importance of early treatment
    27–8
  late-onset 109
  and learning disability 104
  long-term 35–42
  maintenance therapy 31–3, 36, 41
  non-compliance with medication
    35, 45
  patient education 35–6, 55
  and pregnancy 117–18, 120
  prodromal signs monitoring 45
  rehabilitation 31, 40, 53
  relapse 33
    and expressed emotion 43–4
    prevention 35–6
    rates 35
    signature 45

treatment resistant 30, 36
  unresolved negative symptoms
    38–9, 44–5
  unresolved positive symptoms
    36–8, 44–5
  welfare benefits 54–5
seclusion 9
secondary outreach services for
  homeless people 83
selective serotonin reuptake
  inhibitors (SSRIs)
    association with NMS 22
    in breast-feeding 121
    in dual diagnosis 91
    in psychiatric disorder with
      learning disability 106
self-esteem and learning disability
  103
serotonin receptors, action of
  antipsychotics at 18
serotonin syndrome 24
sertindole 29, 30, 32, 37
service development approach 49,
  50
sexual abuse and learning
  disability 103
sexuality in learning disability 104
social therapy in schizophrenia 29
speed *see* amphetamine
speedball 93
SSRIs *see* selective serotonin
  reuptake inhibitors
staff safety 9
stimulant misuse 93–9
substance misuse 86
  assessment 97
  complications 89
  preferential use 87
  and psychosis 86–7, 92
    extent of dual diagnosis 87
    implications of dual diagnosis
      88–9
    management 89–91
    reasons for 87–8
  and self-medication 88
  stimulants 93–9
sudden death
  acutely disturbed patients 6
  associated with antipsychotic
    treatment 6, 7, 16
  MDMA-related 98–9
suicide and postnatal psychiatric
  illness 121
sulpiride 29
  in acute disturbance 4
  association with NMS 22
  daily oral maximum dose 10, 14
  elderly patients 111
supervision register 76, 77, 84

tardive dyskinesia associated with
  antipsychotics 16, 113–14
TCL 58–9

temazepam misuse 91
tenuate dospan 94
tetrabenazine 21
thioridazine 29
  daily oral maximum dose 10,
    14
  dose–occupancy profile 18,
    19
  in rapid tranquillisation 8
  side-effects 8
Thorn psychosocial intervention
  training 46–7, 68–9
training in CBT techniques 46–7
Training in Community Living
  58–9
tranquillisation, rapid 5, 7–8, 10
tranylcypromine 94
tricyclic antidepressants
  association with NMS 22
  and breast-feeding 121
  in psychiatric disorder with
    learning disability 106
trifluoperazine 10
trimipramine, association with
  NMS 22
tuberous sclerosis 101
12-step model of treatment 90

valproate in learning disability
  107
vigabatrin
  in learning disability 107
  side-effects 103
violence
  associated with high-dose
    antipsychotics 16
  in dual diagnosis populations
    67
  management following incidents
    11–12
  management of 5
  pharmacological management
    3–4
  in schizophrenia 39
visual impairment and learning
  disability 102
voir dire 129
voluntary sector, service provision
  for homeless people 83

welfare benefits
  for homeless people 82
  for people with schizophrenia
    54–5
whizz *see* amphetamine

ziprasidone 29, 37
zotepine 37
zuclopenthixol
  in acute disturbance 4, 10
  daily oral maximum dose 10
  intramuscular 10
  in rapid tranquillisation 5